Kingship

Kingship

The Politics of Enchantment

Francis Oakley

Blackwell
Publishing

10-17-2006
WW
$ 34.95

BLACKWELL PUBLISHING
350 Main Street, Malden, MA 02148–5020, USA
9600 Garsington Road, Oxford OX4 2DQ, UK
550 Swanston Street, Carlton, Victoria 3053, Australia

First published 2006 by Blackwell Publishing Ltd

1 2006

Library of Congress Cataloging-in-Publication Data

Oakley, Francis.
Kingship : the politics of enchantment / Francis Oakley.
p.   cm.
Includes bibliographical references and index.
ISBN-13: 978-0-631-22695-6 (hardcover : alk. paper)
ISBN-10: 0-631-22695-8 (hardcover : alk. paper)
ISBN-13: 978-0-631-22696-3 (pbk. : alk. paper)
ISBN-10: 0-631-22696-6 (pbk. : alk. paper)
1. Kings and rulers—History. I. Title.

JC375.O35 2006
321'.6'09—dc22
2005013798

A catalogue record for this title is available from the British Library.

Set in 10/12.5pt Galliard
by The Running Head Limited, Cambridge, www.therunninghead.com
Printed and bound in India
by Replika Press Ltd

For further information on
Blackwell Publishing, visit our website:
www.blackwellpublishing.com

To Will, Charlotte, Ryann,
Kevin, Erin, Joslyn

Contents

Illustrations

Series Editor's Preface

History is one of many fields of knowledge. Like other fields it has two elements: boundaries and contents. The boundaries of history first acquired their modern shape in early modern Europe. They include, among other things, such basic principles as the assumption that time is divisible into past, present, and future; that the past can be known by means of records and remainders surviving to the present; that culture can be distinguished from nature; that anachronism can be avoided; that subjects are different from objects; that human beings are capable of taking action; and that action is shaped by circumstance. Above all else, of course, they include the assumption that history does actually constitute a separate field of knowledge that is in fact divided from neighboring fields – not merely a hitherto neglected corner of some other field whose rightful owners ought ideally, and are expected eventually, to reclaim it from the squatters now dwelling there without authorization and cultivate it properly with the tools of, say, an improved theology or a more subtle natural science.

A prodigious harvest has been gathered from the field bounded by those assumptions. Making a tentative beginning with the humanist discovery of antiquity, gaining confidence with the enlightened critique of religion, and blossoming into full professionalization in the nineteenth century, modern historians have managed to turn their produce into an elementary ingredient in democratic education and a staple of cultural consumption. They have extracted mountains of evidence from archives and turned it into books whose truth can be assayed by anyone who cares to follow their instructions. They have dismantled ancient legends that had been handed down through the ages and laid them to rest in modern libraries. They have emancipated the study of the past from prophecy, apocalypticism, and other providential explications of the future. Pronouncements on the past command respect no longer unless they have been authenticated by reference to documents. Myths and superstitions have given way to knowledge of unprecedented depth, precision, and extent. Compared to what we read in older books, the books of history today are veritable miracles of comprehension, exactitude, and impartiality.

Success, however, has its price. None of the assumptions defining the modern practices of history are self-evidently true. The more they are obeyed, the less it seems they can be trusted. Having probed the realm of culture to its frontiers, we cannot find the boundary by which it is supposed to be divided from the empire of nature. Having raised our standards of objectivity to glorious heights, we are afflicted with vertiginous attacks of relativity. Having mined the archives to rock bottom, we find that the ores turn out to yield no meaning without amalgamation. And having religiously observed the boundary between the present and the past, we find that the past does not live in the records but in our imagination. The boundaries of history have been worn down; the field is lying open to erosion.

The books in this series are meant to point a way out of that predicament. The authors come from different disciplines, all of them specialists in one subject or another. They do not proceed alike. Some deal with subjects straddling familiar boundaries – chronological, geographical, and conceptual. Some focus on the boundaries themselves. Some bring new subjects into view. Some view old subjects from a new perspective. But all of them share a concern that our present understanding of history needs to be reconfigured if it is not to turn into a mere product of the past that it is seeking to explain. They are convinced that the past does have a meaning for the present that transcends the interests of specialists. And they are determined to keep that meaning within reach by writing good short books for non-specialists and specialists alike.

Constantin Fasolt
University of Chicago

Acknowledgments

When writing a wide-ranging essay of this type one's indebtednesses tend inevitably to exceed one's ability to recognize, let alone acknowledge, them. But some debts are clear. Let me convey my appreciation, then, to the following: to Tessa Harvey, Blackwells Publisher, and Constantin Fasolt, general editor of the "New Perspectives on the Past" series, for inviting me to undertake the project and for their warm encouragement and support as I grappled with the challenges it entailed; to the generations of fine students whom I have been privileged to teach here at Williams College in my seminars and tutorials on medieval political thought, and whose insight, tenacity, and good cheer as they wrestled with Eusebius, Augustine, the canonists, John of Paris, the conciliarists, Marsiglio of Padua, and the like never failed to inspire me; to my colleagues Bill Darrow and Bill Wagner, of the Religion and History departments respectively, for their kindness in casting an expert eye on some of these pages, and to my other colleagues in the weekly fellows' seminar at the Oakley Center for the Humanities and Social Sciences with whom I was able to share drafts of some of the following chapters and who also aided me with their criticism and advice; finally, and yet once more, to Donna Chenail and her fine staff in our faculty secretarial office for their characteristically prompt and accurate work in preparing the manuscript for the press. It is to my grandchildren that the book is dedicated, and with much love. They bring joy to an old historian's heart.

F.O.
Williamstown, Massachusetts
July, 2005

Prologue
Matters of Perspective

To establish the connections, in principle and in detail, directly or mediately, between politics and eternity is a project that has never been without its followers. . . . Probably there has been no theory of the nature of the world, of the activity of man, of the destiny of mankind, no theology or cosmology, perhaps even no metaphysics, that has not sought a reflection of itself in the mirror of political philosophy, certainly there has been no fully considered politics that has not looked for its reflection in eternity.

Michael Oakeshott[1]

"That kings are sacred" has been said to be "an anthropological and historical truism,"[2] and kingship and its embedment in the sacred is unquestionably a topic that beguiles. But the enormity of the challenge involved in any attempt to come to terms with it on a global scale is not to be gainsaid. And especially so if one is trying to do so within the confines of a brief interpretative essay. For that is my endeavor. It calls, then, for a preliminary exercise in intellectual throat-clearing. Or, put differently, and imagining the topic as one riding elusively at anchor in a well-protected historiographic safe-harbor, it is not one to be approached without attempting first some methodological and metahistorical minesweeping, both definitional and perspectival.

So far as definitions go, the overlapping meanings of three words must be teased apart. The first, *monocracy*, not quite an archaism but rarely used today in English and (following here the *Oxford English Dictionary*) denoting simply "government by a single person" or "autocracy." The second, *monarchy*, denoting "undivided rule by a single person, sole rule or sovereignty," or, more narrowly (and more recently) rule by "a sovereign having the title of king, queen, emperor, or empress, or the equivalent of one of those." The third, *kingship*, denoting "the office and dignity of a king . . . the rule of a king; monarchical government," with a king being defined as a

1

"male sovereign ruler of an independent state, whose position is either purely hereditary, or hereditary under certain legal conditions, or, if elective, is considered to . . . [possess] . . . the same attributes and rank as those of a (purely or partly) hereditary ruler."

It is possible, by assimilating *monarchy* to *monocracy*, to distinguish fairly sharply between monarchy and kingship. This is the tack taken by Roger Mousnier, who uses *monarch* to refer to "any man who exercises the supreme power of decision in its fullness . . . whatever his legal title may be." He deploys it, therefore, as a category capable of embracing the "tyrants" of Greek antiquity (seventh–sixth century BCE), the "dictators" of republican Rome, the shoguns of Tokugawa Japan (despite the contemporaneous existence of an emperor), as well as such modern dictatorial leaders as Mussolini (despite the contemporaneous existence of an Italian king), Hitler, Stalin, and Franco, and even "at certain moments" the presidential leadership of Charles de Gaulle. Kingship (*royauté*) he treats as a distinct and less inclusive category on the grounds that the king, while "in principle a monarch," "possesses a legitimate, reputable power instituted by consent, recognized by custom" and mediated by "organized dynastic inheritance."[3]

That is not the definitional approach I propose to take. In contemporary English usage *monarch* has come, in effect, to be a synonym for *king* or regnant *queen* (it has the advantage of not being gender specific), and, that being so, Mousnier's proposed distinction does more to confuse than to clarify. *Monarchy*, then, I will take to be a category identical with that of *kingship/queenship* and one, further, that embraces the office of those rulers of large territories or of a number of peoples or subordinate kingdoms whom we have been accustomed to calling *emperors*, or whose titles (Roman *imperator* from the time of Caesar Augustus, Byzantine *basileus*, Russian *tsar*, German *Kaiser*, Chinese *huang-di*, Japanese *tennō heika*) are customarily rendered in English as *emperor*.

It is not only definitional tactic, however, that calls for comment. So, too, does the very choice of devoting a book to kingship. After all, if we exclude from purview those contemporary African kings whose titles no longer confer upon them any formal political role or standing and who are, in effect and at law, private citizens of their respective states, and if we limit our focus to the 191 states around the world whose independent standing has been recognized by the extension to them of membership in the United Nations, only a mere handful today possess monarchical regimes of any sort. And most of the monarchs involved are constitutional monarchs, reigning rather than ruling, serving as essentially formal heads of state charged with representing the nation to the world at large and with the performance of ceremonial duties. Regimes in the bulk of the free-standing states of the early twenty-first century range instead from the non-monarchical but authoritarian, via the non-democratic but still constitutionalist or quasi-constitutionalist, all the way to the liberal democratic forms pioneered in North America and north-west Europe. If one aspired to identify the constitutional wave of the future, kingship would hardly come to mind, whereas one might be able to mount a reasonably persuasive case for democracy. It is true that in 1970 there were probably no more than 30 democracies worldwide. By 2001, however, that number may even have quadrupled. As a result, we are beginning to encounter in the press the casual attribution of something approaching a manifest political destiny to the forms of liberal democracy that have tri-umphed in the West. We are also hearing expressions of hope that similar governmental forms might prevail even in societies still bereft of effective constitutional mechanisms capable of preventing the abuse of executive power by measures short of force. But if our ears now ring to the clamor of voices in high places calling for the planting of democratic ideals in new (and sometimes improbable) settings across the world, we would do well to bring to the evaluation of such calls the hard-won measure of perspective afforded by the tragic history of the past century, and, beyond that, by the longer course of world history.

In the first place, it is surely too soon to put out of mind the harsh lessons to be learned from the apocalyptic rigors of twentieth-century political life – not only in the world at large but also in old European countries which had already logged considerable mileage with liberal democratic institutions. At the start of that century it was easy enough for progressive historians to take it for granted that the established course of history would continue to move the world naturally towards the realization of a governmental norm that would be essentially constitutionalist. To their more chastened successors at the end of the century, however, that degree of confidence was no longer available. The flowering in the first half of the century, and in the very heart-land of Europe, of totalitarian despotisms of the most squalid type, the later failure in so many parts of the decolonized world of the newly-minted, Western-style constitutional forms so breezily bequeathed to them by their erstwhile imperial masters, the mounting challenges confronted by the coun-tries of Eastern Europe, Central Asia, and Latin America as they attempted (with varying degrees of conviction) to consolidate liberal democratic regimes and to create the institutions and practices of a viable civil society – such bracing realities scarcely encourage one to take at all for granted the flowering on the world-historical scene of constitutionalism itself, let alone the growth of that more exotic plant that we call "liberal democracy."

Moreover, invoking in the second place the longer world-historical record, it would appear to be the case that the classical republican tradition in general, and the Athenian achievement of the fifth and fourth centuries BCE in particular, have together contrived to cast so long a shadow over our Western habits of thinking about the political past as almost to blind us to one fundamental and really quite startling fact. Namely, that for several millennia at least, it has been kingship and not more consensual governmental forms that has dominated the institutional landscape of what we today would call *political* life. For that certainly appears to have been the case from the time of the "Neolithic revolution" (c.8000–c.5000 BCE), marked by the rise to prominence of agricultural modes of food production, all the way down to the acceleration in the nineteenth century of the Industrial Revolution and the concomitant shift of a growing percentage of the world's population into essentially urban modes of occupation.

"Tyranny is the normal pattern of human government," Adlai Stevenson is reputed once to have said. And the claim is not an implausible one. But substitute for "tyranny" the words "kingship" or "monarchy" and the plausible hardens into the indubitable. In terms, that is to say, of its antiquity, its ubiquity, its wholly extraordinary staying power, the institution of kingship can lay strong claim to having been the most common form of government known, world-wide, to man. Consigned thereby to merely *provincial* status (world-historically speaking) are the consensual, representative, republican, and democratic forms that bulk so large on our contemporary political landscape, and to which those of us concerned with political philosophy and its history have tended to devote by far the greater part of our attention.

That being so, kingship and what it involved or presupposed, ideologically speaking, clearly deserves a far greater measure of attention than it has in fact received. Certainly, it warrants a degree of scrutiny at least commensurate with that lavished, since the Renaissance, so obsessively and misleadingly upon the classical *polis* or city-state. What should equally not be taken for granted, moreover, and what calls with equal urgency for historical illumination, is the eventual marginalization of kingship in the modern Western world, as well as its parallel decline in the world at large as that world has progressively been drawn into the disenchanting orbit described by the corrosive forces of Westernizing modernization. Nor should we ignore, even more fundamentally, the dramatic collapse of – or drainage of legitimacy from – the ideological pattern that in one form or another had for long millennia sustained that monarchical institution. For in terms at least of its ubiquity and longevity, that ideology can lay strong claim to having been nothing less than the *political commonsense* of humankind. And, like the institution of kingship itself, that commonsense turns out to have been deeply embedded in the sacred and thoroughly informed by it.

Such thoughts, I recognize, are fated to sit uneasily with what has long since come to function, for those interested in political philosophy and its history, as a sort of constitutive narrative of the course of Western political thinking. No more than implicit, that narrative has served nonetheless to determine the periods to which most attention has characteristically been paid (classical Greece of the fifth and fourth centuries BCE and Europe of the seventeenth to twentieth centuries), to foreground the texts on which students have habitually been encouraged to focus (Plato and Aristotle, Machiavelli, the great contract theorists from Hobbes to Kant, the nineteenth-century Utilitarians, and so on), and to frame the interpretative perspective from which those texts have usually been understood.

In that formative narrative, it need hardly be emphasized, the institution of kingship and the element of sacrality attaching so persistently to it get pretty short shrift. For political philosophers at least, and the contributions of anthropologically and historically inclined specialists notwithstanding, late antique and medieval notions of sacral kingship have yet to find a place under the bright lights of center stage. Nor, until recent years, have the theories of divine right advanced in the seventeenth century by such thinkers as James I of England, Sir Robert Filmer, and Bishop Bossuet fared all that much better. So little so, indeed, that having cited the remark of a contemporary that "never has there been a doctrine better written *against* than the divine right of kings," John Neville Figgis a century ago was moved tartly to observe that "those, who have exhausted their powers of satire in pouring scorn upon the theory, have commonly been at little pains to understand it."[4]

One of the reasons for this, I would suggest, is that we tend instinctively to take the predominantly *secular* nature of our modern political life as something *natural* to humankind, an unquestionable norm towards which all societies, whatever their history, may properly be expected to tend. From that point of view, of course, what constitutes grounds for puzzlement and calls for explanation, is not the emergence on the world-historical scene of that familiar secular norm, but rather the persistence on into the present of societies to which the distinction between the religious and the political has contrived somehow to remain stubbornly alien. And yet, as Giambattista Vico, Jean-Jacques Rousseau and J.S. Mill all famously suggested, and as the beleaguered Muslim world today continues plaintively to insist, it is not the interpenetration in public life of what we in the West have become accustomed to classify as the "political" and the "religious" that needs explaining, but, rather, the novel Western distinction between the two, and the concomitant insertion into public discourse of a political vocabulary that takes such a distinction simply for granted.

Unmoved, however, by such demurrals, and unmindful, it seems, of the findings of modern classicists, anthropologists, and students of archaic and comparative religion, those whose interests focus tightly on political philosophy and its history still resonate, by and large, to older scholarly frequencies. In their writings, that is to say, one catches distinct echoes of the views so dear to the German and English Hellenists of the eighteenth and nineteenth centuries. Peering eagerly into the mists of the classical past, those pioneering Hellenists had been persistently prone, with a glad if often overhasty recognition, to discerning in the political life of the classical Greek *polis* and in the writings of the Greek political philosophers, the looming outlines of their own cherished ideals.[5] And, "modern political thought and anxieties . . . [being] . . . brought to bear on the Athenian democratic experience," the political ideals the Hellenists believed themselves to have encountered in that experience understandably took on a predominantly secular cast.[6]

Hence the perspective so deeply encrypted in our histories of political thought as to have become almost subliminal. In accord with that perspective some sort of fundamental continuity is assumed to exist between the modes of political thinking characteristic of the modern and those characteristic of the classical world, both periods being taken to be committed to the sort of natural and secular modes of rational explanation appropriate to truly *political* thinking. In contrast, what is seen as standing out in the history of Western political thinking is the medieval period. It is seen, in effect, as constituting something of an exception, as a sacralizing deviation from the norm, a period during which the natural categories of political philosophy as we know it were pushed to one side by motifs of *supernatural* bent. Such, for example, was the perspective embedded in the late Walter Ullmann's approach to the history of political thought, which was taken, accordingly, to possess a secular–religious–secular rhythm, with the medieval *religious* phase being the one that needed explaining.[7] Nor was Ullmann alone among historians of political thought in adhering to that point of view. Thus we hear about "the essentially *secular* unity of life in the classical age," and (after its decline) "the Hellenistic propensity for *introducing* the supernatural into politics." We are reminded that Christianity made "*purely political* thought impossible," and that "the peculiar problem of Church and State," which Christianity introduced, involved "the greatest perturbation which has ever drawn men's thoughts about the state *out of their proper political orbit.*" We are even assured, long years of specialized work in other fields to the contrary, that "Medieval Europe offers *for the first time in history* the somewhat paradoxical spectacle of a society trying to organize itself politically on the basis of a spiritual framework," or, again, that it was only with the collapse of the medieval "ideal of a Christian Commonwealth" that there occurred "*a return to a more purely political* conception of the State.*"[8]

Clear enough, I suppose. But that perspective I have come over the years to view as a fundamentally flawed one. The historical "rhythm" I detect in the ebb and flow of ideas is not a secular–religious–secular one, but, rather, religious–religious–secular. Almost a century and a half ago, writing even before anthropology and sociology had emerged as formal academic disciplines and in a compelling evocation of the centrality of religion to the life of the ancient city state, Greek no less than Roman, Fustel de Coulanges warned his own contemporaries of the ever-present danger of anachronism, of historical narcissism, of finding their own attitudes reflected all too readily in those of ancient peoples whose characteristic modes of thought were in reality fundamentally alien to theirs. Since he wrote, moreover, the findings of the classicists, the cultural anthropologists, the students of archaic and comparative religion have converged in such a way as to confirm the precocity of his vision and to make clear that the transition from the archaic and classical to the Christian outlook was a shift not so much from a secular to a religious viewpoint as from one ancient and widespread mode of religious consciousness to another and radically different one.[9] And, as we shall see, the same was to be true of the later transition in Western Europe from the world of Celtic and Germanic paganism to that of early medieval Christianity.

Once this is understood it is no longer, of course, the *religious* nature of medieval political thinking that cries out for explanation but, rather, the degree to which it called the age-old pattern of regal sacrality into question, as also the subsequent (if gradual) emergence in the modern era of the uniquely secularized political vision that has so succeeded in shaping the commonsense of the modern Western world that we are persistently tempted, even at the cost of rampant anachronism, to see it as something grounded in the very nature of humankind. But historians being, as Eric Hobsbawm once remarked, "the professional remembrancers of what their fellow citizens wish to forget," it is properly their task to deliver us from such delusions. And I would suggest that an attempt to grasp the significance attaching to the early emergence, global reach, and extraordinary longevity of the institution of sacral kingship and of the ideological pattern that sustained it is not a bad place to make a start on that process of deliverance.

Kingship, as we shall see, emerged from an "archaic" mentality that appears to have been thoroughly monistic, to have perceived no impermeable barrier between the human and divine, to have intuited the divine as immanent in the cyclic rhythms of the natural world and civil society as somehow enmeshed in those natural processes, and to have viewed its primary function, therefore, as a fundamentally religious one, involving the preservation of the cosmic order and the "harmonious integration" of human beings with the natural world.

The ancient kings, as a result, and their analogues later on across the globe, were regarded as sacred figures – often priestly, sometimes divine – and forms of sacral kingship, with all that they presupposed and entailed, have well been described as together constituting "the archetypal pattern of the archaic culture which underlies all the most ancient civilizations of the world."[10] Nowhere were the lineaments of that archetypal pattern more strikingly evident than in ancient Egypt, where the Pharaoh was regarded as a god incarnate whose task it was to ensure the cyclic rhythm of the seasons, to guarantee the fertility of the land, and to secure the prevention of any disharmony between human society and what (reaching instinctively and misleadingly for a word that did not make its appearance until well into the Christian era) we are tempted to call the *supernatural* forces. Egypt was an extreme case, but similar prerogatives were claimed in greater or lesser degree by the other sacral monarchs of the ancient Near East. Via the Hellenistic Empire of Alexander the Great and its successor states, moreover, the ideology undergirding such monarchies was to exert a profound influence over the political thinking of the late classical world, Roman as well as Greek, and it was able to do so because it came not as an alien heterodoxy but as a return to a way of thinking whose ideologically underpinnings had survived the long centuries of republican rule and had never been fully dismantled.

If that dismantling was, indeed, eventually to take place, it was to do so much later, amid the religious and civil wars, political revolutions, scientific, commercial, and industrial developments that were to characterize the modern European centuries. Many complexly interrelated factors contributed, of course, to that destabilizing process – not least among them the undermining of the confessional state by the stubborn growth of religious pluralism, the secularizing thrust of scientific reason and technological progress, the powerfully transformative impact of economic and bureaucratic rationalization. But while in no way minimizing the importance of such developments it will be my purpose to focus on a factor that was more fundamental, more enduring, more gradual in its working and more corrosive in its ultimate impact. That factor constituted what amounted, in effect, to a necessary condition in the absence of which the contours of our political life today would have been unimaginably different. And what was it? Nothing other (perhaps counter-intuitively) than a *religious* one, the disturbing impact upon archaic and Hellenic modes of thought of the singular conception of the divine nature that was basic to Judaic, Christian, and Muslim belief.

Involved in that belief was a restriction of the meaning of the divine in a manner that would have been no less incomprehensible to the ancients than is the archaic pattern of thought to us. If we ourselves find that pattern so hard to grasp today, we would do well to remember that that is the case precisely because our very idea of what it is to be divine has been radically reshaped by long centuries of Judaic, Christian, and Muslim thinking with its obdurate insistence on the unity, omnipotence, and transcendence of God, centuries during which the meanings ascribed to such words as *god, divine, religious* and so on have, by archaic standards, been narrowed down to a degree bordering on the eccentric. In shattering the archaic sense of the divine as a continuum running through the worlds of nature and society, the dominant belief patterns characteristic of Judaism, Christianity, and Islam undercut also (and therefore) the very ontological underpinnings for archaic and worldwide patterns of sacral kingship. In so doing, they exposed the very institution of kingship to a slow but persistent desacralizing, demystifying, and (ultimately) delegitimizing process, one that such later European attempts at accommodation with the past as the early modern divine-right theory proved powerless in the end to halt.

If these are admittedly large claims, they are not made without deliberation. They presuppose and stem from a bracing effort to approach and judge the European and Western political experience from the outside as well as from the inside, and to see it, especially, from the broader perspective afforded by a reflective encounter with the millennial unfolding of universal or world history. And that encounter, I should acknowledge, has been very much conditioned by one of the intuitions central to the comparative civilizational thinking of Max Weber, the great pioneer of historical sociology, as well as by the subsequent elaboration of that intuition by such others as Peter Berger, Marcel Gauchet, and Gianni Vattimo.[11] Our characteristically Western modes of life and thought, Weber repeatedly insisted, are not simply to be taken for granted. However numbingly familiar they may well be to us today, they are far from representing any *natural* or inevitable culmination towards which all civilizations strive or have striven. They represent, instead, only one very particular line of development, one possibility out of several radically different ones. To appreciate that crucial fact it is necessary for us to try to envisage them as they might appear to alien eyes. Once we make that effort, succeed in raising our heads high enough to be able to peer out over the parapet of our own particular cultural trench and to engage the multiple histories of the larger world that stretches out endlessly beyond, we are inevitably led with Weber to ponder the odd concatenation of circumstances that came to determine the civilizational trajectory that has made us what we are. To such an effort, then, focusing specifically on what we are accustomed to classifying under the category of the *political*, it is time now to turn.

1
Gate of the Gods
Archaic and Global Patterns
of Cosmic Kingship

The roots of the institution of kingship reach so deeply into the past that they are lost to us in the shadows of prehistory. Historians have sometimes speculated that some of those roots might extend even into the hunting and gathering cultures of the late Paleolithic era, to the powers accruing over countless generations to wonder-working shamans and to the heads of clans or lineages. It is doubtless conceivable that such proto-royal figures may have emerged in the centuries prior to the Neolithic invention of agriculture. And it is certainly the case that a dwindling monarchical cohort has lingered on into the increasingly urbanized and industrialized world of the late twentieth and early twenty-first centuries. But historiographic prudence suggests that one might be wise to rest content with the observation that kingship enjoyed what was to be its heyday during the long millennia stretching from "the Neolithic revolution" and the spread of pastoral and agrarian modes of subsistence around the eastern Mediterranean (c.8000–c.5000 BCE) down to the late eighteenth-century onset of the Industrial Revolution and the accelerating shift of a growing segment of the world's population from the land and into essentially urbanized modes of occupation.

Kingship: Ubiquity, Longevity, Sacrality

Certainly, by the beginning of the third millennium BCE when, with the invention of writing, the historiographic shadows begin finally to lift, we find that kingship had already established itself in the ancient Near East. It had done so along the Nile valley in Egypt and in the Tigris and Euphrates basin in Mesopotamia, as well as in the flatlands that stretched between them. If in Egypt society appears always to have been organized along monarchical lines, in Mesopotamia the Sumerian kingship was preceded by more broadly participatory forms of governance centered on temples and sanctuaries. But there, too, it soon became the universally dominant system of government. As such, it was to leave its imprint also on the modes of rulership characteristic elsewhere in the ancient Near East and in the lands bordering on the eastern Mediterranean – on the Syrian, Canaanite, and Minoan kingships of the mid-third to mid-second millennia BCE, as well as on the types of kingship to be found in Crete and Greece during the Mycenaean era (c.1600–c.1100 BCE). By the latter period, altogether independently and at the other end of the world, kingship had made its appearance on the Chinese mainland. It had done so with the establishment of the Shang dynasty (c.1500–1027 BCE), and it was destined to attain its classic shape a thousand years later during the Ch'in and Han periods (221 BCE–222 CE). The following centuries saw its appearance and consolidation also in Japan, Korea, Polynesia, and central, south, and south-east Asia, in most parts of which it was fated to persist down into the nineteenth and even twentieth centuries. During the same era, the same was to be true of the Christian kings of western, central, and eastern Europe, successors alike of the late Roman emperors and of the Celtic and Germanic kings of the pre-Christian era. And across the Atlantic, during the centuries traditionally labeled in Eurocentric historiography as late antique, medieval, and early modern, the lands of Mesoamerica and South America witnessed the wholly independent emergence of the extraordinary Olmec, Maya, Toltec, Aztec, and Inca monarchies. Similarly, the "medieval" and sub-sequent centuries down to the twentieth were punctuated in sub-Saharan Africa by the rise, persistence, or fall of a myriad of kingdoms, great and small, from that of the Shilluk in the north to that of Swaziland in the south, or those of Benin and Yorubaland in the west, to the kingdoms that flourished to the east in Tanzania and Uganda.

On the world-historical stage, then, the career of kingship as a form of government has certainly been characterized by ubiquity and longevity. But it has been distinguished also by its sheer variety. Variety, that is to say, both in the shapes it has assumed and in the functions and responsibilities with which it has characteristically been burdened. If in many instances, ranging from the Pharaohs of ancient Egypt or the Inca rulers of fifteenth- and sixteenth-century Peru to the French and English monarchs of early modern Europe or some of the African rulers of the same period, kingship involved the full panoply of governing roles – administrative, military, judicial, economic, religious, in others the role was a much more limited, focused, or specialized one.

At one end of the spectrum, and reflecting the turbulent conditions prevailing in this or that region, the emphasis lay heavily on the king's military role as lord of hosts or leader in war. This was true of kings as far separated by time and space as the Mycenaean and Homeric kings of ancient Greece, the Hebrew kings of the early first millennium BCE, the Germanic kings of early medieval western Europe, the early Inca kings of South America, and the warrior Bemba kings who, during the eighteenth century and much of the nineteenth, carved out by conquest and overawed by their military prowess something of an empire in Tanganyika.

At the other end of the spectrum, however, one encounters no difficulty in identifying a host of kingships, dispersed equally widely in space and time, to which hardly any remnant of what we today would call "political" power attaches, though they do tend to be possessed of (or burdened with) extensive ceremonial or ritual functions. For European historians the classic instance of this type of kingship is to be found in the "do-nothing" Frankish monarchs of the Merovingian dynasty who, from 687, at least, to 751 CE, characteristically stood to one side as recognized bearers of the *mana* of royal legitimacy, while the actual power of the kingship was wielded by the successive Carolingian "mayors of the palace." And if, in the end, the latter succeeded in appropriating the mantle of legitimacy and making themselves kings of the Franks, they were not able to do so without some difficulty. Only a little less familiar is the situation at the other end of the world in Japan where, whatever one's judgment on the earlier centuries, from the late twelfth century onwards under first the Kamikura and then the Tokugawa shogunate, the real governing power resided with the generalissimos or "shoguns" headquartered eventually at Edo (Tokyo). During those centuries, while deferred to as the theoretical source of the shogun's authority, the emperors remained nonetheless secluded in the imperial capital of Kyoto, cut off from direct contact with the *daimyo* or provincial nobility, limited in their official activities to the performance of traditional ritual functions, bereft themselves of military power, and "protected" instead by a garrison under the command of a military governor responsible directly to the shogun.

These two cases, however, are simply the most familiar among a whole series of instances worldwide of kings who, whatever the prominence of the symbolic role they played in their respective kingdoms, were (or, across time, had become) well-nigh powerless in what we today would recognize as real political terms. Courtesy of Christopher Marlowe's "mighty line" and his pioneering play *Tamberlaine the Great*, Timur, the fourteenth-century upstart conqueror of central Eurasia and a good deal of the Near and Middle East, is a name that has reverberated down the centuries. But we should not miss the fact that the sweeping powers he wielded were those of a shogunlike substitute for a long-forgotten puppet, a direct descendant of the great Chingis Khan, who actually bore the title of king (*khan*) of Persia. Similar instances of do-nothing (or seemingly do-nothing) kings are to be found at times and in places as widely separated one from another as the eighth-century (CE) Kingdom of Axum (in Ethiopia), or the nineteenth-century South Pacific island kingdom of Tonga, or the tenth-century king of the Volga Bulgars whose feet were not permitted to touch the ground and whose duties had to be discharged by a viceregal deputy.[1] More generally, focusing on the traditional Balinese kingdoms of the late nineteenth century, Clifford Geertz has painted an arresting picture of what he calls the "theatre state," involving an essentially expressive form of kingship in which "power served pomp, not pomp power," and in which "mass ritual was not a device to shore up the state, but rather the state, even in its final gasp, was a device for the enactment of mass ritual."[2]

Unless one recognizes the centrality of the sacred to the archaic forms of kingship, wherever and in whatever historical era one encounters them, it will be impossible to make much sense of such singular institutional phenomena. Nor will it be any easier to come to terms with so many other arresting parallelisms that one finds connected with the institution of kingship in parts of the world and periods of history so widely separated by place and time from one another as to preclude explanation in terms of diffusion outward from some central point of origination. Thus, for example, the ritual slaying of kings (or substitute figures) in the aftermath of bad harvests or if (or before) they had lost their vigor and become weak is evidenced not only in ancient Assyria and, later on, in sub-Saharan Africa, but also in Europe among the Celtic and Scandinavian peoples. Or from Tonga and Africa to India, Nepal, ancient Sparta and pre-Christian Germany, the archaic institution of dual kingship, with the two royal partners affiliated with different divinities and charged with different functions and cultic responsibilities. Or, yet again, the commonplace linkage of kings with the sun-god and, more generally, their association with sun symbolism. In this respect, Louis XIV's self-portrayal as *le roi soleil*, and the sun symbolism permeating the iconographical program at his palace of Versailles, and the Roman emperor's adoption of *sol invictus* (the name of the invincible sun-god) as a title are simply instances from classical and European history of a phenomenon that crops up again and again in settings as disparate as Japan, India, Persia, Mesoamerica, Hellenistic Greece, and, quintessentially, of course, ancient Egypt where the Pharaoh came to bear the title of "Son of Ré" (the sun-god). It was common in many parts of the world for kings to be conceived of as bearers of light, suns who rose over and with their beneficent beams illuminated their realms. Their royal regalia had similarly cosmic associations – the throne with the cosmic mountain as axial center of the universe, the mace or scepter with the thunderbolt, the crown with the very sun itself. And the rooting of kingship in such forms of cosmic religiosity found further reflections in practices that we tend to misconstrue because we see them as transparent matter-of-fact gestures devoid of any connotation that could readily be labeled as "religious."

Thus, to take a commonplace example, scholars like Chadwick, Schlesinger, and Wallace-Hadrill have taken the old Germanic practice of initiating a king by raising him up on a shield as simply reflecting the origin of such kings in their election as military leaders by their armed followers. But it turns out that the Germanic practice was not an isolated one and other instances suggest (perhaps counter-intuitively) that it may well have been grounded in the sacral sphere. At his coronation, the Byzantine emperor, too, was lifted up on a shield and that practice was still being interpreted in sacral terms as late as the thirteenth century, for it was understood as involving his ascension as a "great sun" to the heavens, the (star-studded) shield being taken to symbolize the cosmos and the emperor being viewed as the cosmocrator.[3] A certain parallelism to this may be detected in the royal accession ceremony indigenous to the Mongol and Turkic peoples of central and north-east Asia (and passed on, for a while, to China itself). For there, too, kings (*khan, khagan*) were viewed as making a symbolic ascent to the heavens when, at their accession, they were solemnly raised up on a black felt carpet by seven dignataries. All such arcane practices point insistently, of course, to the degree to which what we would call the state was conceived in some sense as an "embodiment of the cosmic totality," and the institution of kingship itself was embedded in one or other species of the cosmic religiosity that for long millennia constituted something approximating the religio-political commonsense of humankind. It was the cosmic nature of that religiosity that determined the cosmic character of kingship. It was the source from which the latter drew its ideological sustenance. And with its fate the fate of kingship was destined to be inextricably entangled.

It is time, then, without making any impossible attempt to trace all the intricate variations evident in its multiple manifestations or, indeed, to signal the areas of greatest uncertainty about it,[4] to map out the dominant contours, at least, of that mysterious but beckoning ideological landscape.

Cosmic Religiosity and the Sacral Kingship

The cartography of the mind is an endeavor fraught inevitably with challenge. And those challenges grow understandably more severe when the mind in question is one so frustratingly remote from us today. Remote not necessarily in time (though, for shorthand purposes, I will use the terms "premodern," "primitive," or "archaic" to denote it) for variants of the cosmic religiosity persisted in some parts of the world right down into the nineteenth and twentieth centuries. Remote, instead, in its distance from the modalities of thought long since habitual to those of us nurtured, intellectually speaking, in the disenchanted cradle of Westernizing modernity.

In contrast with those modalities of thought, the "primitive," "archaic," or "premodern" mentality characteristically attempts to penetrate the encompassing mystery of being along an essentially symbolic, analogical, or associational rather than a strictly causal axis of explanation.[5] Actors in what has been called an ongoing "drama of being," and participants, as they certainly intuited themselves to be, in a richly variegated community that reached out from humankind to encompass the world of nature and its countless denizens as well as the more enduring realm of the divine, the peoples of "premodern" societies appear instinctively to have been moved by the explanatory power of symbol and analogy. "The mainspring of the acts, thoughts, and feelings of early man was the conviction that the divine was immanent in nature and nature intimately connected with society."[6] The mentality involved was thoroughly monistic and the degree of consubstantiality of those who composed the extended community of being was such that it tended to marginalize any distinction or separateness of substance among them. As a result, the sharp distinctions that we are accustomed to make between nature and supernature, between nature, society, and man, between animate and inanimate, were almost wholly lacking. Archaic man was encompassed by darkness, mystery, and a natural world that he apprehended almost instinctively in terms of his own psyche. "In the significant moments of his life," it has been said, "[he] was confronted not by an inanimate and impersonal nature – not by an 'It' but by a 'Thou.'"[7]

Nature was alive; it was to the peoples of the Classical world "full of gods" or "full of Jupiter"; it expressed, both in its benign cyclical rhythms and in its intimidating and catastrophic upheavals, the movements and indwelling of the divine. Hardly surprising, then, that man himself should be conceived less as an individual standing ultimately alone than as an integrated part of society, deriving therefrom whatever value he possessed. Hardly surprising, either, that society itself should be conceived as imbedded in nature, as entangled intimately with the processes of the natural world. Hardly surprising, again, that its primary function should be something that exceeded the powers of any individual – namely, the preservation of the cosmic order by a complex system of ritual and taboo, the prevention of natural catastrophes, the seasonal regeneration of the world via the ritual elaboration of New Year festivals, and the "harmonious integration" of humankind with nature. That is to say, nature being but a "manifestation of the divine," it is hardly surprising that the *primary* function of society (the family, the tribe, and ultimately what *we* would call "the state"), the first object of its anxious, daily solicitude, should be what *we*, again, would call "the religious."

15

Characteristic of the form of religiosity involved was the symbolization of our familiar "profane" space and time via the analogy of the all-embracing spatial and temporal order of the cosmos itself to which it was typically related as microcosm to macrocosm. To that cosmic order, to the repetitive movements of the heavenly bodies and the cyclic rhythms of vegetative nature, the forms, laws, and procedures of terrestrial political society were, then, intuited as analogous. So far, indeed, as mundane objects in the external world and human acts alike were concerned, they were understood as deriving whatever value they possessed from their participation in the celestial archetypes and forms of "reality" that transcended them.

Thus terrestrial structures like temples, sacred places, royal palaces, cities, were regarded as having been fashioned on the model of celestial or cosmic prototypes. They were often assimilated, ideologically speaking, to the cosmic mountain which was understood to have emerged from the primordial waters at the creative moment when a god or gods had rescued cosmos from chaos. They were understood, moreover, to be situated at the very *axis mundi*, the hub, center, or navel (*omphalos*) of the world, the numinous intersection of heaven and earth. In Maya terms the portal of the Otherworld; in Mesopotamian terms the point of contact with the gods. The name Babylon (Bāb-ilāni) itself means "gate of the gods," and the ziggurats of Mesopotamia as well as the pyramids of Egypt and Mesoamerica symbolize the primal cosmic mountain and represent the numinous *axis mundi*.

If this was the case with terrestrial structures something similar was true of human acts. "Just as profane space is abolished by the symbolism of the Center, which projects any temple, palace, or building into the same central point of mythical space," Mircea Eliade has said, "so [too] any meaningful act performed by archaic man, any real act, i.e. any repetition of any archetypal gesture, suspends duration, abolishes profane time, and participates in mythical time."[8] This was exemplified quintessentially by the New Year festivals of the ancient Near East which were devoted to the symbolic "regeneration" of time, and which characteristically involved a dramatic ritual in which the king, as earthly representative or son of the creative god, was understood not merely to *memorialize* the primordial creative act, the establishment of cosmos and the defeat of the forces of chaos, but also in some profound sense to "reactualize" that great cosmogonic moment. For it was the king who, as himself a divinity (thus Egypt, Japan, Mesoamerica) or as son or earthly representative of the divinity (thus Mesopotamia, China, and elsewhere), was burdened with the heavy responsibility for ensuring by a ceaseless round of ritual and sacrifice the good order, not merely of human society, but of the cosmos at large in which human society was so deeply embedded.

At the heart of primitive and archaic "politics," then, lay one form or another of the cosmic "religion" – so much so, indeed, that for the greater part of human history it is an egregious anachronism even to make use of those words, the very definitions of which presuppose our modern Western distinction between the religious and the political and evoke misleading intimations of the modern church–state dialectic. This becomes unmistakably evident if one takes the trouble to examine archaic concepts of kingship, which were conceived in China and Mesoamerica no less than in the ancient Near East and elsewhere as an institution "anchored in the cosmos." "If we refer to kingship as a political institution," Henri Frankfort has said,

> we assume a point of view which would have been incomprehensible to the ancients. We imply that the human polity can be considered in itself. The ancients, however [and as we have seen], experienced human life as part of a widely spreading network of connections which reached beyond the local and national communities into the hidden depths of nature and the powers that rule nature. The purely secular – insofar as it could be granted to exist at all – was the purely trivial. Whatever was significant was imbedded in the life of the cosmos, and it was precisely the king's function to maintain the harmony of that integration.[9]

Frankfort was speaking here with explicit reference to the ancient Near East, but evidence for the existence of sacral kingship and versions of the cosmic religiosity that sustained it is broadcast across the globe in regions as far distant one from another as Ireland and the Sudan, India and Peru, Scandinavia and Polynesia, West Africa and China. The Chinese empire, indeed, the successive geologic deposits of Taoist, Confucian, and Buddhist patterns of thought notwithstanding, proved in the long haul to be the most stable and enduring manifestation of what has been called the "ontocratic state" or state as "the embodiment of the cosmic totality," with the emperor "identified with the cosmic center, which was also the place of the ancestors."[10] Thus, for two millennia and more, and independently of analogous developments elsewhere in Eurasia and Mesoamerica, it remained the emperor's duty, as Son of Heaven and possessor of the mysterious "mandate of Heaven," to bridge the gulf between heaven and earth and, by scrupulously performing a cyclic round of rituals and sacrifices, to secure the maintenance of order, cosmic no less than natural, natural no less than societal. As late as October 6, 1899, the *Peking Gazette* carried a decree in which the emperor confessed his own sinfulness as the likely cause of drought in the land.[11] The structure of the altars of earth and heaven to the north and south of the imperial palace at Beijing, at which the emperor offered sacrifice at the summer and winter solstices respectively, was "meant to indicate the cosmic totality at the center of which the emperor dwells as the all-commanding axis [*mundi*] on which both the order of the universe and that of society and the state depend."[12] Comparable arrangements prevailed at the Vietnamese imperial capital of Hué, and the ceaseless round of imperial sacrifices at both Beijing and Hué were destined to continue on into the twentieth century (until 1912 and 1915 respectively).

What was presupposed by all of this, and despite the successive religious and ideological accretions of centuries, was clearly a variant of what we have called the cosmic religiosity. And such, indeed, was the quasi-universality of one or other version of that cosmic religiosity, and of the royal cultic practices grounded in it, that commentators of Jungian sympathies have understandably been tempted to see them as reflecting Jungian "archetypes of the collective unconscious," patterns hard-wired, as it were, into the very structure of the human psyche itself. From that point of view "the cosmology of myth" can be understood as nothing other than "the exteriorized self-portrayal of the inner psychic world," and "the complex ritual of renewal in the seasonal festivals of archaic times" viewed as "composed of the same elements as the reconstitutive process in the psyche, the one faithfully mirroring the other."[13] But however marked the universality of such phenomena, it must be insisted that it is not without its limits. And those limits preclude the acceptance of views so all-embracing in their reach. The origins of the institution of cosmic kingship and religiosity may well be lost to us in the deep shadows of prehistory, but their decline and demise in the modern era are not. They have taken place, instead, in the unforgiving glare of contemporary scrutiny. They form a recognizable part of the historical record and that fact is not to be ignored.

Rather than being wired, then, into the unchanging uniformities of nature, cosmic kingship and its attendant religiosity are lodged instead amid the shifting contingencies of history. But if their formidable lifespan, however remarkable, has proved in the end to have met its term, it has proved also to have been distinguished over the years and across the distant reaches of the globe by an impressive measure of creative variety. In what has gone before, we have been able to select for scrutiny only a few central threads of what developed over millennia into an intricate and richly variegated tapestry. It is time now to take a look at a few of the sub-patterns which came, over the vastnesses of time and space, to be woven around those central threads. We will do so by focusing briefly and in turn on several cases of sacral kingship drawn from widely scattered locations around the globe and spanning (collectively) no less than five millennia of the human odyssey. The exercise will be the more valuable in that it will serve also to highlight disparities in the types and amounts of evidence available to us as we seek to come to terms with the cases in question.

East Asia: Imperial Japan (Seventh to Twenty-first Centuries)

Although they are compilations which draw on earlier documents now lost to us, as well as on much more ancient oral traditions, the oldest Japanese writings extant are the earliest chronicles – the *Kojiki* or "Record of Ancient Matters" (711–12 CE) and the *Nihongi* or "Chronicles of Japan" (c.720). Along with the later *Kogoshūi* (806–7), and via a combination of myth, legend, and history, they together trace the origins of the Japanese empire all the way back to the primordial decision of the *kami* or great ancestral deities to send down to earth from heaven the grandson of the sun-goddess, Amaterasu-ō-mikami, charging him with the conquest of the realm and promising him that the imperial succession would continue "unbroken and prosperous, coeternal with heaven and earth."[14] The legendary first emperor, Jimmu (660 BCE), his equally mythical prehistoric successors, and those who, from the sixth and seventh centuries CE, we can begin at last to discern in the intermittent light of recorded history stretching forward right down to the present, all came to be viewed as members of an imperial family with an unbroken and divine lineage stretching back to that originating moment of cosmic condescension.

The primordial divine promise and the endlessly repeated claims that the Japanese imperial office had remained in the same imperial family down through the ages to the present have naturally tempted observers to attribute a comparable degree of continuity to the lineaments of the imperial institution itself. Politicians, certainly, have not infrequently succumbed to that temptation. Thus Nakasone Yasuhiro, for example, sometime Prime Minister of Japan, did not hesitate to assure the Budgetary Commission of the Diet's Lower House in March, 1986, "that Japan has had the same tradition and culture for two thousand years and that the lives of the Japanese people have centered on the emperor throughout that history."[15] Similarly, the great imperial pageants of the era of Meiji restoration (1868 onwards) – the national holidays celebrating the emperor's birthday or the legendary accession of the Emperor Jimmu in 660 BCE, the Empire Festival celebrating the inception of rule over the nation by the sun-goddess's imperial descendants, the triumphal military reviews, the imperial funerals and weddings, the great imperial progressions throughout the nation's provinces (a practice renewed by the Shōwa Emperor Hirohito in February, 1946, less than two months after being forced publicly to disavow his divine status) – all such imperial ceremonial performances served as devices strengthening the cult of the emperor as the still point of the turning Japanese world, the very pivot or axis of the national unity and identity. Of course, all was not quite as it seemed. No less than the seemingly timeless pomp and ceremony surrounding the British monarchy (a good deal of it the work of imaginative and resourceful court liturgists during the last quarter of the nineteenth century), much of the "traditional" ceremonial round associated with the modern Japanese emperors represents, in fact, a quite self-conscious "invention of tradition" responding to contemporary European court practice and dating back no further into the past than the era of Meiji restoration itself.[16]

Much, it may be, but by no means all. Revisionism undoubtedly has its place, but on this matter, as on others, it can easily be taken too far. The controversy that broke out in Japan in 1990 concerning some elements of the accession rituals planned by the imperial court for the new Heisei emperor (the former Crown Prince Akihito) may serve as a salutary reminder that the Meiji inventors of tradition (in common with their counterparts in Britain) could hardly have been so successful in their endeavors had they not inherited an ancient core tradition on which they could readily build.

The English coronation liturgy used in 1953 to solemnize the accession of Queen Elizabeth II had, in fact, a millennial history stretching all the way back to the tenth-century Anglo-Saxon "Edgar *ordo*." An even greater antiquity has to be recognized in the elaborate imperial enthronement or accession ceremonies of Japan. At the accession of the Shōwa emperor those ceremonies were spread across the better part of two years (December 25, 1926 to November 30, 1928). They began with the *senso*, or formal transfer of the (divinely donated) imperial regalia and announcement of the succession before the sanctuary of the imperial ancestors and the shrines of the Sacred Regalian Mirror and of the gods of heaven and earth. And they proceeded via two other major moments. First, the *sokui-rei*, or ceremony of ascending the throne and announcing the succession to the gods of heaven and earth, to the spirits of the imperial ancestors, and to the nation and world at large. Second, the *daijō-sai*, or "Great New Food Festival," which was then followed by culminating ceremonies of sacred dances before the shrine of the Sacred Regalian Mirror and of worship by the emperor and empress at the shrine of the gods of Heaven and Earth and at the sanctuary of the spirits of the imperial ancestors.[17]

Although this whole round of accession ceremonies was suffused with the spirit of the ancient nature- and ancestor-oriented folk religion still embedded in state Shinto, public controversy in 1990 came to focus specifically on the *daijō-sai*. To that ceremonial moment representatives of the Christian denominations and of the socialist and communist parties all objected on the grounds that it involved an unconstitutional extension of state support to religion and,

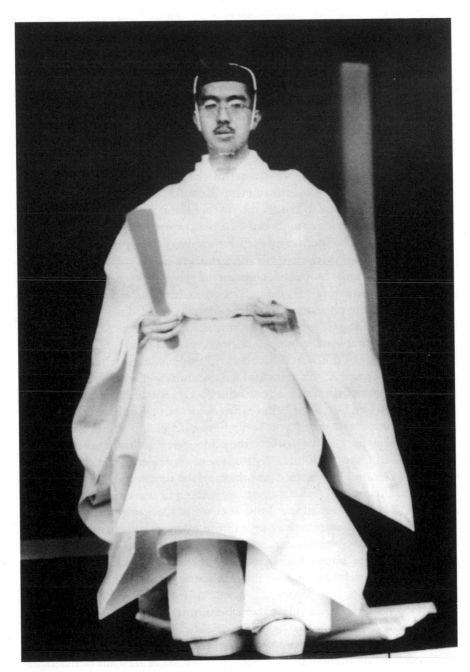

Figure 1 Japan. Emperor Hirohito during his enthronement in 1928. (Keystone, Hamburg)

as the Christians chose to put it, the transformation of "a ceremony of one specific religious sect [Shinto] into a state function."[18] Brushing off all such criticisms and claiming (without, one suspects, much conviction) that the ceremony in question was primarily a secular one, the government committed some 20 million dollars to fund the event, and it was attended (though at a requisitely discreet remove) by the Prime Minister himself, the members of his cabinet, and a goodly number of other Japanese public figures as well.

The outcome of the whole imbroglio was the focusing of a good deal of public attention and curiosity (some of it mildly, if anachronistically, prurient) on one of the most ancient and mysterious of Japanese imperial rites. If the ceremony of ascending the throne involves worship of the sun-goddess, Amaterasu-ō-mikami, and recalls the mythological dispatch to earth of her grandson, the first emperor, along with the imperial regalia, the *daijō-sai*, Holtom says, "and its [purifying] preparatory rites are deeply stamped with an interest in safeguarding the growth and fertility of crops." On that occasion, it was traditionally understood, the emperor, screened from the intrusion of any profane gaze, and acting "as the great representative of the people before the *kami*, by the act of presenting food [the specially planted and harvested first fruits], and by the partaking thereof himself," entered "into an intimacy of communion with spiritual powers." He was viewed as becoming, in effect, the very "repository of the sacred Rice Spirit," and, as such, "the sacred living *kami* in whose magical person is enfolded the entire welfare of his people."[19]

Do such archaisms, however engaging, warrant the degree of attention given to them here? Clearly I believe they do, and not simply because of their intrinsic interest. For they throw some light on a phenomenon that cannot simply be taken for granted, namely, the odd survival across the centuries and as a supposed fount of political legitimacy of an imperial office that, more often than not, and long before the advent of the Kamikura shogunate of the twelfth century, was in fact bereft of any real political power. Already in the Nara era (710–94), not all that long after the holders of the imperial office first emerge from the shadows of legend and myth into the light of recorded history, dictatorial leaders or regents drawn from the Soga and Fujiwara families had begun to arrogate to themselves the real governing power. By so doing they had established a governmental pattern that, with periodic fluctuations, was to dominate Japanese history down to the nineteenth century. Absent its crucial religious role, to which the accession rites continue powerfully to attest, the office of emperor could well have been destined to disappear altogether. But it did not do so, and its legitimating function was eventually to find regular and formalized symbolic expression in the accession ceremonies at which each successive Tokugawa shogun assumed his executive role. This tradition whereby the emperor (theoretically) delegated executive authority to the shogun alone made credible the way in which the Meiji restoration of 1868 was represented by the oligarchs who had engineered it, namely, as the moment when the emperor took back into his own hands the power he and his predecessors had previously condescended to confer on the shogunate. It served also to afford at least a thin veneer of credibility to the subsequent representation of the Meiji constitution of 1889 (as also, more surprisingly, that of 1947) as one "granted" by the emperor to the nation ("a gift of the emperor and his one line of ancestors"), thereby suggesting or affirming that he himself transcended it. An unmistakable echo, surely, of the traditionally mystical, reverential, and grandiose understanding of the nature of the imperial office.[20]

Equatorial Africa: The Kingdom of Kuba (Seventeenth to Twentieth Centuries CE)

Now incorporated into modern-day Zaire, the kingdom of Kuba (a name given to it by its neighbors to the south) occupied in its late nineteenth-century heyday an area roughly the size of Belgium. Its territory was bounded approximately by the Sankaru, Kasi, and Lunna rivers. With an overall population falling somewhere between 100,000 and 150,000 persons, it was ethnically diverse, including among others, and along with the dominant Kuba people, the aboriginal Keta and the pygmoid Cwa. Although a careful analysis of the oral traditions reveals that the Kuba had had a growing presence in the region stretching back already for hundreds of years, before the early seventeenth century they appear to have been organized simply as a congeries of chiefdoms. At that time, however, the outlines of a coherent kingdom begin to emerge. Indeed, the distinguished Africanist Jan Vansina has been able to trace the succession of kings belonging to the Matoon dynasty from Shyaam a Mbul a Ngong (c.1620, and much celebrated in the traditions) all the way down to his twentieth-century successors.

Since 1900 when the capital city fell to European invaders and the kingdom itself was absorbed into a colony, it has been devoid of any independent, sovereign status. Such was the unforgiving fate of many another African kingdom, of course, but some of them – the Shilluk, for example, of the Nilotic Sudan, or the Ashanti of Ghana, or the kingdom of Benin in West Africa – had already attracted the attention of Europeans and European scholars. As a result, they possess to this day a degree of name-recognition that Kuba still lacks. But the latter's achievement, it had been said, is "in many ways . . . comparable" with that racked up by "the kingdom of Benin from about 1500 onward," and it has, in effect, "been underrated in the history of Africa."[21] It was unique in having ridden out the great upheavals

23

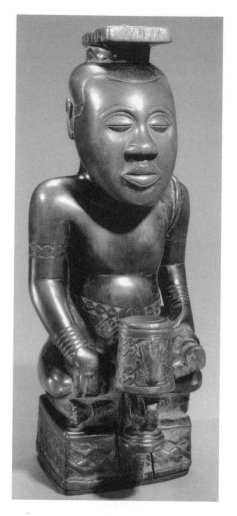

Figure 2 Africa, Kingdom of Kuba. *Ndop* portrait of King Mishe miShyaang maMbul. Eighteenth-century Bushoong Kuba, Democratic Republic of Congo, wood (*crossopterix febrifuga*), 19 1/2 × 7 5/8 × 8 5/8 in. (Brooklyn Museum. 61.33. Purchased with funds given by Mr and Mrs Alastair B. Martin, Mrs Donald M. Oenslager, Mr and Mrs Robert E. Blum, and the Mrs Florence A. Blum Fund)

Ndop wooden carving of King Shyaam aMbul aNgoong, Kuba-Bushoong, probably late eighteenth century, from the Democratic Republic of Congo (formerly Zaire). (© Copyright The Trustees of The British Museum) that had brought down other Central African states, leaving it, by the late nineteenth century, as the sole surviving kingdom in the region, and one possessed of a distinguished artistic tradition capped by a celebrated series of dynastic statues or revered royal "doubles." As a kingdom, it stands out also for its organizational and institutional complexity, as well as for the comparative clarity of what historians have been able to learn about its development from the oral traditions, from linguistic and ethnographic data, and from the written record which (apart from one or two earlier documents) becomes available only for the period from 1880 onwards. Whatever the case, by focusing on Kuba, it is possible to come away with a reasonably good sense of the nature of kingship in a "premodern" Central African setting – though (the evidence about it being quite fragmentary) with a less coherent sense of the pattern of religious thinking that that kingship presupposed.

The king, in whose person all governmental hierarchies culminated, was head of the centrally situated Bushoon chiefdom, the largest and most powerful of the country's several chiefdoms. Flanked on the east and west by much smaller and subordinate chieftaincies, it formed by 1880 the very core of the kingdom and accounted for somewhere in the neighborhood of 40 percent of land and population alike. No less than 10 percent of that overall population lived in the capital city which was itself capable of fielding enough military power to dominate the entire kingdom. Within the core region, and on a day-to-day basis, a constabulary composed of about 40 royal slaves and commanded by one of the king's sons sufficed to ensure that the government's edicts were respected. For emergency situations, whether within the kingdom at large or along (or beyond) its borders, the royal government could activate a formally organized and officered military force in excess of 2,000 men. That was enough, the record suggests, to maintain the real, effective unity of the kingdom and to ensure that it could properly claim to being something more coherent, governmentally speaking, than a merely loose-limbed confederation of chiefdoms.

That coherence is reflected in the kingdom's sophisticated apparatus of conciliar, administrative, judicial, and economic institutions and practices. This it was that made possible the achievement of a fine balance between two potentially competing phenomena – on the one hand, a high degree of participation by the various power groups in the several councils of the city and of the realm, and on the other, the ability of the king, acting via a "bureaucracy of title holders" (the *kolm*) and a judicial system of city tribunals and village moot-courts, to ensure that the rule of law prevailed, that his own edicts were enforced, that taxes were paid, that the required labor on public works was performed, and that the growing agricultural surpluses needed to support this whole governmental apparatus and to enlarge the royal treasury were indeed achieved. The introduction in the seventeenth century of higher-yielding American crops (maize, cassava, beans, chili peppers, etc.) and their rise to dominance by the nineteenth, the maintenance of trading connections with the Portuguese–African commercial network, the existence of a well-organized, well-protected, and well-policed system of internal markets, and the steady and effective application of pressure from the governmental center[22] – all such developments helped to generate those vital economic surpluses and to secure, thereby, the power of the king.

But if the kings of Kuba were possessed of a very considerable measure of power and were not afraid, if need be, to use it, the degree of support they appear to have received from their subjects was so strong and so enthusiastic as to suggest that it stemmed less from fear of punishment or hope for reward than from some deeply ingrained conviction concerning the fundamental legitimacy of the royal authority. And, as in so many other African kingdoms, the roots of that legitimacy were unquestionably engaged in what we would classify as "religious" soil.

We are not at all well informed about the nature and history of the Kuba religion, and the fragmentary quality of the evidence surviving precludes any truly confident grasp of its development across time. By the nineteenth century an earlier cult of the ancestors appears to have become marginal, or even to have disappeared, and been replaced by a belief in metempsychosis. Similarly, although the worship of the *ngesh* (nature-spirits), believed to dwell in forests, rivers, and springs and to have a degree of control over fertility, was still alive and well into the 1950s, those spirits appear, across time, to have increasingly been seen as subordinated to the power of the supreme creator-deity, Ncyeem, to whom ritual sites located in every village were dedicated. For our purposes, it must suffice to note that both the *ngesh* and the creator-god figured centrally in the ideology of kingship. And about that, at least in its nineteenth- and early twentieth-century form, we are somewhat better informed than we are about Kuba religion at large.

The king of Kuba was the lineal descendant of the great Shyáám, the early seventeenth-century king who was portrayed in the traditions as the great culture-shaper of Kuba and as a great shaman-like figure possessed of some of the attributes of a priest of the nature spirits. He was also the allegedly lineal descendant of the man whom the nature spirits had chosen to be "chief of chiefs." To those potent forms of legitimation had come to be added, in the post-seventeenth-century "age of kings", the belief that the king was to be identified with Kap aNgaam, the nature spirit (and Bushong ethnic spirit) who dwelt in the sun, and, further, that he had received his power from the creator-god himself.

Thus the poem:

26

My eagle is the eagle of the *ngesh* of the forest,
My kingship stems from Nyony a Mboom,
It is Ncyeem who has given this kingship
   into my hands.[23]

The solemn rituals involved in a royal installation reflected the significance of such credentials. They were spread across an entire year and involved, among other things, the king's meeting in the forest at night with *muyum*, the keeper of what may be described as the royal regalian charms (including the skullcap of one of the royal predecessors) which were regarded as yet another source of royal power.

The Kuba king, then, was unquestionably a sacred figure. Despite the disappearance of an ancestor cult among the Kuba at large, there had persisted (or emerged) a cult of the nature spirits of the deceased royal ancestors, and that cult may have involved the display of the celebrated dynastic statues (or doubles). The king was encumbered by ritual prohibitions (he could not eat in the presence of his wives, could not cut across a field, could not seat himself on the bare ground, and so on). These taboos were viewed as necessary to protect the powers he possessed over rain, the fertility of the land, and the fertility of women. Such powers were viewed as similar to those of the moon, which, as elsewhere in Africa, was itself linked with the fertility of the land. At the new moon every month, the king was called upon to perform in the seclusion of the royal compound a ritual sacrifice for the wellbeing of the kingdom. The order of things, which it was his duty to guarantee, was viewed as extending well beyond the political, legal, social, and economic, reaching into the depths of nature and touching the cosmos itself. It comes as no surprise, then, that a "patterned anarchy" should ensue upon the announcement of a royal death, for without a king, it was believed, society itself would wither away. In the late nineteenth century, at least, the king was clearly something more exalted than "the lieutenant of God," which was all that Mbop Mábíínc maMbéky (the royal incumbent in 1953) was willing to claim to be. Instead, he was *Ncyeem akwoonc,* "god on earth," a being in some profound sense responsible, it may be, for life itself. As one man put it: "If I sleep it is the king; if I eat it is the king; if I drink it is the king."[24]

Mesoamerica: The Maya Kingship of the Classic Period (250–900 CE)

Of the great Mesomerican civilizations that trace their roots back to the ancient Olmec "mother culture," the Maya has emerged in recent years as in some ways the most striking. Not least of all because "as much as 85 percent of the total body of Classic Maya inscriptions can now be 'read'," and "the ancient Maya . . . [have become] . . . the only truly historical civilization of the New World, with records going back to the third century after Christ."[25] Their civilization flourished, somewhat improbably, in the swampy lowland of what is now Belize, in Guatemala, and part of southern Mexico, as well as in the drier and thin-soiled lowland of the Yucatan peninsula, and in the uplands and Pacific coastal region embracing stretches of modern Guatemala, Honduras, El Salvador, and Chiapas, Mexico. After a long formative period stretching back to the beginnings of forms of settled village life in the early second millennium BCE, the Maya civilization entered on what is usually described as its Classic Period (250–900 CE), and endured until the traditional order slid into decline and eventual dissolution under conditions marked by mounting population pressure, environmental degradation, incessant warfare, and what is sometimes described as a transition to more "secular" cultural forms.

That traditional order, which crystallized in the late pre-Classic and early Classic era, was anything but secular in character. It centered on a multitude of small city-states with constantly shifting rivalries and alignments and ruled by kings. At the height of the Classic Period there were more than 50 of these independent states, embracing altogether an area in excess of 100,000 square miles and ruling over a population of farmers, merchants, skilled urban craftsmen, warriors, and aristocrats running into the millions. These Maya kingdoms pivoted on capital cities organized around cultic or ceremonial sites often of considerable grandeur and maintained or serviced by urban populations running into tens of thousands (in the case of Tikal, at its peak the largest of the kingdoms, probably somewhere in excess of 60,000). Prominent among the kingdoms in the late pre-Classic and Classic eras were Tikal, Uaxactún, El Miradur and Palanque in the southern lowlands, Copán to the east, and Cerros to the north.

Once viewed, at least in comparison with the Aztecs, as a peace-loving, somewhat Utopian, society ruled by priests, the Maya have emerged in recent years, as their complex writing and the programs of hieroglyphs on their monuments have progressively been deciphered, as a somewhat more typical people. They were socially hierarchical and extremely warlike; human sacrifice and ritual (auto) bloodletting played a very important role in their cultic life, and they appear in the Classic Period not to have had a distinct priestly "order." That mediatorial role was played, instead, by the kings themselves. Possessed of extensive powers, the kings were charged with a broad array of military, administrative, judicial, economic, and, above all, ritual and religious functions. These last occupied a central place in the life of the Maya, and the kings' ability to discharge such crucial functions was the key factor serving to legitimate their rule. In their drive to erect the great acropolises that dominated their capital cities, they must have made on aristocrats and commoners alike truly enormous demands. And yet they seem not to have felt the need to maintain either police forces or standing armies. Instead, they clearly felt themselves able to rely on the willingness of their subjects to commit themselves to such vast and burdensome enterprises. Hence the obvious question: whence came that willingness?

The answer almost certainly lies in the nature of the Maya kingship, in the sacral status the Maya characteristically accorded to their king as "great sun lord" (*Mah K'ina*), "Holy Lord" (*ch'ul ahau*), or "Lord of Lords" ("an *ahau* of the *ahauob*"). "The rituals of the *ahauob* [nobility]," Schele and Freidel have said,

> declared that the magical person of the king was the pivot and pinnacle of a pyramid of people, the summit of a ranking of families that extended out to incorporate everyone in the kingdom – from highest to lowest. His person was the conduit of the sacred, the path of communication to the Otherworld, the means of contacting the dead, indeed of surviving death itself. He was the clarifier of the mysteries of everyday life, of planting and harvesting, of illness and health. . . . The people reaped the benefits of the king's intercession with the supernatural world and shared in the material wealth his successful performance brought to the community.[26]

If that performance was certainly played out on the battlefield or in the negotiation for his subjects of favorable trade agreements, it was enacted quintessentially in the rites and sacrifices that punctuated the year (with a New Year's festival being probably the central moment) and called for the erection of the great complexes of platforms, pyramids, plazas, and temples upon which so much royal attention was lavished. For "like the trees of the four directions, which raise up the sky over the earth, the king was the central pillar – the Tree of Life who raised the sky that arched over his entire realm."[27]

This last statement is a revealing one. It is pertinent both to the nature and function of the pyramids and temples and to the ceaseless round of rites and sacrifices the kings themselves performed in those settings. These ceremonial centers were constructed as microcosmic images of the macrocosm, "stylized representations of the four-quartered universe," oriented to "astronomical events such as the solstices, equinoxes, and Venus cycles," aligned with points on the horizon where the sun and Venus (the latter recognized as both the morning and evening star) would predictably make their appearance.[28] Looking back to the primordial sacred landscape as it had appeared at the creation, the pyramids or platforms on which they built their temples

29

Figure 3 Maya. Tikal, Temple One; Archaeoastronomy teaches us that this planetary alignment of Jupiter, Venus, and Mars above Temple One at Tikal will not occur again for some 300 years. The Classic period city in the jungle of the Guatemalan Peten region was one of the most powerful imperial cities of the Maya. Today, Tikal is a destination atop the list of travelers who wish to study the ancient culture of the Maya. (Kenneth Garrett)

represented the sacred mountain. Each centered on an *axis mundi* (or hub of the world), the World Tree, which the divine father had used at creation to lift the sky up above the earth, and which constituted the numinous point of contact with the divine, the conduit between the celestial overworld, the earthly middle world, and Xibalba, the dark underworld of the dead.

With that World Tree, as monumental representations make clear, the king was himself symbolically identified. He was, in effect, "the axis and pivot made flesh."[29] If the physical layout and orientation of the temple mount evoked in microcosm the lineaments of the macrocosm, so, too, embedded as they were in the cyclicity of time, did the ritual performances of the king reiterate the archetypical divine gestures of the mythopoeic past – such as the lifting of the sky above the earth, or, again, the "harrowing of hell" by the Hero Twins, their defeat by trickery of the Dark Lords of Death, and their subsequent ascension into the sky where one of them, like all subsequent Maya kings, became identified with the life-giving jaguar sun-god, the other with Venus. Thus, at the dedication of the temple, it fell to the king to preside over the erection of the World Tree, a ceremony by which the cosmogonic moment was reactualized. And by the ritual acts he performed on the temple mount, some of them witnessed by his subjects assembled in the great plaza surrounding it, whether those acts involved the letting of his own blood, or the offering of human or animal sacrifices, or both, he opened up the portal of the Otherworld and, as the great mediator for his people, drew into ecstatic communion with him the ancestors, gods, divine forces, upon whose benevolent engagement success in war, the fertility of the land, the wellbeing of the kingdom, and the very order of the cosmos itself all depended.

About the Maya pantheon itself, various uncertainties remain. And it is certainly the case that the "cosmovision" we have been discussing is an exceedingly complex and sometimes quite baffling affair.[30] In order, then, to convey a reasonably accurate "feel" for what was involved, it may be preferable to refrain from further generalization about the Maya religious vision at large, and to conclude instead by focusing briefly, and by way of illustration, on the cultic performance of the king in just two of the multiple kingdoms about which historians and anthropologists have, over the past several decades, become increasingly well informed. The first is Cerros, a kingdom which came into existence in the late pre-Classic period; the second, Palenque, a kingdom of outstanding importance during the Classic period, one which enjoyed its golden age in the seventh century CE, and one for which the archaeological record established in the past half-century is particularly rich and revealing.

So far as Cerros is concerned, let me simply draw attention to the fact that the construction, astronomical alignment, and emblematic program of the first temple (c.50 BCE) was such as to align with the celestial path of the sun and of Venus the (clockwise) ceremonial progression of the king from an inner sanctum in the east to the entrance to the temple at the front of the pyramid on which it was built. Into the façade on the "front" or plaza side, were set four great masks. Two of them represented the jaguar sun-god as he rose and as he set; the other two represented Venus in the guise, respectively, of the morning and the evening star. The decoration of the temple, then, was "a model of the sun's daily path," and something more than that. It was also "a depiction of the Ancestral Twins," one of whom, it will be recalled, was symbolized by the sun, the other by Venus. And the whole was so designed and presented that it could be read in that way by the king's subjects assembled in the plaza below. In effect, when, having completed his ritual bloodletting on their behalf and showing himself now to the people,

> the king stood upon the stairway between the four great masks [on the front face of the pyramid], he represented the cosmic cycle of the day, but he was simultaneously at the center of a four-part pattern representing the lineage cycle of the Hero Twins as his [divine] founding ancestors.[31]

The ancestral Hero Twins also figured large in the Temple of Inscriptions which Pacal, the great, long-reigning king of Palenque, constructed in the last decade of his life, and which remains one of the most celebrated of the many extraordinary monuments surviving in the Mesoamerican region. How could it not be such, when the king-lists which decorate the pyramid-temple-tomb were extended by Pacal's son, Chan-Bahlum, to encompass not only the mythical founder of the dynasty but also "the divinities who established the order of the cosmos at the beginning of this current manifestation of the [cyclical] universe"?[32] Many of those royal ancestors are depicted on the richly decorated lid of the great sarcophagus which Pacal had himself provided for. And the central image on that lid represented Pacal's fall at death

> down the great trunk of the World Tree into the open jaws of the Other-world. At the same time . . . a sense of resurrection [is incorporated] into this death image. As Pacal falls, he is accompanied by a bowl of sacrifice marked with the glyph of the sun. . . . Like the sun, the king would rise again in the east after his journey through Xibalba. He was, after all, the living manifestation of the Hero Twins who had set the example of how to defeat the Lords of Death.[33]

Those of us endowed by nature with a robustly commonsensical temperament (though commonsensical, we should not forget, in a specifically modern, Western fashion) may well be tempted to dismiss such classic Maya cultural moments as mere pieces of esoterica, in themselves, no doubt, intriguing enough, but with no more than marginal pertinence to the gritty realities of political life. We would be unwise, however, to yield to any such temptation. The extraordinary investment of time, effort, economic resources, artistic creativity, and religious energy made throughout the Maya world in order to frame and set the stage for such royal performances and events attests powerfully to their importance and to the cultural and political significance attaching to them. It attests also to the fundamentally sacral nature of the Maya kingship and to the centrality of the mediatorial role Maya kings were called upon to play in their cyclically repeated ritual efforts to align the microcosm of human society with the divinely constructed macrocosmic order, and to integrate humankind into a "natural" order that was itself impregnated with the divine.

Western and Northern Europe: Celtic and Germanic Kingship prior to the Advent of Christianity (from the Fourth to the Eleventh Centuries CE)

It was during the period stretching from the fourth to the eleventh centuries that Christianity became the dominant religion in western and northern Europe. It took hold first in the lands that were (or had been) provinces of the Roman Empire, spread thence into Ireland, Scotland, and (later) northern Europe, with the culminating evangelization of Norway and Sweden gathering momentum in the tenth century and reaching its term by about 1100. Historians attempting to assess the nature of Celtic and Germanic kingship in the pagan era prior to those centuries of evangelization have often found themselves, given the nature, provenance, and paucity of the evidence surviving, confronting interpretative challenges of an unusually testing kind. Generalization has proved frequently to be difficult, agreement often elusive. But if a nervous caution nips persistently at the heels of those seeking to address the continental center, a higher degree of confidence is available to those whose interest is focused on the insular or the northern periphery. It is with the periphery, then, that we would be wise to begin.

The sacral character of the kings of pre-Christian Ireland is not in dispute. In common with their Celtic counterparts elsewhere, the pagan Irish did not themselves commit their lore to writing. One has to quarry the pertinent information instead from the ancient Irish law tracts, and from the historical traditions and epic tales recorded for posterity by later Christian redactors. But whatever the degree of Christian "overpainting", those writings are far from having been completely depaganized, and the outlines of the picture that emerges when the overlay is removed, while less complete than one might like, is comparatively clear and consistent.

33

"The Irish law tracts," Binchy tells us "still show a rural society consisting of a congeries of petty kingdoms, each governed by a *rí* (king),"[34] who was selected from among "the royal kindred," those possessed of the inherited royal blood. The priestly and judicial functions of kingship passed, with time, into the hands of castes of learned specialists. But it seems likely that in the small Irish *tuath* (or primary territorial unit) the king originally functioned not only as its leader in war, to whom his subjects owed military service and tribute, but also as its lawgiver and judge; and not only as its representative in dealings with other kingdoms but also as its representative before the gods, its sacral mediator with the divine forces upon which the wellbeing of his people depended.

The importance attaching to the solemn royal rites of inauguration speaks powerfully to the centrality among the king's responsibilities of that religious function. Those inaugural rites took place at multiple sites scattered across Ireland and traditionally viewed as sacred. In a manner familiar to us from other cultures, each of them was identified as the center of the world, marked by the *bile* or great tree which stood in microcosm for the *axis mundi* or hub of the universe itself. Of these sites the most celebrated was that at Tara, located in *Midhe* (i.e. "middle"), the central province of Ireland, at the confluence of the other four provinces, and functioning as the center of "a cosmographic schema which has parallels in India and other traditions." Indeed, "the traditional accounts of the disposition of the court of Tara," reveal it to have been "conceived as a [microcosmic] replica of this cosmographic schema."[35] And at that center or numinous point of contact with the divine, was periodically held the great "feast of Tara" (*Feis Temhra*) at which was celebrated the inauguration of a new king and his ritual or symbolic mating with the (earth) goddess Medb. Appropriately enough, the inauguration is referred to as *banais ríghi*, "the wedding-feast of kingship."

Comparable rites of inauguration and related fertility rites took place in the other Irish kingdoms (as also, at the other end of the Indo-European world, in India). They affirmed the sacral character of the king, encouraged, doubtless, the well-attested constriction of his freedom of movement by taboos of one sort or another, and strengthened the degree to which he was held responsible for the fertility of the land, the favorable nature of the weather, and the abundance of crops.[36] And while it would be improper simply to suppose that Irish patterns of thought and behavior were identical with those of the Brythonic Celts of Wales or the Celts of continental Europe, the shards of evidence we do possess for the lives of those related peoples in the pre-Christian era strongly suggest that their kings, too, were sacral figures.[37]

Something similar may be said about the kings of the Scandinavian north.

Though late in date, and subject to Christian influences, the evidence concerning them is comparatively plentiful. As a result, there is enough scholarly consensus for one scholar to insist "That kingship in Old Scandinavia is entirely sacral is nowadays considered as a mere matter of fact."[38] That may be a little over-confident, but in a traditional society possessed of its own version of the cosmic religiosity, with the cosmic tree Yggdrasill marking the center of the divine world, upholding the universe while at the same time reaching down with its roots to both the world of man and the world of death, it is hardly surprising that the Scandinavian monarchs played a prominent role in the religious cult. They performed *blót* or sacrifice not simply "in order to provide for a good and fertile year . . . but [beyond that] to provide for a year to come" serving thereby as the "creator of a new year."[39] Regarded as being of divine descent, they were sometimes revered as gods after their death and, in accord with the pattern familiar to us from so many other parts of the world, were held responsible for the rotation of the seasons, the fertility of the land, and the general wellbeing of their subjects. Such notions were so deeply ingrained, indeed, and their half-life so very long, that as late as 1527 King Gustav Wasa could complain bitterly at a meeting of the Reichstag of Västerås that "the Swedish peasants of Dalarna blamed him if bad weather prevailed – as if he were a god and not a man."[40]

Consensus evaporates, however, when one turns to the Germanic kingship in western and southern Europe during the late imperial age and the subsequent age of barbarian migration. It being a period of great turbulence, the picture that emerges is understandably more complex and confused. The evidence from which it has to be reconstructed is much more fragmentary, and the interpretive challenge exacerbated by the fact that the scanty written record is powerfully shaped by the essentially Roman and/or Christian preoccupations and perceptions of the various authors involved. Given the fact that the Germanic peoples shared a common Indo-European inheritance with the Celts and were also, over an extended period of time, close enough neighbors (or even intermingled) with them for some of their traditions to develop in tandem, it would seem natural enough to assume the presence of sacral kingship among them in the pre-Christian era. The more so, indeed, if one takes into account the testimony of cultural anthropologists and students of comparative religion to the ubiquity of that institution. In the past, however, historians of late antique and early medieval Europe have proved to be somewhat resistant to any such conclusion. They have tended to take their stand on the paucity of direct evidence available to sustain it, and, while so doing, to deny the legitimacy of any appeal either to the later Scandinavian evidence or (still less) to cross-cultural analogies.

Here, however, one of the brisk methodological observations that the late anthropologist A.M. Hocart was prone to making is particularly apposite. Commenting admiringly on the way in which the astronomer "coolly reconstructs the history of the solar system for millions of years from observations of the present only," he slyly contrasted that celestial endeavor with the way in which the terrestrial historian insists, in distinctly sublunary fashion, on pinning "his faith to direct evidence, to the writings of eyewitnesses, to coins, to ruins." Distrusting circumstantial evidence, the historian, he says, persists instead in clinging "to his direct evidence as a timid sailor to the coast."[41] The point is well taken and it encourages one to insist, given the ubiquity and longevity of the sacral monarchy, that the burden of proof should properly lie, not (as historians have tended to assume) on the shoulders of those who claim its presence among the Germanic peoples of the pre-Christian era south of the Baltic, but rather on those who stubbornly persist in denying it, by so doing insisting on the historical "exceptionality" of the Germanic political experience.

Behind that reluctance, one cannot help feeling, lurk shadowy remnants of the old Teutonic racial myth, the belief – as Bishop Stubbs had put it in 1880, evoking the authority of Caesar's *De bello gallico* and Tacitus's *Germania* – that the English somehow inherited freedom with their Germanic blood, and that in "the common germs of German institutions" were to be found the origins of the elements of representation and consent destined ultimately for so glorious a future in the providential flowering of English constitutionalism.[42] But, then, there is no good reason for assuming that because Germanic kings were so often "elected", or because limitations of various sorts were placed upon their power, they might not also be regarded as truly sacral kings.[43]

After all, in what has been dubbed "the first Indo-European contribution" to the development of ideas of kingship, the Hittite *pankuš*, or assembly of nobles, which we know to have existed at least in the Old Kingdom (c.2700–2200 BCE), *may* have had a voice in "the making of the Hittite kings" and certainly "had jurisdiction over the king if the latter committed a crime." And this despite the fact that the Hittite king was unquestionably a fundamentally sacral figure "regarded during his lifetime as the incarnation of his deified ancestor" and worshipped after death as a god.[44] Nor should we indulge the anachronistic assumption that the *thing*, or popular assembly, which is described as choosing the Germanic or Scandinavian kings, was necessarily itself some sort of "secular" or "democratic" body, lacking a sacral status and bereft of sacral functions. Nor, again, should we assume that the act of "election," even apart from the limitation of choice to members of royal families claiming divine descent, was itself devoid of a sacral dimension.[45] And as for limitations on the power of pagan Germanic kings in western and southern Europe, the most definite evidence that has come down to us again suggests very strongly that such limitations, like those suffered also by Irish and Scandinavian kings, sprang precisely from their sacral status. The king of the Burgundians, as the fourth-century Roman historian, Ammianus Marcellinus, tells us

> according to an ancient custom, lays down his power and is deposed, if under him the fortune of war has wavered, or the earth has denied sufficient crops; just as the Egyptians commonly blame their rulers for such occurrences.[46]

Despite, then, the grumbling persistence of scholarly disagreement on the matter, there really seems to be no compelling reason for denying to the Germanic kings of the pre-Christian era in the territories south of the Baltic a sacral status in some sense analogous to that which we know their neighboring Celtic counterparts to have possessed, as also, if centuries later, their royal counterparts in Scandinavia. "When the Germanic peoples entered the sphere of Christendom," Otto Höfler has rightly insisted, "they did not arrive as a 'religionless' multitude, but [as a people] shaped by an order of life in which the operation of religious forces and experiences can still be recognized."[47] So far as kingship is concerned, the operation of such forces can most clearly be recognized in the care with which a whole series of Germanic peoples – from the Ostrogoths to the Anglo-Saxons – handed down genealogies tracing the ancestry of their royal families back to mythical divine progenitors. It can be recognized, too, in the notion of sacred qualities inherent in the blood by virtue of which the election of kings was in fact limited to choice from among the members of the divinely descended royal dynasties – those, in effect, who were possessed of the royal *mana*, or what German historians have called *Geblütsrecht* or *Geblütsheiligkeit*. How seriously this was taken is strikingly illustrated by the story which Procopius relates concerning the two successive embassies that the Heruli, then living in Roman territory, sent back to their original homeland in the Germanic north in order to find among the members of the ancient royal family the king they needed. This king's perceived legitimacy turned out to be so potent that the entire army of the rival Heruli king, whom the Roman Emperor Justinian had meanwhile seen fit to appoint, proceeded to desert him and to go over to the contender possessed of *Geblütsheiligkeit*.[48]

The Ancient Near East: Kingship in Egypt and Mesopotamia (Third to First Millennium BCE)

In treating of institutions and ideologies possessed of nothing less than millennial careers it would be all too easy to "retroject" later, highly developed forms into their related, but much more inchoate predecessors. This is particularly easy in relation to the Egyptian and Mesopotamian civilizations, given the wholly extraordinary span of time during which they flourished, one which by comparison reduces the later lifespan of the Roman Empire to almost provincial proportions. The insensible transformation of institutions and ideologies from within; the repeated waves of invasions from without; in Egypt, the stately succession of dynasties punctuated by intermediate periods of chaos and confusion; in Mesopotamia, the bewildering succession of Sumerian, Akkadian Kassite, Hurrian, Assyrian, Chaldean (or neo Babylonian) rulers – clearly a great deal of change must inevitably have occurred under the carapace of institutional and ideological forms that from millennial distance can easily seem static and timeless. And change was no less celestial than terrestrial. Thus in Mesopotamia the Babylonian god Marduk came eventually to be assigned some of the roles the Sumerians had earlier assigned to Enlil, son of the sky-god, Anu. And in Egypt, where the earliest kings succeeded in uniting what came to be called Upper and Lower Egypt, they came also in some of the earliest texts to be identified not only with the sky-god Horus but with both Horus and Seth in their capacities as the rival gods of those "two lands." Similarly, later on, under the Old Kingdom (2815–2298 BCE) and with the rise to prominence of the sun-cult among the priests of Heliopolis (situated near the capital of Memphis), the Egyptian king came to be identified in life also with the sun-god, Ré and entitled "Son of Ré," just as, at death, he was identified with Osiris, the god-king who had died, been resurrected, and was linked with fertility and the restorative or "resurrective" function of the Nile.

Such shifts and developments are not to be ignored, and with them in mind I should acknowledge that what is said here will apply most accurately, so far as Egypt is concerned, to the Pharaohs of the Old Kingdom, and, so far as Mesopotamia is concerned, to the period of the Assyrian and Chaldean or neo-Babylonian empires (c.1300–539 BCE). At the same time, however, I should also acknowledge that one of the most striking features of these two archaic civilizations is the remarkable degree of continuity, stability, and uniformity they both manifested across the *longue dureé* of their millennial histories. During that extraordinary span of time they cherished and handed down in Mesopotamia an ideological framework that was essentially of archaic Sumerian provenance, while stolidly maintaining in Egypt a cluster of fundamental belief-structures whose origins can be traced back to those early years marked by the union and consolidation of the "two lands."

Both countries, of course, disposed of complex and sophisticated sets of institutions – legal, judicial, administrative, bureaucratic, military, and priestly. All of these institutions reflected an extensive delegation of functions and authority to subordinate officials, with the institution of the palace growing in importance across time in Mesopotamia, as also did the office of *tjaty* (or vizier) and *nomarch* (or provincial governor) in Egypt. All were subordinated ultimately to the king whose powers, in Mesopotamia, were extensive, and, in Egypt, all-embracing – so much so, indeed, that person, rank, status, liberty, even "private" property were all understood as royal "gifts." In the absence of more than a handful of surviving legal and administrative documents, about the exercise of that all-embracing power and the day-to-day functioning of the Egyptian kingship we know very little. About the functioning of the Mesopotamian monarchy, at least in its later Assyrian form and from the time of Hammurabi onwards (c.1792–58 BCE), we are much better informed. Royal correspondence, collections of laws, and official documents open a revealing window on the king's wide-ranging and detailed concern with governmental activities. In effect, it has been said, the sources permit us to see the Mesopotamian king "in active control of even subordinate officials stationed in distant cities of his empire, . . . investigating quite trivial complaints and disputes among the humbler classes of his subjects, and often sending back a case for retrial or for further report."[49]

In this respect the contrast evident between the Egyptian and Mesopotamian version of kingship may conceivably be, as much as anything else, an artifact produced by the differential survival rate in the two countries of the pertinent documentation. Whatever the commonalities, however, and we will touch upon them later, fundamental differences between the two kingships certainly did exist. From Rekhmire, the vizier of Thutmose III (c.1490–1436 BCE), has come down to us a classic definition of the Egyptian kingship, one that reflects enduring Egyptian attitudes towards their rulers. "What is the king of Upper and Lower Egypt?" he asked. And the answer: "He is a god by whose dealings one lives, the father and mother of all men, alone by himself without an equal." The king, in effect, was a god incarnate whose coronation, it has well been said, was not merely "an apotheosis" but rather, "an epiphany".[50]

The Egyptian kingship, then, was divine. It dated back to the very creation of the universe. It was embedded eternally in the cosmic order itself. Just as his dead father was identified with the god Osiris, the reigning king was at the same time the "Son of Ré," that is, royal successor to the sun-god, and the living incorporation of the sky-god, Horus. His very divinity precluded any

Figure 4 Egypt. The gold mask and trappings of the mummy of Tutankhamun. (Jürgen Liepe)

direct approach to his person and even any direct reference to him. To avoid the latter, resort was had to circumlocutions of one sort or another, prominent among them (and note the way in which we refer to the "White House") *per-aa* or "the Great House," from which our word "Pharaoh" derives. In Mesopotamia, in contrast, where the institution of kingship had been forged during the third millennium BCE in the crucible of internecine conflict among a congeries of city-states, the king, or *lugal*, was no more than a man. He was, nonetheless, a very "great man" (the literal meaning of the Sumerian *lugal*), a priestly figure, no incarnation of the gods, admittedly, but representative of them and wielding an authority that they were understood to have delegated to him.

Egyptian and Mesopotamian kings were often depicted as warrior kings, heroic leaders in battle, and we know some of them, certainly to have flourished in that role. But perhaps the most frequent and most significant battles in which they took part were symbolic ones, ritual battles of cosmogonic import. For whatever the differences between the two monarchies, and we have seen them to be real, both were underpinned by the enduring adhesion of their peoples to styles or variants of the cosmic religiosity.

Their most important responsibilities, then, extended far beyond what we today would classify as the political. Thus when we read that in Egypt Amenhotep III (c.1398–1344 BCE) strove "to make the country flourish as in primeval times by the designs of Maat" (a word usually rendered as "truth" or "right order"), we have to realize that what *maat* denoted was not simply human or societal justice but, rather, "the inherent structure of the cosmos, of which justice is an integral part." It was personified as a goddess – daughter "of the sun-god Ré whose regular circuit is the most striking manifestation of . . . [that] . . . established cosmic order." The rotation of the seasons, the annual rise of the Nile, the reinvigoration of the soil and the abundance of the crops which that ensured – all were understood to depend on the Pharaoh's faithful discharge of his ritual responsibilities. Playing a central role at all of the major agrarian rituals, "he was the god who brought fertility to Egypt." At his specific command, committed to writing and cast upon its waters, the Nile began each year to rise. "The Nile is at his service," it was said, "and he opens its caverns to give life to Egypt."[51]

The kings of Mesopotamia were called upon to shoulder similar responsibilities, though given the less predictable and frequently hostile physical environment in which they lived as well as the less exalted status which they themselves enjoyed, a greater anxiety attended upon their efforts. For them, the link between their person and the fertility of the land was a less direct one; it stemmed not from their own divinity but from the success with which they discharged the task of looking after the gods on behalf of their people.

41

This they did via a formidable cycle of cult festivals, rites, and offerings, one of the oldest of them being a fertility rite. Linked with the accession of a new king, it involved a sacred coupling of king and priestess, taking the roles, respectively, of the shepherd-god Dumuzi-Tammuz and the fertility-goddess Inanna, a marriage, in effect, "of the creative powers of Spring."[52]

The Sumerians and their successors often built their temples on imposing ziggurats or artificial mountains, and the Egyptians characteristically situated the holy of holies in their temples in a high place raised above the entrance. In so doing, both were echoing the symbolism of the cosmic or primeval mountain which, at the moment of creation, had emerged from the waters of chaos to become the center of the world. And it was the purpose of some of the most striking of the rites in which the Egyptian and Mesopotamian kings played a central role to "reactualize" that cosmogonic moment. In Egypt, the creation was ascribed to various gods, but quintessentially to the sun-god Ré, who, prior to his creation of the primeval or cosmic mountain, could be quoted as having said: "Only after I came into being did all that was created come into being. . . . The sky had not come into being; the earth had not come into being. . . . I found no place where I could stand." "The analogy with Ré," Frankfort notes, "is stressed especially at the coronation [of the Pharaoh], which can be regarded as the creation of a new epoch, . . . a situation, therefore, which partakes of the quality of the creation of the universe."[53] In Mesopotamia, similarly, the king played a central role in the protracted New Year's Festival celebrated at Babylon. On that occasion and at that city, the "gate," after all, "of the gods," was solemnly recited and in its entirety the great Babylonian creation myth, the *Enûma Elish*. The festival evoked, therefore, the analogy between the renewal or "recreation" which each New Year involved, and solemnly "reactualized" the cosmogonic struggle between cosmic order and primordial chaos – rendered as the great victory of the valiant king-god Marduk over "raging Tiamat," the terrifying sea-monster who represented the watery chaos. And it should be noted that the latter's very name is cognate to the Hebrew word *tehom* – "the deep" referred to in Genesis 1:2, itself part of the priestly account of creation woven into the post-exilic redaction of that book, and claimed by some scholars to have, in fact, been modeled on the opening lines of the *Enûma Elish*.

With that putative bridge between a remote Near Eastern civilization long since dead and the book that has endured on into the Western present as the revered focus of a living religious tradition, we must bring our series of case studies to a close. These brief studies will have served their purpose if, while illustrating the varied forms of sacral kingship that have contrived to flourish across the millennia and around the globe, they have also succeeded in con-

42

veying the degree to which one or other variant of what I have called the cosmic religiosity functioned throughout as the ideology undergirding all those forms. It is a matter of no little significance that that should have been true not only of the forms of kingship native to Egypt and Mesopotamia but also, in some measure at least, of those that came to the fore in the eastern Mediterranean region as a whole during the late antique era of cultural syncretism and cosmopolitan empire. For that is the background against which both Hellenistic and Hebraic ideas of kingship must be seen if they are properly to be understood. To those ideas we must now turn, as we begin the process of tightening the orbit of our inquiry and shifting the focus of attention from the global to the regional, from the world as a whole to the experience of Europe and the West.

2
Royal Saviors and Shepherds
Hellenistic, Roman, Biblical, and
Islamic Views of Kingship

As we begin the process of shifting the focus of attention from the world at large to Europe and the West, while we must necessarily dwell on Hellenic, Hellenistic, Judaic, and, in some measure, Muslim roots, in so doing we have to be careful. So far, at least, as patterns of kingship are concerned, we would be unwise simply to assume that we are destined to encounter any truly decisive departures from the archaic pattern of cosmic kingship that was so deeply entrenched in the ancient Near East and, during the late antique era of cultural syncretism and cosmopolitan empires, so widely diffused throughout the eastern Mediterranean region as a whole. Given the ubiquity and longevity of that pattern and of the cosmic religiosity that undergirded it, it is appropriate once more to insist, as we did with reference to the world of German paganism, that the burden of proof should properly be placed on the shoulders of those who argue for radical discontinuity or marked exceptionalism rather than of those whose interpretative instincts resonate to the more chastened frequencies of merely evolutionary change. If, methodologically speaking, that is a justifiable posture to adopt when approaching the political commitments of the classical or "Hellenic" period and of the "Hellenistic" centuries stretching from the ascendancy of Alexander the Great (d. 323 BCE) to the birth of Christ, it will surely be appropriate also when we come to address the Israelite kingship that emerged at the start of the first millennium BCE, and no less appropriate when we attempt to come to terms with the comparably uneasy notions of kingship prevalent later on among the followers of those other "Abrahamic" religions, Christianity, and Islam. That said, it is with Hellas that we must begin.

Hellenistic and Roman Sacrality

Of Plato, Mircea Eliade once perceptively remarked that "he could be regarded as the outstanding philosopher of 'primitive mentality,' that is, as the thinker who succeeded in giving philosophic currency and validity to the modes of life and behavior of archaic humanity."[1] Anyone who has read Plato's great dialogue, the *Timaeus*, in conjunction with the Babylonian *Enûma Elish* or the Egyptian *Memphite Theology* (all three of them creation myths embracing a theogony, cosmogony, and anthropogony) would, I suspect, be inclined to concur in that appraisal. Recognizing how often the long, retrospective Western engagement with the experience of the classical *polis* has lapsed into rampant anachronism, we might well be wise to approach that experience, as Eliade's insight suggests, rather from the perspective of what went before than from what came to be made of it in later centuries.

Given the fragmentary nature of the available evidence, this is, of course, easier to say than to do. And yet, in the context of the history of kingship, at least, and despite any affinity we may well feel for their republican way of life, it would be improper to regard the Greek city-states of the classical era as having marked any truly decisive break with the archaic sacral pattern so deeply ingrained in the ancient Near East and in greater or lesser degree throughout the eastern Mediterranean world. By the third millennium BCE a complex civilization had emerged on the island of Crete, which was linked commercially not only with the Greek mainland but also with Egypt and Asia Minor. By the mid-second millennium, under the influence initially of Minoan Crete, a civilized way of life had emerged also on the Greek mainland. It pivoted on a group of strongly fortified towns, the most prominent among them being Mycenae, like Crete a center of maritime commercial enterprise reaching out across the whole eastern Mediterranean. And although the great Homeric epics (in the form in which they have come down to us) are usually dated to around 750–650 BCE, scholars have commonly, if variously, argued that the world so vividly evoked in the *Iliad* and *Odyssey* is an older one. It may be, they have said, that it harks back to the Mycenaean Age of c.1400–1150 BCE, or, alternatively, that of the later "Dark Age" of Greek migration (c.1050–900 BCE) which witnessed the destruction of the Mycenaean civilization, or, yet again, that it reflects some complex amalgam evocative of conditions prevailing in both of those ages.

Whatever the case, it does seem that the political organization of both the Minoan and Mycenaean civilizations hinged upon a form of sacral monarchy which had much in common with that to be found broadcast right across the ancient Near East.[2] The Homeric kings, though their power was comparatively limited, are portrayed as hereditary kings, descendants of Zeus, himself

45

viewed as supreme king of the gods. They not only led their people in battle but served also as their chief priests, performing sacrifices on their behalf. So integral a part of their royal status were their sacral functions, indeed, that when, from the eighth century BCE onwards, the kings were in most places nudged to one side (Macedonia being a notable exception) and aristocratic *poleis* or city-states came to dominate the Hellenic political landscape, "the new states continued to regard the divine cult as one of the main bases on which the state should be built."[3]

As a result, it was now necessary for the chief magistrates to execute the priestly duties discharged formerly by the kings, and Plato himself notes that in some states – Athens being but one "striking example" – a special prominence was accorded to a particular officer who still bore the title of "king" (*archon basileus* or king-archon) and who was charged with the task of performing "the most solemn ancestral sacrifices" of the *polis*, in this respect functioning as "the heir of the Mycenaean priest-king."[4] In some of the city-states, moreover, the degree of continuity with the Mycenaean religio-political tradition is underlined not only by the fact that such religious ceremonies were still being performed by a kingly figure, but also by the specific types of ceremony being performed and by the particular sites at which they took place. Thus in many of the city-states the palaces of the former kings became, or were replaced on the same sites, by temples of the city's god. At Athens itself, Aristotle tells us in his *Constitution of Athens*, there remained a king or *archon basileus* who, among his other duties, supervised the Eleusinian mysteries with the assistance of four "curators," two of them chosen, respectively, from the Eleusinian Eumolpidai and the Eleusinian Kerukes – old priestly families which may have been of royal descent. At the Dionysian festival of the Anthesteria, moreover, the king-archon's wife was still required to contract a sacred marriage with the god Dionysus in the Boukolion, a building on the Acropolis which had once been the royal residence.[5] It was possibly on this occasion, E.O. James comments,

> that her marriage with the king was celebrated, and its object seems to have been to renew and ensure the processes of fertility over which Dionysus had control, as in the other sacred marriages of the king and queen in the seasonal ritual.

And his conclusion? Nothing other than the claim that

> the widespread and very deeply-rooted fundamental theme of the sacral kingship persisted in Greece in myth and ritual long after the monarchy had ceased to function as a political institution in the city-states.[6]

That being so, the ease with which during the Hellenistic era a return was made, albeit in more philosophical guise, to something roughly akin to the archaic pattern of sacral kingship hardly calls for the type of elaborate explanation which historians have frequently felt obliged to proffer. With the triumph of the Macedonian king Alexander the Great (336–323 BCE) over the Persian empire and its incorporation along with other territories into a vast Hellenistic empire, belief in the divinity or sacrality of emperors and kings came to exert a profound influence over the whole late classical world. Rooted already in the several successor kingdoms to Alexander's empire it went on, further to the west, to establish itself in the emerging empire of Rome. And it was able to do so precisely because it came not as an alien heterodoxy but as a return to a form of politics the ideological underpinnings of which had never fully been dismantled. That was no less true of Greece in the fourth century BCE than it was to be, later on, of Rome. The celebrated refusal in 327 BCE of the Greek and Macedonian soldiers at Alexander's coronation to perform the traditional Persian *proskynesis,* or act of obeisance in the presence of the god-king, can be explained as readily by the fact that they were being confronted with what was to them an innovation of alien Persian provenance as by any unambiguous antipathy to the ruler-cult as such. A strong case, indeed, can be made for believing that the idea of divinizing a living ruler as well as the very ruler-cult itself were by no means unfamiliar to them, but were rooted in traditional modes of Greek hero- and ancestor-worship. They drew sustenance also from the charismatic character commonly attributed to members of the Macedonian royal dynasty which in Alexander's own day still continued to trace its line of descent back to Heracles, son of Zeus.[7] More surprisingly, perhaps, even during the age of the *polis,* such notions and traditions lurked on the fringes of the really quite extensive discussion of the strengths of the monarchical governmental ideal that rumbled on at Athens during the course of the fourth century BCE and was fed by the contributions of such notable writers as Xenophon, Theophrastus, and (above all) Isocrates. While, then, archaic associations of the king's ritual performances with the fertility of the land and the abundance of crops had begun to fade, other echoes of the old cosmic religiosity were still to be heard.

Certainly, in the Hellenistic notion of the state as an analogue of the universe, with the king himself as an incarnate *epiphaneia* or manifestation of the divine ordering *logos* (or reason conceived to be immanent in the universe and analogous to the reasoning power in man), the Greeks themselves fashioned out of Pythagorean and Platonic as well as oriental materials their own more consciously philosophized version of sacral kingship. Bearing "the same relation to the state as God to the world," and the state being "in the same ratio to the world as the king is to God" (Diotogenes),[8] the king was conceived as "a dynamic and personal revelation of deity," a "living law" (*nomos empsychos; lex animata*), "himself the state, its constitution and its link with the world order." That vision was reflected in the writings of such Hellenistic theorists as Diotogenes and Ps.-Ecphantus the Phythagorean. It was reflected also in those of Plutarch later on, a man well acquainted with Hellenistic political literature in general, as also with some pertinent writings now lost to us. It was reflected again in the claims of the Hellenistic kings, Ptolemaic, Seleucid, and Parthian alike, to be themselves, the "shepherds" and "saviors" of their peoples and to be deserving of such elevated titles as "Benefactor," "Mediator," "*Theos Epiphanes*" – "god manifest" or, perhaps, "god incarnate."[9] It was a vision of regality that was destined for centuries to awaken potent memories in the Western political consciousness and to do so, above all, because it had proved capable of exerting a profound and progressively deepening influence upon Roman legal and political thinking.

That influence, and the general process of Hellenization of which it was but a part, were to reach their peak in the third century CE. By that time, however, they had already been at work for several centuries – from the latter part of the first century BCE, certainly, perhaps earlier. Even Octavian, react negatively though he might to Mark Antony's embrace of Hellenistic monarchy, did not prove himself to be altogether immune to the lure of such Hellenistic ideas. It is conceivable that his adoption as a *praenomen* of the title *imperator* (which we translate as "emperor") was modeled on the use which Hellenistic rulers were accustomed to make of *basileus* (king) as a first name. Similarly, in his decision to attach his official residence to the temples of Apollo and Venus we may again detect signs of eastern influence. Certainly, in the subsequent growth of the imperial cult and of the practice of divinizing emperors, that eastern influence remains unquestionably apparent.

As early as the first century BCE it was becoming commonplace for the Hellenized peoples of the eastern provinces of the empire to pay divine honors to their Roman proconsuls. In those provinces Julius Caesar and even Octavian were worshipped in their own lifetimes, and Cicero tells us that as proconsul of Cilicia he himself was hard put to prevent such honors being paid to him.[10] But as time went on and as Hellenistic and oriental influences were felt ever more forcefully in the western provinces, reservations of that type became increasingly unfashionable. To the reserve of Cicero succeeded ultimately the emperor Diocletian's eager sponsorship and conscious orientalization of what had become, by the end of the third century CE, a well established imperial cult. As Cochrane reminded us a full half-century ago, that cult could hardly have rooted itself so firmly in Roman soil had it come as something "foreign or exotic."[11] In republican Rome, as in Athens, the break with the archaic pattern of sacral kingship had never been complete. The very foundation of the commonwealth remained in some profound sense what we would call "religious." Although "king" had become a dirty word and the era of kingship in a "political" sense was gone, it had still been felt necessary for religio-political purposes to retain the office and title of king in the form of the priestly *rex sacrorum*. And when Caesar Augustus attached to his office of *princeps* ("first citizen") the priestly function and title of *pontifex maximus* ("supreme pontiff" – an old republican office) it is conceivable that he was moved as much by memories of the cultic role of the ancient Roman kings as by any specifically Hellenistic practice.[12]

Whatever the specific source of the thinking that lay behind it, it is important to recognize that the practice whereby the Roman Senate could choose to deify an emperor after his death is not to be dismissed anachronistically as "mere ritual" or a "transparently political" gesture possessed of no truly religious significance. Nor indeed should the obligation to perform public worship to "Rome and Augustus" or the elaborate public ceremonies involving the *consecratio* or apotheosis of deceased emperors be similarly dismissed. In his novel *I, Claudius*, it is true, Robert Graves was able to have some good derisive fun at the expense of the *consecratio*, and viewing (with him) the whole ritual as something of a charade, historians when writing about the period have tended generally to bracket it and to focus instead on what they clearly view as the "realities" of power – war, politics, administration, and diplomacy. But in this they may in some measure have missed the point. For, it turns out, contemporaries appear to have viewed the *consecratio* "with complete seriousness," and it constituted nothing less than "the central focus of imperial ideology at Rome for [no less than] three hundred years."[13]

A similar seriousness attached to emperor-worship, the imperial cult which seems to have reflected, especially in the eastern provinces, a genuine piety – though, of course, a piety of the antique civic mode.[14] Its eventual spread throughout the empire owed less, it seems, to governmental enforcement than to popular sentiment. If it was, indeed, a *political* act, it was political, not in the modern and (historically-speaking) impoverished sense of that term, but in the older, broader, more inclusive sense that bore the clear, continuing imprint of the archaic religio-political vision. City-state, republic, Hellenistic kingdom, Roman empire – all of them still remained something more than "states" in the modern sense. Despite our anachronistic inclination to cynical dismissal of the old civic piety, political thinking and practice in the classical world continued to acknowledge no real distinction between the political and the religious. The loyalty men owed to their state was equally a loyalty to their civic gods, and that loyalty was in general conceived to be an ultimate loyalty from which there could be no appeal to any higher norm. If the irruption into that world of the biblical religions was eventually to call into question that age-old way of thinking, it had that effect only centuries later, and long after Judaism and Christianity alike had first proved themselves to be in some degree responsive to the allure of the archaic cosmic religiosity and had been drawn accordingly and irresistibly into the strong magnetic field it continued to exert.

Abrahamic Unease (i): The Israelite Monarchy

By the eleventh century BCE, after the most recent of a devastating series of barbarian invasions from the north, the powers which had long maneuvered warily for advantage in the Fertile Crescent stretching from the Sinai peninsula to the headwaters of the Euphrates were either removed from the scene or reduced momentarily to comparative impotence. Egypt and Assyria were left in badly weakened condition and the mighty Hittite empire had been utterly destroyed. In Canaan or southern Syria, conditions were ripe for the emergence of an array of petty independent states or kingdoms. And the kingdom that is of concern to us is that of the Hebrews, a semi-nomadic pastoral people, an entity which came into being just before the beginning of the first millennium BCE.

In the twelfth century the Hebrews had begun to migrate from the surrounding desert into Canaan and to settle among the agrarian population long since established there. By the eleventh century the strength of their presence had become such as to lead them into a bitter struggle for control of Canaan with the sea-faring Philistines established in city-states strung along the Mediterranean coast. And it was in response to the demand for organization and cooperation evoked by that great struggle that they began to relinquish their old traditions of tribal independence and, under two successive warrior leaders, Saul and David, to accept a form of monarchy. During the long reign of Solomon, David's son and immediate successor, an attempt appears to have been made to develop the Hebrew kingdom, now pivoting on the cultic center of Jerusalem, into something more closely akin to a despotism of the traditionally Mesopotamian type. The attempt, however, failed, and to the united or confederated kingdom succeeded upon Solomon's death in 933 BCE two smaller entities – the kingdom of Israel (or Ephraim) to the north, with its capital at Samaria, and that of Judah to the south, with its capital at Jerusalem. The subsequent revival of Assyrian power meant that their days would prove to be numbered. In 722 BCE the Assyrians conquered Israel. In 586 BCE their Chaldean or neo-Babylonian successors destroyed Judah, deporting many of its more substantial citizenry to Babylon. There they endured in exile until 538 BCE, somehow surviving as a distinct (and distinctive) people capable of handing down to posterity its most enduring legacy: the remarkable collection of narratives, laws, poems, and meditations which together form the Jewish Bible/Christian Old Testament.

In the context of the ancient Near East at large all of this amounted to very small beer indeed. That in the narrow compass of this essay we are compelled to devote any space at all to the Israelite kingdoms speaks less to their intrinsic political importance or the significance of their essentially provincial secular histories, than to the powerfully formative influence that the biblical account of their religious beliefs, hopes, and yearnings was destined to exert over European and Western modes of life and thought. In a profound sense that is not true of the histories of the other peoples of the ancient Near East, our history in the West is continuous with the history of the ancient Hebrews – or, rather, with their own retroactive and providentialist understanding of their remarkable odyssey through time. So much so, indeed (traditional histories of political thought to the contrary), that our own history is not fully comprehensible unless we undertake to come to terms with that singular fact.

To make that attempt, however, is no easy undertaking, and especially so if one's concern (as is ours) is with the Israelite kingship. In trying to make *historical* sense of that institution one has to grope one's way through a fog of later theological commentary that can easily screen from us the differing historical contexts in which the various "books" of the Bible were produced. One has to wrestle also with extremely intricate problems concerning the precise dating of the narratives in the "historical" books of the Jewish Bible/Christian Old Testament that speak to the introduction of kingship into Israel. And, further than that, one has to take into account the degree to which those historical narratives may themselves have been shaped at the time of their composition or later redaction by considerations essentially theological in nature.

With those craven caveats duly posted, let me boldly suggest that the best point of entry into discussion of the Israelite monarchy is along the trajectory followed in the mid-twentieth century by the English and Scandinavian scholars whose names were associated with what are commonly referred to as the "myth and ritual" and "Uppsala" schools of interpretation.[15] Both schools were intent on making the case that the ideology which undergirded the Israelite kingship was in its essentials the same as that which we have seen to lie behind the Egyptian and Mesopotamian kingship and which extended also to other regions of the ancient Near East. Not least among those regions was the land of Canaan among whose inhabitants the Hebrews settled and with whose religious and institutional forms they came into intimate contact.

The evidence available to support that case, it should be acknowledged, is quite substantial and not lightly to be dismissed.

Thus, many of the attributes ascribed to the coming Messiah and the epithets heaped upon him by Isaiah and the author usually referred to as Deutero-Isaiah – righteousness, love of justice, "Mighty God," "Everlasting Father," "Servant of God," and so on – are now said to be of Sumerian, Babylonian, or Egyptian provenance.[16] Similarly, persuasive parallels have been drawn between Deutero-Isaiah's suffering Servant of God, a kingly, Messianic figure destined not only to "raise up the tribes of Jacob and to restore the survivors of Israel" but also to atone by his death for the sins of others, and the role which the Babylonian king played on the day of atonement that formed part of the New Year's Festival. For on that occasion, acting as the representative of his people and as "Servant of God" (a title explicitly accorded to him) he sought ritually to expiate the wrongdoings of his people.[17]

I do not choose these illustrations at random. The relationship between the Messianic motif and the Hebraic or the later Christian political vision is more direct than it might at first seem. If the epithets which the prophets applied to the Messiah or the imagery and symbols associated with him betray parallels with Egyptian and Babylonian court style, they do so because some of them, while conveying or being susceptible of an eschatological meaning, were actually applied to or associated originally with the real-life pre-exilic kings of Israel and Judah. Of the developments in Old Testament studies over the course of the past century the one that is most pertinent to our concern here is the discovery that a whole series of the psalms (the language and imagery of which echo through Deutero-Isaiah) together form a distinct group. Those psalms, which have since come to be known collectively as the "royal" psalms, are not "original expressions of personal or collective piety written in post-exilic or perhaps even post-Maccabaean times, but derive from hymns, liturgies, prayers, and oracles to be used in the sacred cult of the pre-exilic [Hebrew] monarchy."[18] As a result, whether or not they are inclined to take at face value the extraordinary statement addressed to the *king* in Psalm 45:6 ("Thy throne, O God, endures for ever and ever"); some scholars have certainly taken the evidence yielded by these royal psalms, as well as additional evidence gleaned from the historical books of the Old Testament, as disclosing the lineaments of a pre-exilic Hebrew monarchy in style and status well-nigh indistinguishable from the other sacral monarchies of the ancient Near East.

A couple of examples must suffice. In the first place, in this context it is tempting to attach a heightened significance to the fact that the great temple which Solomon erected with Phoenician help in Jerusalem reproduced the cosmological symbolism we have seen to be common to the temples and royal palaces of the ancient Near East and elsewhere – a symbolism in accordance with which the structure of the temple reflects in microcosm the structure of the macrocosm. Similarly, and in the second place, Sigmund Mowinckel and others have detected in the autumnal festival at Jerusalem a New Year's Festival comparable to that of the Babylonians. At that festival, or so they argue, there occurred a symbolic repetition by the king of the work of creation in which Yahweh triumphed once more over the primeval forces of chaos, and, having been ritually proclaimed as universal king, showed to his followers "that he was prepared to restore their fortunes in the year that lay ahead, . . . in particular, to bestow upon His people the gift of rain and all the blessings of fertility." In the ritual of that festival, they further claim, the Hebrew king played a cultic role comparable to that played by his Babylonian counterpart, an absolutely central role as superhuman representative of his people, sacral mediator between them and Yahweh, "the channel through which the divine blessings flow to the people."[19]

It has to be acknowledged, however, that such attempts to draw firm parallels between the autumn festival at Jerusalem and the Babylonian New Year's Festival have since been subjected to severe evidentiary criticism. There is, moreover, considerable dispute about the nature and extent of any priestly role to be ascribed to the pre-exilic Hebrew kings, and few scholars, indeed, would now be tempted to read Psalm 45:6 as attributing divine status to those kings.[20] Mowinckel, moreover, has been criticized on the grounds that "he interprets the Old Testament religion as a whole by working inwards from the wide circle of a primitive and general Semitic *Umwelt* [milieu], instead of outwards from the centre of the prophetic consciousness." And he himself was led to concede somewhat to such criticisms by acknowledging that whatever the "phenomenological 'parallels'" detectable between notions of kingship in Israel and in the ancient Near East as a whole (and clearly there are many), "the essential question" that has to be asked "is what significance has been imparted to a borrowed idea in its new context, what the religion of Israel has made of it."[21]

Ask that question, of course, and fundamental differences begin to emerge between the Hebrew political experience and that of the Babylonian, Egyptian, Canaanite, and other peoples in the ancient Near East. And, in the contexts of world history and of the development of specifically Western notions of kingship during the Latin Middle Ages, it is to those differences rather than to all the admitted similarities that true significance attaches. And here, I would suggest, a pertinent parallel is to be found in the way in which the post-exilic priestly redactors transformed the "priestly account" of creation (Genesis 1:1–2:4A). The parallel material on which they drew to inspire them in their work appears to have been drawn from the verses of the Babylonian *Enûma Elish*, but unlike the latter the Genesis text is nowhere merely "allusive, 'symbolic,' or figuratively poetic." Instead of featuring a bewildering succession of gods, good and evil, the Genesis account "is dominated by the monotheistic concept in the absolute sense of the term."[22] It asserts (or assumes), in effect, not simply the oneness of God, but also his transcendence and omnipotence – themes that run through the pages of the Old Testament and find, of course, particularly powerful and eloquent expression in the pages of Deutero-Isaiah. As a result it involves also the assertion, in Kierkegaard's words, of "an infinite qualitative difference" between God and the world. That world, by simple *fiat* or an untrammeled exercise of his will, he had drawn out of nothingness (or so Genesis came eventually to be interpreted) and into being. Hence, whatever the use made of Babylonian materials, in the priestly account they are subordinated to the exigencies of an understanding of the divine differing radically from that to be found in the *Enûma Elish* or the other creation myths of the ancient Near East. Hence, too, the concomitant reshaping of the very notion of creation itself into something much more radical than the archaic notion of the imposition of cosmos (or order) upon some sort of preexisting chaos.

The link between the Genesis creation account and the ideas and practices attaching to Hebrew kingship extends, moreover, well beyond a pertinent parallelism in the ways in which attitudes and notions absorbed from the surrounding Near Eastern cultures were gradually, under the transformative impact of the Yahwist religion, transmuted into something very different. It extends also, in fact, to the substantive. The biblical notion of creation, that is to say, and the notion of God as one, transcendent and omnipotent which it both presupposed and entailed, inevitably imposed severe limits on the degree of sacrality that could properly be accorded to any truly Israelite king. By destroying the archaic sense that there existed a consubstantiality between God, nature, and man it de-divinized or de-sacralized the two last. As a result, it had a desacralizing effect also on human society and on the political institutions necessary for the maintenance of that society. In negating the fundamental primitive or archaic notion of a divine *continuum* linking humankind with nature and the state with the cosmos, it undercut as well what we have been calling "the cosmic religiosity," itself the very foundation for the archaic pattern of divine or sacral kingship and the understanding of the state as "the embodiment of the cosmic totality." And, in undercutting that pattern, it shifted the arena in which the relationship between the divine and the human is played out from that dominated by the cyclic rhythms of nature in which "there is nothing new under the sun" to that constituted by the open-ended succession of unique events in time that we call "history." In

that arena it envisaged the millennial unfolding across the unpredictable vastnesses of time of a salvific dialogue between the uncreated and transcendent
God on the one hand and, on the other, the human creatures who owed
their very existence to his inexplicable generosity. In that dialogue kings were
assigned no inevitable or stable role. The central players, instead, were God
himself and his chosen and covenanted people.

It should be emphasized, however, that such judgments are comparative
in nature. If, in retrospect, there is indeed a marked contrast between the
developed religio-politico vision of the Hebrews and that of the surrounding
peoples, it was to take centuries before the nature of the discontinuity
involved was fully to be comprehended. There seems no good reason, for
example, to deny that the pre-exilic Hebrew kings performed *some* functions
of a priestly nature. Even if we were content to indulge in anachronism, we
would encounter great difficulty if we tried to distinguish in any of the
Israelite regimes, whether pre- or post-exilic, discrete "religious" and "political" spheres analogous to the modern categories of church and state. It is
the case, then, that we have to be careful not to exaggerate the extent to
which (and the speed with which) the ancient Hebrews actually broke away
from the archaic sacral pattern of things. Nonetheless, it is extremely unlikely
that even the pre-exilic kings laid claim to any "divine" status. Nowhere in
the Old Testament, Mowinckel conceded, do we meet "with a 'metaphysical'
unity of Yahweh and the king or a really mythological idea of the king's relationship with Yahweh."[23] Had such an idea been advanced, that fact would
surely have been reflected in the form of yet another charge of blasphemy
embedded in the protracted polemic which the prophets directed against
their kings. And the very existence and strength of that prophetic polemic
itself reflects, after all, the peculiarly uneasy status of the Hebrew kingship
and the fragility of its relationship with the divine.

The presence of two different attitudes towards the kingship in those parts
of the books of Samuel concerned with its introduction into Israel discloses,
perhaps better than anything else, this fundamental uneasiness in the position
of the Hebrew kings and goes some way towards illuminating its nature. On
the one hand, God is described as having readily accepted the popular desire
for kingship and as having anointed Saul to be "ruler over his people Israel"
(1 Samuel 10:1; 12:1–5). On the other, he is portrayed as having regarded the
demand of the Israelites that they should have a king to govern them and fight
their battles so that they might be "like other nations" as nothing less than a
betrayal, a quasi-blasphemous demand derogating from his own eternal kingship. After all, the Lord tells Samuel, by that request "they have not rejected
you, but they have rejected me from being king over them" (1 Samuel 8:4–9,
19–22).

This marked ambivalence in attitude towards the kingship is by no means unique to Samuel. It is evident at many points in the Old Testament. "They made kings," said the Lord to Hosea, "but not through me, they set up princes, but without my knowledge" (Hosea 8:4). The religious syncretism consequent upon the Israelite penetration into Canaan, the degree to which the Hebrew monarchy did indeed become like that "of other nations" – the focus of a royal cult, the mediatorial pivot of a state envisaged as "the embodiment of the cosmic totality" – these things (much emphasized by the adherents to the "Myth and Ritual" school) seem increasingly to have stimulated among the Israelites themselves criticism, first, of royal behavior when kings went "whoring" after the alien fertility gods of the Canaanites, and then, eventually, of the monarchy itself. As a result, that very institution came to be portrayed as a failure, a great aberration, a foreign importation incompatible with the Hebrew religious vision, a veritable betrayal of the covenant between God and his chosen people, something irreconcilable with the supreme kingship of Yahweh himself. Again and again, prophetic voices were raised defending the true kingship of Yahweh against those deluded human upstarts who, worshipping in the "high places," sought to "ascend to heaven," to "raise their throne above the stars of God," to make themselves "like the Most High" (Isaiah 14:12–14). And the hostility thus engendered, enshrined in the writings (or redactions) of exilic or post-exilic times, survived the destruction of the kingship in Judah no less than in Israel. It informed the thinking of the Hebrews to such a degree indeed, that not even the revival of the monarchy in 103 BCE could overcome it or rally the support of the entire nation behind the (non-Davidic) Hasmonean kings who, by their military prowess, had been able to revive the old kingdom of Judah and, for more than half a century, to guarantee its renewed independence.

Despite any earlier flirtation with the cosmic religiosity and cosmic kingship, then, the Hebrews finally resisted their blandishments. The Hebraic conception of God and the understanding of creation that flowed from it were determinative in undermining the structure of the archaic sacral pattern. But they were not by themselves strong enough to destroy it. If the archaic pattern of divine or sacral kingship was excluded, it was excluded, after all, in the name of kingly divinity. And Yahweh alone being recognized eventually as truly king, the Israelite governmental ideal remained what the Hellenistic Jewish writer Flavius Josephus was later on to label as "theocracy."

The point is an important one, and for more than one reason. Among other things, some measure of insight into the history of the idea of the kingship of Yahweh is vital for an understanding of the political attitudes one finds expressed later on in the New Testament, and especially of those clustering around the notion of the "Kingdom of God" or "Kingdom of Heaven." As suggested earlier, the relationship between the Messianic motif and the Christian as well as Hebraic political vision is more direct than at first it might seem. Side by side with the growing sense that the reign of the earthly Israelite kings derogated from the supreme kingship of Yahweh lay the anticipation of the latter's final victory over his enemies, the expectation that in the providential unfolding of history the "day of Yahweh" would eventually dawn when his kingship would finally be vindicated and the Kingdom of God gloriously realized on earth.[24] Bound up, moreover, with that belief in the coming of the kingdom was a set of teachings concerning the "anointed one" (Hebrew: *Messiah*; Greek: *Christos*; Latin: *Christus*), the future mediator between God and his people, the leader whose coming would inaugurate that glorious event. And, as the name itself suggests, the Messiah came to be envisaged as a royal figure, an ideal king sprung from the House of David, a royal warrior who would recall the Israelites from their decadence, restore their loyalty to the covenant with God, and lead them into glorious victory over their enemies. "Behold," proclaimed the prophet Jeremiah (23:5–6),

> the days are coming, says the Lord, when I will raise up for David a righteous Branch, and he shall reign as king and deal wisely, and shall execute justice and righteousness in the land. In his day, Judah will be saved, and Israel will dwell securely. And this is the name by which he will be called: "The Lord is our Righteousness."

Such Messianic teachings, then, certainly bore in their train and passed on to future generations a familiarity with the attributes, epithets, and images long associated with the actual sacral monarchs of the ancient Near East. But those teachings evolved in complex ways during the post-exilic centuries and, by the dawn of the Christian era, they had come to take on some very different forms. As a result, the Christian appropriation of the Messianic hope, which was to shape the early Christian attitude towards kingship, proved to be a selective and highly specific one.

Abrahamic Unease (ii): The Christian Reaction

Given the destruction of the kingdoms of Israel and Judah, the burden of the Babylonian exile, and the turbulence and disappointments of the subsequent history of the Israelite people, it is hardly surprising that the traditional version of the Messianic longing that remained dominant right down to the lifetime of Jesus should have been robustly this-worldly in nature. It pivoted, that is to say, on the hope against hope that from the House of David would spring the ideal king who, by delivering the chosen and covenanted people once more from alien domination and by restoring the national kingdom, would vindicate the kingship of Yahweh and inaugurate the reign of righteousness of which the prophet Jeremiah had so eloquently spoken. Indeed, the picture of the Messianic king which is conveyed by the poems known as the "Psalms of Solomon" and dating to the period after the extension of Roman control over Jerusalem (63 BCE) would suggest that the years of renewed Israelite independence under the Hasmonean kings (168–63 BCE) had actually strengthened and rendered more concrete the traditionally this-worldly nature of the Messianic hope.[25] Certainly, in Christ's own lifetime the extremists among the Israelites were drawing from the teaching that Yahweh alone was king of his people the radical conclusion that they should tolerate no other king, and that it was through his priests alone that Yahweh's wishes would be communicated. On the basis of this conclusion, these extremists (the Zealots) adopted a posture of unyielding opposition to Roman rule. It ranged from hostility towards the payment of tribute to the empire all the way to advocacy of the violent overthrow of what they regarded as a blasphemous and alien tyranny.

But if the members of the Zealot faction were growing in importance in Christ's own lifetime, they were not the sole bearers of the Messianic legacy. From the core notion of Yahweh's supreme kingship a whole range of differing conclusions could be drawn and had, in fact, been drawn. Side by side with the position adopted by the Zealots must be placed at least two others. Running in opposition to the revolutionary activism of the Zealots was the strain of Messianic quietism which was shared by Pharisees and Sadducees – though, doubtless, in differing ways. And in opposition to Zealots, Pharisees, and Sadducees alike – all of whom shared the traditionally this-worldly understanding of the Messianic kingdom – was that subsidiary complex of Messianic ideas, glimpses of which can be had in Deutero-Isaiah (Isaiah 40–6), in Daniel 7:13–14, in the Jewish Apocalypse known as the Book of Enoch (first century BCE), and in the writings of the Qumran sect (c.200 BCE–70 CE).[26] These disparate works were by no means the bearers of any single, unified, or coherent system of thought. Insofar, however, as they ignore the traditionally this-worldly version of the Messianic expectation and emphasize instead the heavenly, semi-divine character of the Messiah and the universal and spiritual nature of his kingdom, they do share at least a common tendency. And it is in the context of all three of these positions that one must strive for an understanding of the ideas about kingship and the political life embedded in the several books of the New Testament.

Any analysis of those political ideas, exegetical pitfalls notwithstanding, must necessarily begin with those which Christians, as early as the Apostolic Age (30–110 CE), themselves believed it correct to attribute to Jesus, for those are the ideas ascribed to him in the gospels. Once we begin, we are immediately forced to confront the fact that,

> taken as a uniform, consistent, and literal record of Jesus' teaching, the gospels are a collection of puzzles. Jesus' teaching, life, death, resurrection was basic to them – but the gospels also give us the later *interpretations*; and the only possible way toward a solution of the inconsistencies is a frank recognition of the *variety* of interpretation reflected by the gospels and their underlying sources.[27]

Grant issues this warning while attempting to elucidate the meaning of the expression "the Kingdom of God." It is one which occurs about a hundred times in the New Testament, which conveys a notion that clearly lies at the very heart of Jesus's teaching, and which constitutes the key to his attitude towards kingship in particular and matters political in general. On this point "variety of interpretation" is certainly very evident. In many passages of the gospels the general emphasis is eschatological, the Kingdom of God thus being identified as the state of righteousness destined by God's will to arrive at the end of time and Christ's career being regarded as the compelling witness to the certainty of its ultimate arrival. But there are also a few passages (e.g. Matthew. 13:41ff.; 16:18–19) that seem to suggest at least some sort of tentative equation between the Kingdom of God and the congregation of the faithful or visible Church. And if the former – eschatological – emphasis is the safer guide to an understanding of the teaching dominant in the gospels, it has in some measure to be qualified by the sense expressed in very many gospel passages that "the time was fulfilled," that "the decisive eschatological turning point" had "already begun in Jesus the Christ,"[28] that the Kingdom was already at hand, was already in some degree a present reality, albeit one destined to develop and grow over the long course of history until the moment of the final consummation (thus Matthew 5:3 and 10; 11:11–12; 12:28; 13:24ff.; 18:4; 23:13; Mark 10 14–15; Luke 17:21).

But if the Kingdom was at hand, was already breaking in by gradually extending its empire over the souls of individuals, what sort of a kingdom or kingship was involved? Here the evidence of the gospels presents fewer obstacles to understanding. And it reveals a Christ who, while accepting the role (if not the title) of Messiah, drastically reinterpreted its meaning, setting his face against the dominant and traditionally nationalistic and this-worldly understanding of the Messianic kingdom, appropriating instead the more spiritualized version that we have seen ascribed to Deutero-Isaiah, Daniel, the Book of Enoch, and the Qumran documents, at the same time clarifying,

deepening, and extending its meaning. Thus we should not miss the significance of the fact that the gospels represent Jesus as having lost no opportunity
to underline the spiritual and universal (i.e. supranational) character of the
kingdom whose advent he was proclaiming. For it was a kingdom that was to
transcend all national and racial preferences and to embrace the righteous
from among all peoples – Jewish, Samaritan, and Gentile alike (Matthew
13:31–8).

The celebrated reply to Pilate: "My kingship is not of this world" may
occur only in the Gospel according to St John (18:36) but the attitude it
expresses is reflected again and again in the other three ("synoptic") gospels.
Thus the kingdom belongs above all to "the poor in spirit," those who "have
been persecuted for righteousness' sake" (Matthew 5:3 and 10), those who
are "the servant[s] of all" and have become as little children (Mark 9:35–7;
Luke 9:47–8). In that kingdom leadership will properly belong to those who
serve, and there will be no lordship of the type claimed by the quasi-divinized
Hellenistic kings of the day who were bold enough to title themselves
"Benefactors" (Luke 22:24–30). That last text is one of several in the New
Testament that appear to voice an oblique deprecation of the contemporary
portrayal of the king as a "living law," the state's "link with the world order,"
titled appropriately not only as "benefactor," but also as "shepherd," "mediator," and "savior."[29]

What was involved, clearly, was a conception of the Kingdom of God that
differed radically from that associated with the Messianic views dominant in
Jesus's own lifetime. To that fact attests the evident bewilderment both of his
own followers, at least one of whom appears to have been a Zealot (Luke
6:15), and of his Jewish opponents, who certainly were not, but who at the
end sought to convince Pilate that he had to be something, at least, of a
Zealot fellow-traveller. But Jesus's frequent disparagement of the kings and
governments of this world and of their coercive methods had little in
common with Zealot views. It was directed, after all, against *all* the governmental structures with which he came into contact, Jewish no less than
Roman. And it was also balanced by a relative (if modest) approval of governmental authority. The latter found its most explicit endorsement in
Christ's famous statement concerning the tribute money, a statement which,
if it evaded the trap being set for him by the Pharisees and Sadducees, must
certainly have scandalized the Zealots. For if the things that were God's were
to be rendered unto God, the tribute money, nevertheless, was identified as
Caesar's, and Christ insisted that it had to be rendered unto Caesar
(Matthew 22:17–21; Mark 12:14–17; Luke 20:22–5). That position was
wholly in keeping with his insistence that the Kingdom of God which he was
preaching was "not of this world," thus implying (in modern terms) an alto-

gether novel separation of "religious" from "political" loyalties that, in the fullness of time, was to be fraught with revolutionary implications.

If Jean-Jacques Rousseau was later to lament that fact, saying that it "made the State no longer one, and brought about the internal divisions which have never ceased to trouble Christian peoples," Fustel de Coulanges was later to take a more positive view. Lauding the degree to which the sharp distinction between political and religious loyalties liberated the individual conscience from the omnipotence of the state, he proclaimed that

> Christianity completes the overthrow of the local worship; it extinguishes the prytanea [sacred fire], and completely destroys the city-protecting divinities. It does more: it refuses to assume the empire which these worships had exercised over civil society. It professes that between the state and itself there is nothing in common. It separates what antiquity had confounded. We may remark, moreover, that during three centuries the new religion lived entirely beyond the action of the state; it knew how to dispense with state protection, and even to struggle against it. These three centuries established an abyss between the domain of government and the domain of religion; and, as the recollection of this period could not be effaced, it followed that this distinction became a plain and incontestable truth, which the efforts of even a part of the clergy could not eradicate.[30]

Both claims have merit. But both overestimate the immediacy of the change involved. And both grievously underestimate the difficulties which Christians were to experience in perceiving and internalizing the full implications of the new teaching, once they had ceased to be an intermittently persecuted minority and had come to occupy the favored position of adherents to a religion first tolerated by the empire and then accorded the privilege (or burden) of official establishment. Those difficulties were certainly grounded in the sheer novelty of the new teaching which (at least in retrospect) can be seen to have run counter to the political commonsense of millennia. But they were grounded also, it must be conceded, in the challenge involved in attempting to identify in the New Testament, taken as a whole, any univocal or fully integrated teaching on matters political.

It is true that if one stands back from the admitted complexities of the gospel teaching, two things do stand out in comparatively bold relief. First, that archaic notions of sacral kingship have been nudged to one side and, so far as they implied the actual divinization of kings, bluntly rejected. Second, that if such notions survive at all in the gospel setting it is by being drawn into the magnetic field exerted by Jesus's central teaching on the Kingdom of God and by being transmuted, as a result, into something radically different.

If, however, one opens up the scope of the inquiry and looks beyond the teaching ascribed to Jesus in the four gospels to the New Testament texts taken as a whole, one finds marshaled around those comparatively clear central commitments a varied array of positions. And those positions reflect in many ways the particular and changing circumstances in which the various New Testament authors found themselves at the time they were actually writing.

So far as kingship itself goes, nowhere, it is true, does one encounter any real recession from the deprecatory attitude which Luke and some of the Pauline epistles evinced towards the claims for sacrality embedded in the Hellenistic regal philosophy. Under the threat of persecution, indeed, that attitude can be seen to have hardened, developing in an apocalyptic direction, implying that the last days were at hand, and postulating an open and inevitable opposition between the Kingdom of God and the established (fundamentally Satanic) powers of this world. Hints of that development appear in the fourth gospel and in St John's First Epistle. And it moved into the foreground during the persecution by the emperors Nero and Domitian at Rome when, in the name of the Kingship of God, the "Apocalypse of John" denounced as Satanic the blasphemously divinized emperors of Rome.[31]

Elsewhere, however, though not with specific reference to the institution of kingship, we encounter an attitude towards political authority that, while still negative in comparison with archaic and classical views, is a good deal *less* negative. Writing as he was in the earlier part of Nero's reign (54–68 CE), when stable government prevailed and the persecution of the Christian community at Rome had yet to be instituted, it is understandable that Paul, himself a Roman citizen, should take Christ's injunction that we should render to Caesar the things that are Caesar's in a very positive way. Thus in Romans 13:1–7, the text that was destined to play so formative a role in the shaping of Christian thinking about political authority through the centuries, Paul insisted that obedience to governmental authority is required, not simply by fear but also by conscience. In the Gospel of John (19:11) Jesus is reported as having said to Pontius Pilate "You would have no power over me unless it had been given you from above." And here Paul, expressing the same conviction that political authority is itself of divine institution, goes on to insist that rulers, even when they punish the evildoer, are acting as the ministers of God. "Pay to all what is due them," he concludes (v.7), "Taxes to whom taxes are due, revenue to whom revenue is due, respect to whom respect is due, honor to whom honor is due."

The emphatic nature of these exhortations (cf. I Timothy 2:2; Titus 3:1–2), as also those to be found in Peter's First Epistle (2:13–17 – "Fear God, honor the Emperor"), may reflect a need, shared by the Protestant reformers later on, to worry about the drawing of unwarranted and *politicized* conclusions from the notion of Christian liberty. Whether or not it did, it laid the basis, when taken as the point of entry into Christian thinking about the state, and once Christians were accorded toleration, for a much more positive view of political authority than that suggested by Christ's teaching on the Kingdom of God. Certainly, when taken in conjunction with another element in the New Testament which was in itself of historical rather than explicitly political import, it served to ease the way for those Christians who, long before Constantine's conversion in the early fourth century, first dared to look forward to a more positive relationship between Roman empire and Christian Church. That element was the frequency with which Luke correlates the gospel story with the history of the empire at large, noting in particular the coincidence of the birth of Christ with the reign of the first emperor, Caesar Augustus (Luke 2:1ff., 3:1ff.; Acts 11:28, 18:2). The latter correlation, and as early as 127 CE, Melito, Bishop of Sardis, saw as nothing less than providential. So, too, at the beginning of the fourth century, did Eusebius, Bishop of Caesarea. And, moving along that axis, while managing also to appropriate for his own purposes many an element of the Hellenistic philosophy of kingship, Eusebius proved able (see below, ch. 3, pp. 69–76) to accomplish what the biblical notion of the divine and the New Testament's revolutionary separation of the religious from the political would seem to have rendered altogether impossible – namely, a species of Christian accommodation with the archaic pattern of sacral kingship.

Abrahamic Unease (iii): The Islamic "Political" Tradition

A similar, if somewhat more qualified accommodation began to emerge later on in the seventh and eighth centuries CE. It did so in the whole vast region stretching from the Pyrenees in the west to north-west India in the east that had become by then the sphere of Islam, the third of the great Abrahamic religions. That accommodation (or, more accurately, set of accommodations) was the outcome of a complex process spanning the periods of Umayyad and 'Abbāsid ascendancy (c.661–850), as Islamic thinkers gradually felt their tentative way into an essentially monarchical mode of polity. As they did so, they were of course guided by the fugitive hints to be found in the Qur'ān itself and in the *hadīth* – the body of traditions, reports, or narratives conveying to posterity the sayings and actions attributed to Muhammad and his companions, which the emerging cadre of '*ulamā* (scholars and teachers) assembled, largely in the mid-eighth century, and of which they eventually succeeded in constituting themselves the authoritative interpreters. But it has to be recognized that those Muslim thinkers and leaders on whose shoulders, during the

63

centuries immediately subsequent to Muhammad's death (632), descended
the burden of framing a mode of polity congruent with Islamic aspirations,
drew also (perhaps rather) on the vast repertoire of inherited bureaucratic
practices in the conquered territories, as well as on ideological, ceremonial,
and iconographic motifs elaborated over previous millennia in the kingdoms
of the ancient Near East – especially those of pre-Islamic, Persian origin.[32]
For Islamic political life, whether one is thinking of the mode of kingship
attaching in the early centuries to the Umayyad or 'Abbāsid caliphs or that
attaching in the modern period to the sultan/caliphs of the Ottoman Empire
or to the Safavid shahs of Persia, that ancient Near Eastern inheritance was of
great importance. That fact must not be overlooked or swept, anachronistically, to one side.

The point deserves emphasis. When, at Persepolis in 1971, the Shah of
Iran ("*ShāhānShāh*"; "King of Kings") unwisely made a point of lauding the
virtues of 2,500 years of Persian kingship, his future nemesis, the Ayatullāh
Rūh-Allāh Khumainī (d. 1989) tartly responded from exile by attacking as
unIslamic the very title "King of Kings." In so doing, he was reflecting the
worried ambivalence towards kingship in general that was early embedded in
the Islamic tradition,[33] and, beyond that, echoing the early Muslim juristic
view that that particular title represented a profane human usurpation of a
prerogative that belonged rightly to God alone. "The title King of Kings,"
he said, "is the most hated of all titles in the sight of God." But when he
went further and asserted that "to the whole notion of monarchy. . . . Islam is
fundamentally opposed," thereby dismissing the long centuries of absolute
monarchical rule in the Muslim world at large as some sort of deviation or
declension from an original and more purely Islamic norm, he was in effect,
and like so many of the *'ulamā* before him, rewriting history to bring it into
conformity with the urgencies of his own contemporary religio-political
ideal.[34]

The fact is that the Qur'ān has next to nothing to say about politics or
government as such and the *hadīth* not a great deal more. Moreover, "the
history of the first years of the Muslim polity is particularly obscure" and, by
Khumainī's day, modern writers had long slipped into the habit of taking at
face value the "formal theological disputes and debates over the nature of
political authority" that *medieval* Muslims had eagerly projected (or retro-
jected) onto what was a largely empty and concomitantly receptive screen.
On this point, Aziz Al-Azmeh is particularly insistent. "Muslim forms," he
says, "did not arise *ex nihilo*, nor quite simply from the writ of a Book; to
propose otherwise is absurd in the light of historical reason."[35]

What did arise, however, from the writ of the Qur'ān, was something
destined to impress a distinctive stamp on Muslim "political" thinking, some-

thing that sets it apart from the principles fundamental to the political thinking (if not always the political practice) of the Christian world, and something that eased the way for the partial penetration into Muslim thinking about political life of ancient Near Eastern notions of royal sacrality, despite the conviction conveyed by such as Dhiya' al-Din Barani (d. c.1357) that "between the traditions (*sunnah*) of the Prophet Muhammad and his mode of living, and the customs of the Iranian emperors and their mode of living, there is complete contradiction."[36] What I have in mind is the *umma* or community which Muhammad established at Medina. It was, in Western terms, a "religious" community as well as a "political" organism." "The concept of the *umma* has remained as the one unifying factor amidst the diversity of the peoples of the Islamic empire," and the union of the political and religious that characterized it is "symbolized in the institution of the caliphate as the essence as well as the outward form of the *umma*." So that

> Islam knows no distinction between religious and temporal realm, between religious and secular activities. Both realms form a unity under the all-embracing authority of the *Sharī'a* [the law].[37] . . . Politics is part of religion, so to speak; . . . [it] is the scene of religion as life on this earth so long as the law of the state is the *Sharī'a*. This state is the *Khilāfa* [caliphate] or *Imāma* [imamate or realm of the *imām*, chief or leader in prayer], and if we must operate with our Western terms, it may be defined as a spiritual and temporal unity.[38]

That being so, not even the purity of its monotheism or its adamant insistence on the transcendence and omnipotence of God sufficed to immunize Islam altogether against infection by notions deriving from the archaic pattern of sacral kingship with which it came into such intimate and enduring contact in the conquered territories of the Near East, most notably Iran. It is true that the essential "biblicism" of its basic theological commitments and the traditionalist and juristic temper of the majority Sunni community ("the people of the Community and Tradition," as it was sometimes called) tended to preclude anything more than intermittent flirtation with elements of the cosmic religiosity underpinning that archaic pattern of sacral kingship. The extraordinary claims repeatedly advanced in the Islamic world for the absolutist nature of the type of kingship associated with caliph, sultan, and (under the Ottomans) sultan-caliph, the elaborately mystifying ceremonial practices that served to distance those rulers from subject and foreigner alike, the hyperbolic jumble of titles and laudatory epithets ("King of Kings," "shadow of God, "Caliph of God," "human god," "abode of clemency," "the second Ka'ba" and so on) that served to enhance the ineffability of their dignity – all such things notwithstanding, the ideological reach of Islamic regality was persistently contained in the Sunni tradition by the subordination of caliph no less than sultan to the divinely willed prescriptions of the *Sharī'a* and hemmed in further by the successfully vindicated claim of the *'ulamā* to be the (corporately) authoritative interpreters of that overarching and controlling legal code.

That fact duly acknowledged, it would be improper not to acknowledge also the inroads that elements deriving ultimately from archaic notions of regal sacrality periodically made into Muslim attitudes concerning rulers and rulership. It early became assumed, for example, that the accession to the throne of a new caliph would bring with it rainfall and a general revival of the natural world. Later on, the belief spread that "the person of the caliph was a support of the order of the universe." If he were killed the entire universe would lapse into disorder, the sun would hide its face, rain would cease, and plants would grow no more. If, in Sunni Islam, such notions were little more than "popular conceptions" apt to be dismissed by the "Muslim theologians who . . . [dealt] . . . with the theory of the caliphate,"[39] they found more fertile soil in the Shī-ite branch of Islam, with its proclivity for esoteric interpretations and its fervent stress on the central role of the Imām or leader upon whom the mass of faithful depended for their knowledge and understanding of the revelation. Through his authoritative teaching alone, it was believed, could the *Sharī'a* be determined. He, it was said, is "the pillar of the universe, the 'gate' through whom God is approached." By his blessing "god maintains the Heavens, that they do not fall and destroy their inhabitants." And in the absence of such an Imām representing us here below, or so said the Shī'ite theorist, Jafar al-Sadiq, "verily the earth itself would collapse."[40]

It is not surprising, then, that at times when and in places where Shī'ite rulers grasped the reins of imperial power essentially archaic notions of regal sacrality got something more than rhetorical free play, for example, the Fātimid caliphate centered on Egypt (907–1171) and the Safavid empire centered on Iran (1500–1722). In the early days of the Safavid monarchy claim was made by the Shah to a "bedazzling array of unlimited worldly and supernatural powers" – nothing less, in effect, than supreme authority in matters spiritual as well as temporal. Calling himself "Jesus, son of Mary," Shah Isma'il (d. 1524) went on to identify with God the Imām 'Alī ibn Abi Talib (d. 661, cousin of the Prophet and fountainhead of the Shī'ah i-Alī or partisans of 'Alī). And he went on further to claim that he himself was "of the same essence as 'Alī (for) a man can be a manifestation of Godhead."[41] And it was under the Fātimid caliphate that the degree of veneration of the ruler began to press against the limits set by the fundamentals of Qur'ānic belief. With the portrayal of the Caliph al-Hākim bin Amr Allāh (d. 1021) as an incarnation of the divine, those limits were finally transgressed, leading to the establishment among those known as the Druzes of what was a new syncretistic religion rather than anything properly identifiable as an Islamic sect.[42]

Such exotic phenomena cannot be regarded as anything approximating mainstream Islam. But the important point for us to grasp is that if adherents of Islam, to whom the Christian doctrine of the Trinity constituted a blasphemous denial of the unicity of God, were nevertheless not entirely unresponsive to notions affiliated with the archaic pattern of sacral kingship, it would be surprising, indeed, and despite the astringency of primitive Christian belief, if Christian thinkers proved eventually to be any less responsive. They were in fact no less responsive, and on this matter, at least, it was the remarkable achievement of one notable tradition of patristic thinking to have accomplished the difficult task of filling up with "the new wine of Christianity" what the seventeenth-century English philosopher, Thomas Hobbes, was (engagingly) to describe as the "old empty bottles of Gentilism,"[43] and to have succeeded in so doing without immediately breaking them. In the Latin west that (essentially syncretistic) patristic tradition was eventually to be challenged and subverted. But it was to endure for centuries in the Byzantine east and to leave a clear imprint on the imperial ideology of Tsarist Russia. It is to that tradition that we must now turn.

3

The Eusebian Accommodation
Christian Rulership in Imperial Rome, Byzantium, and Russia

Involving as it did a clear departure from New Testament norms and a truly breathtaking degree of assimilation to archaic patterns of sacral monarchy, the accommodation which Christian leaders made with Roman imperial power at the start of the fourth century constituted a revolutionary event fraught with the most far-reaching consequences for the history of kingship in Byzantium and Russia no less than in the western Roman empire and its Germanic successor kingdoms in western Europe. Less than three centuries earlier, as we have seen, the author of the Book of Revelation/Apocalypse of John had not hesitated to denounce as Satanic the blasphemously divinized emperors of Rome. And no more than a few decades earlier, worried, it seems, by the infiltration of Christian beliefs into the ranks of those holding high civil or military office, and viewing the characteristic Christian refusal to participate in the public worship of "Rome and Augustus" as an intolerable threat to the reconstituted unity of the empire, the emperor Diocletian (284–306) had sought to eliminate the danger by launching, in 303, what was probably the most widespread and thoroughgoing of persecutions. He had done so in vain. But the emperor Constantine's subsequent policy of extending first toleration and then favor to the new faith brought with it for emperor and Christians alike challenges of a different type – challenges, so far as the core commitments of *normative* or *biblical* Christianity were concerned, that were to prove to be no less testing.

By the end of the third century CE the very constitution of the empire had been transformed. That transformation had occurred in the course of more than three centuries during which Hellenistic notions of kingship had progressively reshaped the common Roman understanding of the imperial office. That transformative process had quickened in the wake of the military anarchy that had turned the empire upside down during the disastrous half century running from 235 to 285 CE. As a result, from being a collocation of city-states held together by the imperial *princeps* (or "first citizen") but ruled in collaboration with the Roman Senate, it had been transmuted into something akin to a military despotism. While in deference to Roman tradition the imperial office was presented to the world as technically elective, it had in fact been transformed into an absolute monarchy of quasi-oriental type. In it, certainly, it was the will of the emperor, himself supreme judge and court of last appeal, that was now, in effect, the dominant source of law. And it fell to the military and the imperially appointed bureaucracy – two separate hierarchies operating independently from one another and coming together only in their common head, the emperor himself – to impress that imperial will upon a populace that had now become in character more "subject" than "citizen."

This historic transformation was reflected in the replacement of the term *princeps*, once the emperor's proudest title, by the more accurately descriptive *dominus* or "lord." It was reflected also in the progressive alignment of Roman imperial ideology with the Hellenistic philosophy of kingship. And it culminated in Diocletian's eager sponsorship and intensification of the imperial cult itself, along with his adoption of the court ceremonial, elaborate costume, and other appurtenances of the sacral or divine kings of Mediterranean antiquity. Constantine's grant of toleration to Christians did little or nothing, of itself, to cancel, roll back, or modify that transformation. Christians, it is true, had had to endure for three centuries as a proscribed and intermittently persecuted sect. One might have expected them, then, to have reacted to their own remarkable change of state and to the claims and pretensions of their imperial master with a degree of prudent reserve comparable, at least, to that evident in the writings of the mature St Augustine a century later. But that early fourth-century Christians did not do. Their lack of reserve may be ascribed in part to an understandable euphoria in the wake of the dramatic improvement in their public fortunes. But it has to be attributed also to the less generally recognized fact that the development across time of their own theological tradition had not left them altogether unprepared, ideologically speaking, for their new relationship with (and understanding of) the imperial authority. It is with that development in mind that I choose to employ for shorthand purposes the term "the Eusebian accommodation."

The Transition at Rome to Christian Monarchy

Even at their most positive, the range of political ideas to be found in the New Testament did not equip Christians in the early fourth century very well when they had to find a way to come to terms with contemporary theories of imperial rulership and their characteristic stress on the exalted and sacred nature of the emperor. If New Testament teaching clearly excluded the possibility of ascribing a divine status to any ruler, however exalted, it did more than that. Some scholars, indeed, have detected in the New Testament an explicit deprecation of the characteristically Hellenistic claim that the monarch, being a living law, the very foundation of justice, the kingdom's link with the *logos* and, therefore, with the cosmic order, should appropriately enjoy the titles of "shepherd," "savior," "mediator," "benefactor" and so on.

Also to be found in the New Testament, however, and as we have seen, is an element which, if not in itself explicitly political, may have eased the way for those Christians who first dared to look forward to a more cooperative relationship between Roman emperor and Christian Church. Certainly, it helped Eusebius, Bishop of Caesarea (d. c.340), the Church historian who can sometimes sound like an official court ideologist for the emperor Constantine, to hammer out the critical accommodation between Christian belief and pagan imperial ideology that was to have so important an impact in Rome itself and so long-enduring an influence on the understanding of kingship in the Byzantine world and, later on, it has been claimed, in Russia, too. But in reaching that accommodation Eusebius had reasons other than the historical correlations signaled in the Lukan texts. For the development of his thinking, another and non-historical New Testament usage was relevant – the application to Christ himself of such Hellenistic royal titles as "shepherd," "savior," "mediator." Whether or not that was done by way of polemic against the ruler cult of the day, the very commonality of language that it involved seems to have encouraged Christian thinkers long before Eusebius to edge towards the prevailing theories of sacral rulership, the more so in that they had before them the persuasive example of the Hellenizing Jewish thinker, Philo of Alexandria (c.30 BCE–c.40 CE).

Like his Christian successors, Philo confronted the urgent task of reconciling the Hellenistic and Roman vision of rulership with his own monotheism. He did so, it has been said, by absorbing "all the elements of the Hellenistic doctrine on kings, except their actual deification."[1] Correlating monarchy with monotheism, he argued that as God is in the universe so is the king in his realm. Rulership he saw as being in the image of God and, as if to underline the parallelism, he used of God as the supreme king the royal titles of "savior" and "benefactor." In this something more than a mere parallelism is involved. Even when tyrannically exercised, rulership is a "special gift" of God – hence the king's high-priestly functions and his role as a living law; hence, too, his obligation to live in community with God and to conform himself with the *logos* of God (which, at least in one text, Philo identifies with

70

the divine law). Thus Moses, in whom all royal virtues were exemplified, Philo presents as king and priest, capable of governing "the people because he himself is governed by the Logos."[2] Nevertheless, however sublime his position, no king, not even the emperor himself, should be accorded divine honors. If "he has no equal on earth" and "by the dignity of his office . . . is similar to God who is above all," nevertheless "by his body the king is like any other man" and "as a mortal . . . must not be extolled."[3]

The use which Philo makes of the notion of the *logos* is central to his thinking about rulership. To this term (possessing the twin denotation of "reason" and "word"), which the Stoics had equated with God as the divine ordering reason immanent in the universe, Philo gave more than one meaning. Sometimes he came close to Stoic views, but, more characteristically, he was careful to distinguish *logos* from God. Instead, he spoke of it as "the image of God," a quasi-personification ("shepherd," "first-born son") of the divine reason, the presence of which in God's creation and governance of the universe alone guarantees its order and intelligibility. Later on, of course, Christian writers were to appropriate this *logos* doctrine and to bend it to their own uses. In so doing, they were encouraged by the fourth gospel's identification of the *logos* with Jesus Christ himself (John 1:1–18), and prompted by the challenge of making the New Testament's statements about the nature of Christ and his relationship with the Father coherent and intelligible to themselves no less than to the Hellenistic world at large. From the time, then, of the second-century Apologists onwards, theologians increasingly exploited the doctrine in their ongoing attempt to shape and clarify their Trinitarian beliefs. The complexity and density of their argumentation is formidable, but if one prescinds from the detail one may properly risk the following generalization: that to the extent to which the Hellenizing motif was dominant, the emphasis in the understanding and presentation of Jesus was not on the historical figure encountered in the New Testament accounts – the incarnate Christ, crucified redeemer, heir to the messianic prophecies of the Old Testament, proclaimer of the messianic kingdom, eschatological king. Instead, the emphasis was placed on the vision of Christ as a cosmic figure, eternally pre-existent *logos* or Son of God, mediator between the transcendent God and the created universe, the means by which the ineffable One could come into contact with the concrete Many, the simple with the complex, the unconditioned with the conditioned. He was presented, in effect, as the intermediate vehicle by means of which the abstract deity of the late antique philosophers could be identified with the personal and omnipotent God of the Old Testament who had deigned to create and govern the universe and to reveal himself to humankind. It was, in effect, a precarious insertion of essentially a-temporal philosophical notions of archaic provenance into the ineluctably historical modality of thinking that stemmed from the Bible.

This particular intellectual tendency came powerfully to the fore with Clement of Alexandria (c.150–c.215) and Origen (185–c.254), in whose teaching one may also detect, side by side with an insistence that the Son or *logos* is truly divine, a sense that he is somehow, nonetheless, subordinate to or less than the Father. It was this "weak" or "subordinationist" Christology, along with their view of Christ as primarily a cosmic figure, the eternally pre-existent *logos*, that enabled them to clothe him with royal attributes derived less from the Bible or the tradition of eschatological Jewish messianism than from the contemporary and characteristically Hellenistic picture of the ideal king. In this, these theologians revealed the impress on their thinking of the writings (and especially the political writings) of their great Alexandrian predecessor, Philo Judaeus. "[T]hrough the identification of the Son with the Logos of Hellenistic philosophy," Per Beskow has said, "it becomes possible . . . to apply the ideas and terminology of [Philonic] political metaphysics to Christ."[4] At the same time, the very subordinationism of their Christology left them not wholly averse to following Philo's lead in applying those same ideas and terminology to their imperial rulers, thus lessening somewhat the gap dividing Christ, the eternal *logos* and savior, from those more traditional saviors, shepherds, benefactors, and manifestations of the *logos* who went by the name of emperors of Rome. Thus, despite the degree to which the omnipotence and transcendence of the biblical God might have been expected to exclude the assimilation of ideas associated with the Hellenistic philosophy of sacral kingship, the development of the *logos*-theology by the Alexandrian church fathers served to open up a conduit through which, under the changed circumstances of the early fourth century and however counter-intuitively, such notions were to find their way into Christian thinking. Even under the more chastening circumstances of their own day, both Clement and Origen had already evinced a surprisingly positive attitude towards the Roman empire. Thus Origen subscribed to the providentialist interpretation of the correlation between the rise of that empire and the birth of Jesus. And Clement went so far as to toy with the idea of the good ruler as being akin to Moses, who "was always guided by the best logos," an animate law and the good shepherd of his flock.[5]

The existence of this strand of thinking in the Greek fathers of the church has to be borne in mind when one approaches the political thinking of those later Christians who reacted so enthusiastically to the improved conditions of the Constantinian era. Notable among them Eusebius of Caesarea. However prominent as a churchman, he is hardly a household name in our histories of political thought. But his writings have well been described as "the point of

confluence of all Oriental, Hellenistic, and Ante-Nicene Christian conceptions of kingship," [6] and "the clearly stated . . . political philosophy of the
Christian Empire."[7] To those writings, then, – notably the *Oration . . . in
praise of the Emperor Constantine*, the *Life of the Blessed Emperor Constantine*, and the *Proof of the Gospel* – we must now turn.

The political vision which informs these works is a remarkably positive
one. So much so, indeed, that it is not that far removed from the view
expressed by Eusebius's pagan contemporary, Themistius, who saw earthly
rulership as modeled after the celestial pattern of the kingship of Zeus, that
god being understood, in effect, as the supreme emperor. Eusebius's point of
departure, however, is a different and more historical one, nothing other
than the "Lukan" tradition which had earlier found expression in Melito of
Sardis and Origen. But Eusebius moves beyond Origen. To the Lukan tradition he weds the Philonic belief in the existence of correlations between
monotheism and monarchy, human kingship and the archetypal kingship of
God. It was, he says, as a result of their unhappy addiction to "the delusion
of the polytheistic error" that the men of old lapsed into the chaos and
anarchy that followed ineluctably from the existence of a multiplicity of competing kingdoms and principalities.[8] Such, however, were the miseries
attendant upon that state, that the divine *logos*, "full of compassion for his
human flock," "proclaimed to men the principles and elements of true godliness," the doctrine of the one God and his "sole sovereignty." He did so,
first, by the ministry of pious men, later, by that of the Hebrew prophets,
and finally by his assumption of "a mortal body." "The causes of multiplied
governments being thus removed," the Roman empire "effected an easy
conquest of those which yet remained" and "no one could deny that the syn-
chronizing of this with the beginning of the teaching about our Saviour is of
God's arrangement."[9] Thus

> At the same time one universal power, the Roman empire, arose and flour-
> ished, while the enduring and implacable hatred of nation against nation
> was now removed; and as the knowledge of one God, and one way of reli-
> gion and salvation, even the doctrine of Christ, was made known to all
> mankind; so at the self-same period the entire domination of the Roman
> empire being vested in a single sovereign, profound peace reigned
> throughout the world.[10]

And this "profound peace," this "deepest peace," the *Pax Augusti* which has
lasted "from our Saviour's birth until now," Eusebius considered to be "the
proof irrefutable that the prophet refers to the time of our Saviour's coming
among men."[11]

If such a significance could attach to the rise of the empire under Caesar Augustus, it is hardly surprising that Constantine's inauguration of a *Christian* empire – so much closer, after all, to the archetype of divine monarchy – could be regarded not merely as a fulfillment of the Augustan mission but almost as an extension (or completion) of the work of Christ. Eusebius, certainly, lost no opportunity to stress the sacred nature of Constantine's imperial position or his personal proximity to God. Thus he is portrayed as "like some general bishop constituted by God," a quasi-priestly figure deeply involved in the government of the Church.[12] To him, we are told, have frequently been vouchsafed revelatory visions and "the frequent light" of "the divine presence." So much so, indeed, that it would be presumptuous to instruct him in matters pertaining to the sacred mysteries.[13]

Such assertions are the more surprising in view of the fact that Constantine was still at the time a mere, unbaptized catechumaen. That notwithstanding, his victory over Maxentius at the Milvian bridge is seen to parallel the destruction of Pharaoh and his host in the Red Sea, and on several occasions Eusebius explicitly compares him with Moses, the figure in whom Philo and Clement of Alexandria had seen all royal virtues exemplified.[14] More startlingly, Eusebius seems to be hinting from time to time that with the advent of Constantine the world was witnessing the dawn of the messianic age which, as had been promised, was to follow upon the reign of Antichrist. The great palace banquet at which Constantine "feasted" with those ministers of God whom he had reconciled would seem to be suggestive of the messianic banquet.[15] In one passage of the *Oration*, moreover, attributing to Constantine the victory which in a parallel passage elsewhere he had attributed to Christ, the *logos*, Eusebius presents the emperor as a quasi-messianic figure, "the Servant of God" who has finally vanquished the "numberless" forces of evil.[16]

It seems safe to assume that it was his indebtedness to Philo and his sympathy with the form of *logos*-theology espoused by the Alexandrian church fathers that disposed Eusebius to draw comparisons of this sort which, in terms even of the most positive strand of New Testament political thinking, are really quite startling. His familiarity with Philo's Judaized version of Hellenistic sacral kingship is well attested. So, too, is the "weak" or "subordinationist" nature of his Christology. Both, certainly, are on display in the *Oration*. There God the Father is presented as the supreme royal figure, "the sole and Supreme Sovereign and Lord." "Unbegotten, above and beyond all creation, ineffable, inaccessible, unapproachable, dwelling . . . in the light which none can enter," he is the God of the late antique philosophers and, as such, if he is also to be the God of the Old Testament, creator of all things visible and invisible, he needs "an intermediate Power between himself and them" – that is, between himself and those merely created beings that are so

74

far removed from his supreme authority. That intermediary is Eusebius's second royal figure, "the only begotten Son of God," Christ, the divine Word (*logos*) whom the Father appointed "Lord and Governor of this Universe" and who, "receiving into his hands the reins . . . of the world, turns and directs it as a skillful charioteer according to his own will and pleasure."[17]

Despite these rather uneasy formulations Eusebius does not deny the divinity of the *logos*, nor does he fail to affirm that, without changing his "true godliness" the *logos* assumed "a mortal body," was crucified, and rose from the dead. But in the *Oration* he speaks little of the historical Christ, and it is significant that he explains the incarnation, crucifixion, and resurrection as necessary, above all, if the *logos* was to be able, by assuming "this mortal body as a medium of intercourse" or "communication" with humankind, to overcome their *ignorance* and to fulfill his mission as revealer of the One God, transcendent and omnipotent.[18]

His Christ, then, faithful in this to the Alexandrian tradition, is above all the eternally pre-existent *logos*, creator, governor, "preserver of all things," sole revealer of the Father, but distinct from and subordinate to him. Thus, although the Christ-*logos* is Lord of All, "mighty power," "the Author of Empire itself, and of all dominion and power," Eusebius is able to associate very closely with him the earthly Roman emperor, no less in his task of imparting to humankind "the knowledge of his Father's kingdom" than in that of governing and directing "the visible and invisible Creation."[19] For the Christ-*logos* expresses "by the similitude of an earthly kingdom that heavenly one to which he earnestly invites all mankind, and presents it to them as a worthy object of their hope." And in that hope the divinely favored Constantine, "whose character is formed after the archetypal idea of the Supreme Sovereign," and "who has formed his soul to royal virtues, according to the standard of that celestial Kingdom," partakes "even in this present life," thus standing as Eusebius's third royal figure in a uniquely intimate relationship with the Christ-*logos*, "from whom . . . receiving, as it were, a transcript of the Divine sovereignty, [he] directs, in imitation of God himself, the administration of this world's affairs."[20]

All such sentiments, of course, like Eusebius's further application to Constantine of the ancient oriental sun symbolism, are redolent of the Hellenistic vision of sacral kingship. Nowhere is Eusebius's eagerness to share that vision more notable than in the second chapter of the *Oration*. For in that section, without ascribing divinity to the emperor or stating him to be an incarnation of the *logos* and, as such, a living law, he contrives nonetheless to correlate his powers and functions very closely with those of "his friend," the Christ-*logos*, and to draw an astonishing series of parallels between their respective authorities, salvational as well as governmental. For if, following the scriptures,

Eusebius accords to the Christ-*logos* such Hellenistic royal titles as savior and good shepherd (titles which, he tells us elsewhere, the soldiers had accorded to the emperor), he himself does not hold back here from attributing similar qualities and functions to Constantine. He presents the emperor as an imitator of the "Divine philanthropy," "a faithful shepherd," and, indeed, as a sort of imperial savior, a priestly and Christlike figure who "dedicates to the universal Sovereign a pleasant and acceptable sacrifice, even his own imperial soul . . . as a noble offering, a first fruit of that world, the government of which is intrusted to his charge."[21]

It has well been said that

> Christians in the Ante-Nicene period [pre-325 CE] had for the most part recognized the Roman State, even when it persecuted them, as an order of *creation*, but emphatically not [as it was for the pagans of that era] as an order of *redemption*. . . . But now in the fourth century with the emperor a Christian, the state would seem to have significance as an ally of the Church or indeed as itself a secondary instrument of salvation by fostering . . . Christianity.[22]

In light of Eusebius's thoroughgoing resacralization of the imperial office on quasi-Christian terms that judgment would seem, if anything, to represent an understatement. For he is certainly moved to interpret "the victory of Constantine in terms of the history of salvation." It is not to the earthly, incarnate Jesus Christ whose authority lives on in the Church that he portrays Constantine as being obedient, but rather to the eternal *logos*.[23] It would be idle, as a result, to seek in Eusebius's thinking for any clear distinction between Church and Christian empire. To the contrary, as the subjects of the empire became Christian, Eusebius saw those two social structures move towards unity, the Christian society thus produced by its very existence standing in close relation to the Kingdom of God. Thus when, at the imperial banquet, Constantine assembled around him all the Christian bishops "whom he had reconciled, and thus offered as it were through them a suitable sacrifice to God," Eusebius comments that "one might have thought that a picture of Christ's kingdom was thus shadowed forth."[24]

The Byzantine *Basileus*

To the extent to which the Eusebian political theology was dependent upon a subordinationist Christology, one might expect it to have been undercut in 325 by the Council of Nicaea's insistence that Jesus Christ was the Son of God, consubstantial with (of the same essence as) the divine Father. In some measure at least, that did indeed happen, but not, it would seem, before the more chastening political conditions of the mid-fourth century had begun independently to make clear how vain had been the Eusebian imaginings that the looming silhouette of the millennial kingdom of the prophets was to be discerned in the newly Christianized empire of Rome. For it was under the impact of the emperor Constantius II's espousal of the Arian heresy that such supporters of the Nicene orthodoxy as St Athanasius (d. 373) in the east and St Hilary (d. c.367) in the west began openly to criticize imperial inter-ference in ecclesiastical affairs.

We must not suppose, however, that the willingness to adopt a less uncrit-ical attitude towards the claims and attitudes of the emperors in matters religious necessarily involved any wholesale abandonment of the Eusebian political vision. In the cases of St Ambrose of Milan (d. 397) in the west or St John Chrysostom (d. 407) in the east, it may reflect no more than an anxious attempt to discriminate between the ill-defined type of priesthood ascribed to the emperor and the more exclusive priesthood in matters sacra-mental possessed by the ordained clergy.[25] But even on that score and even in the west more than half a century later, Pope Leo I (440–61), who stands out for having advanced quite striking claims on behalf of the papal primacy, could still attribute to the emperor a semblance of sacerdotal power.[26] Not until the end of the fifth century, indeed, in the celebrated statements of one of his successors, Gelasius I (492–6), do we encounter an unambiguous rejection of that imperial sacerdotal power. For that much about the con-tested views of Gelasius is certainly clear. Little else is, however, and, given the conflicting interpretations that western commentators were to give to his views over the course of the next millennium, his statements call for some-what more extended commentary here.

Before the coming of Christ, Gelasius acknowledged, there had been men who, like Melchizedek, had been both kings and priests. But since that time "the emperor no longer assumed the title of priest, nor did the priest claim the royal dignity." Christ "distinguished between the offices of both powers according to their own proper activities and separate dignities," so that neither would be "exalted by the subservience of the other, and each profes-sion would be especially fitted for its appropriate functions."[27] That argument he sought to bolster with the historically misleading argument that it was only the pagan emperors who had claimed the title of "supreme pontiff." It has to be realized that he was writing under the crisis conditions spawned by the Emperor Zeno's unilateral attempt to impose his own im-perial doctrinal solution to the Christological disputes of the day. It has to be realized, too, that Gelasius was writing at a time when the emperor no longer wielded anything more than a theoretical authority at Rome itself and when the papacy had already begun the process of elaborating in legal terms its own claims to a primacy of jurisdiction in the Church.

That being so, it is perfectly comprehensible that Gelasius, by dismissing the established notion of the emperor's priesthood and by affirming a dualism of powers that was certainly more in keeping with the New Testament vision of things, should seek to eliminate the grounds for imperial intervention in ecclesiastical affairs. What remains a disputed question, however, is how much further than that he intended to go – whether or not, in effect, he intended to claim for the priesthood in general and for the papacy in particular a superiority even in matters temporal. Many a medieval writer in the west certainly believed that to be the case. Similarly, some modern scholars continue to affirm, and on the basis of the most subtle analyses, that that is the conclusion one should properly draw from Gelasius's oft-quoted statement in a letter of 494 to the emperor Anastasius:

> Two there are, august emperor, by which this world [*hoc mundum*] is chiefly ruled, the sacred authority [*auctoritas*] of the priesthood and the royal power [*potestas*]. Of these the responsibility of the priests is the more weighty insofar as they will answer for the kings of men themselves at the divine judgment.[28]

Much of the controversy over this particular text has turned upon the precise meanings to be accorded to the technical legal terms *auctoritas* and *potestas*, but there seems to be little ground for concluding that Gelasius wished to accord an inherently superior authority to the priesthood and a merely delegated power to the emperor even in matters temporal. Little ground, that is, unless one is committed to the prior assumption that when he ascribed a weightier responsibility to the priests in that they will have to answer for kings at the divine judgment, he had in mind not the emperor as a simple member of the faithful but the imperial power itself. The letter as a whole, which is, moreover, extremely deferential in tone, does not lend itself very readily to such an interpretation – the less so, indeed, when read in its historical context and in tandem with Gelasius's other principal statement on the two powers discussed earlier. For that context, it should not be forgotten, was one of crisis in which it was the pope who was on the defensive and the emperor who had broken with tradition by attempting, on his own sole authority, to impose a doctrinal position on the Church.[29]

Apart, then, from Gelasius's denial of any sacerdotal office to the emperor, his views constitute no marked break with Eusebius's half-Christianized version of the Hellenistic philosophy of kingship. In any case, however much papal theorists were to make of his views later on in the west, Gelasius's immediate successors at Rome appear in remarkable degree to have been unmoved by them, preferring to revert instead to fully traditional attitudes.[30] Still less did his limited break with the tradition evoke any echoes in the east. There, the attribution to the emperor of some sort of priestly power was to persist for centuries, defying efforts to disentangle it in clear and definitive fashion from the specific range of powers possessed by the ordained priesthood. To the emperors Constantine, Theodosius, and Justinian a priestly character was routinely ascribed and, as late as the ninth century, the iconoclast emperor Leo III was at pains to remind the pope that he himself, though emperor, was also a priest.

Over the course of time, however, a somewhat greater measure of clarity was achieved on the question of what such claims actually involved. In the thirteenth century, for example, Demetrios Chromatianos, describing the emperor's ecclesiastical status, called him "the general *epistemonarches* of the churches." The term was a technical one suggesting that, so far as the Church was concerned, he was "the wise defender of the faith and regulator of order in the church." "With the single exception of the sacramental office," Demetrios said, "all the other privileges of a bishop are clearly represented by the emperor, and he performs them legally and canonically."[31]

If one were to attempt to understand what he had in mind by calling on the battery of canonistic distinctions which the church lawyers in the Latin west finally hammered out in the twelfth and thirteenth centuries, one might suggest the following. What was being *denied* to the emperor was the "power of order," the power of conferring sacraments which bishops and priests possessed by virtue of having themselves received the sacrament of holy orders. What, on the other hand, was being accorded to the emperor in his dealings with the Church was the "power of jurisdiction in the external forum" or public sphere, a coercive power pertaining to a public authority, exercised even over the unwilling, and directed to the common good of the faithful – in effect, a truly governmental power over the Church.[32] It should be conceded, however, that in the Latin Middle Ages that species of jurisdictional power was viewed as embracing the magisterial power or authority over the defining of true doctrine. And while some Byzantine emperors did indeed make the weight of their imperial authority felt in matters doctrinal, they tended to run into an unyielding wall of clerical (and especially monastic) opposition if they attempted to do so unilaterally, by so doing shattering the *symphonia* or harmony with the Patriarch of Constantinople, the "amicable dyarchy" that represented in such matters the enduring Byzantine ideal.[33]

That qualification duly noted, there seems little reason to fault the characteristic judgment of Norman H. Baynes to the effect that in Eusebius's

Oration we find clearly stated, and for the first time, "the political philosophy of the Christian Empire, that philosophy of the state which was consistently [to be] maintained throughout the millennium of Byzantine absolutism," its basic tenet being "the conception of the imperial government as a terrestrial copy of the rule of God in Heaven."[34] Hence the persistent Byzantine consciousness of the proximity in which the Christian empire stood to the Kingdom of God. Hence, too, the uninterrupted and intimate mingling of the political and ecclesiastical orders in the political life, no less than in the legal and political thinking of the Byzantine world. In the Greek "political" vocabulary "Christianity" and "Christendom" had no cognates. The Church was itself viewed as essentially coterminous with the empire, and Justinian's legislation, accordingly (and quintessentially), extended into almost every nook and cranny of ecclesiastical life.

To acquiesce in such judgments, I should add, is not necessarily to suppose either that Byzantine public life remained undisturbed by the existence of tensions between the clerical authorities and the imperial government or that Byzantine attitudes on matters political were altogether monolithic and resolutely unchanging. Even a nodding acquaintance with the complexities of Byzantine history would serve to disabuse one of any notion that the emperor possessed a degree of control over the apparatus of ecclesiastical life such that the assertion by clerical dignitaries of the ultimate spiritual independence of the Church was totally inconceivable. Such, for example, was the intensity of the monastic opposition to the religious policies of the eighth- and ninth-century iconoclastic emperors that they were finally forced to abandon their prohibition of image-worship.

Despite such shifts and tensions, and despite an identifiable strengthening across time of the spirit of clerical independence, Byzantine thinking about kingship did indeed betray a remarkable degree of stability. It never abandoned the ideal of a fundamental *symphonia* or harmony between the imperial authority and the clerical priesthood to which the emperor Justinian had given influential expression – even if he had not always honored it in the actual exercise of his power. As he put it in one of his decrees, it was his conviction that "the priesthood and the *imperium* do not differ so very much, nor are sacred things so very different from those of public and common interest." And it was equally his conviction that "our chief concern . . . regards the true dogmas about God and the saintliness of the priests." In so speaking he also made clear that he regarded the imperial authority no less than the priesthood as a gift of God to man, and that he believed it to be a fundamental part of his imperial mission to lead his people to God, to concern himself with their spiritual welfare and, acting in harmony with the priesthood, to take whatever steps were necessary to preserve the true faith.[35]

Though Justinian nowhere systematically expounded it, the old Hellenistic philosophy of kingship so powerfully influenced his thinking that in one of his laws, abandoning even the muted qualifications of a Eusebius, he went so far as to embrace the ancient notion that God had sent the emperor to man to serve as an "incarnate law." That being so, it is understandable that remnants of the old vocabulary of imperial divinity, lingering on at Byzantium, were to generate echoes in the legal code itself, or that something approximating a Christianized version of the old imperial ruler cult was to remain embedded in the elaborate ceremonial of the imperial court and in such practices as that of venerating the imperial image in the churches of the empire. It early became common to portray the emperor as a "new David" or a "new Solomon" and to compare him, not only with Moses but also (Gelasius to the contrary) with Melchizedek, the archetypal priest-king of the Old Testament. In the great mosaics of San Vitale, Ravenna, Melchizedek is depicted wearing the robes of the *basileus* and elsewhere David is depicted in similar guise. Nor is it surprising that Byzantine iconography should reflect at least the chastened post-Nicene version of the Eusebian political vision, the imperial majesty thus being brought into close relation with the royal attributes of Christ.[36]

With this last point we return to beginnings. It was their Christological thinking, after all, that had eased the way for theologians like Origen, Clement of Alexandria, and Eusebius to domesticate Philo's version of the Hellenistic philosophy of kingship within the alien and hostile landscape of Christian belief. They had succeeded despite the disruptive impact of the Judaic conception of God and of Christ's reinterpretation of the messianic hope. By so doing, of course, they had succeeded in making possible what Christian political attitudes of the Apostolic era might well seem to have rendered impossible – namely, the construction of a Christianized version of the archaic sacral pattern. That version was to preclude the emergence in the Byzantine east of any firm distinction between what we in the west have become accustomed to calling "church" and "state," and even came close at times to affirming that the realization of the Kingdom of God was to be linked with the expansion of the Christian empire. Across the centuries, certainly, it consistently presupposed that that empire stood in close relationship with the heavenly kingdom.

Thus the emperor Constantine (Eusebius tells us) wrote to the king of Persia in defence of the Persian Christians, by so doing revealing that "he fancied himself the Caesar of every Christian in the world, claiming a power that could only rest on an identification of a universal Church and a universal empire" as well as on the presupposition that "since there was only one God in Heaven, only one emperor should represent him on earth."[37] Another

Figure 5 Byzantium, Constantinople. Hagia Sophia, mosaic in the south vestibule. The Virgin Mary with her child, between the Emperors Constantine and Justinian, end of tenth century. (akg-images/Erich Lessing)

letter, written over a thousand years later and at a time when a shrunken empire possessed no more than tattered remnants of its former power and glory, witnesses powerfully to the remarkable tenacity with which such ideas persisted at Byzantium. Written around 1395 by Antonius IV, Patriarch of Constantinople, to Vasili I, Grand Prince of Moscow, and responding to the latter's assertion that he recognized the authority of the Byzantine patriarch but not that of the [Byzantine] emperor, it bluntly insisted that

> The holy emperor has a great place in the Church: he is not as other rulers and the governors of other regions are; and this is because the emperors, from the beginning, established and confirmed true religion (*eusebeia*) in all the inhabited world (*oikoumenē*) . . . My son, [because of that] you are wrong in saying "we have a church, but not an emperor." It is not possible for Christians to have a church (*ekklēsia*) and not to have an empire (*basileia*). Church and empire have a great unity (*henōsis*) and community; nor is it possible for them to be separated from one another. . . . Our great

and holy sovereign (*autokratōr*), by the grace of God, is most orthodox and faithful: he is the champion, defender, and vindicator of the Church: and it is not possible that there should be a primate who does not make mention of his name.[38]

As we shall see, the gulf between Antonius's outlook and the posture characteristically adopted by his fellow ecclesiastics in the Latin west was to loom large. But however alien his outlook would have been to fourteenth-century contemporaries in the west, it was to prove eventually to be very much at home in the Russian east. Scholars, accordingly, have often been tempted to view the distinctive features specific to Russian kingship and even to the modern Russian state as stemming from the nature, depth, and endurance of Russia's Byzantine inheritance. Such claims, of course, have not gone uncontested. They warrant then, and by way of conclusion, a brief attempt at appraisal.

The Russian Tsar

By the nineteenth century the mantra characteristically on the lips of those who gave expression to the official Tsarist ideology was "Orthodoxy, Autocracy, Nationality." Already, a century earlier, Peter the Great (1682–1725) had abolished the Moscow patriarchate and reduced the Church, legally speaking and in matters administrative and organizational, to a department of state. In his *Articles of War*, he had also made it clear that his will no more suffered limits in temporal affairs than it did in ecclesiastical. "His Majesty is a sovereign monarch," the twentieth article bluntly asserted, "whom no one on earth may call into account for his actions, but who has power to govern his realm and lands, as a Christian sovereign according to his own will and judgment."[39] And that very formulation attests to the degree to which, since the time of Ivan IV ("the Terrible" – 1533–84), the title of *autokrator* had come to be understood as connoting not simply "independence from external or foreign powers" but also "independence from internal, domestic restraints, authority unlimited by laws, institutions, or customs."[40]

Contemplating so aggressive and unqualified an understanding of the reach of royal power, which went well beyond the claims made for the absolute monarchies of western Europe, the late Arnold Toynbee was moved in 1948 to assert that "the Soviet Union today, like the Grand Duchy of Moscow in the fourteenth century, reproduces the salient features of the medieval East Roman Empire." "In this Byzantine totalitarian state," he added, "the church may be Christian or Marxist so long as it submits to

being the secular government's tool."[41] Toynbee's formulation is a characteristically extreme one. In response, scholars have been quick to question
the validity of his characterization of the Byzantine tradition. And they have
also insisted to the contrary that "the seeds of [modern] Russian totalitarian-
ism . . . far from being inspired by Byzantine models" instead reflected
western Lutheran practices and "were sown by Peter the Great" in the eighteenth century.[42]

Such demurrals duly noted, and wherever one comes out on the larger
issue which Toynbee raised, it is indeed on the inheritance from earlier centuries that one should properly focus if one's concern, as is ours, is with the
sacral dimension so persistently attaching to the office and person of the
Russian tsar. But there would be something skewed about that focus if it did
not also embrace, along with the Byzantine inheritance, the legacy deriving
from 240 years of Mongol or Tatar rule or overlordship (c.1240–1480).

The nature and extent of that legacy is not easy to assess. In general, it is
important to recall that a sacral element attached to the office and person of
the Mongol khan (or king). Sacred or divine ancestry, certainly, was ascribed
to the great Chingis Khan, who, in the Chinese fashion, bore the title of
T'ien-tze or "Son of Heaven." He was viewed, and viewed himself, as possessed of the "mandate of heaven," and as divinely charged with the noble
mission of bringing peace to mankind by absorbing the nations into an overarching unity. The very title of Tsar, regularly applied to Russian rulers from
the time of Ivan IV's coronation in 1547 onwards, had earlier been applied
not only to Byzantine emperors but also to the Mongol khans descended
from Chingis Khan himself. Hence the sense that their rule, too, was divinely
ordained. Hence, too, the gradual process whereby in Russia "the image of
the khan overlapped that of the [Byzantine] basileus" and became "vaguely
fused" with it. Hence again, the related process whereby the "golden cap" or
cap or crown of Monomachus – of Central Asian rather than Byzantine
origin and originally "an expression of the sovereign position of the Tatar
khan" – became the primary piece of royal regalia of the Russian state. "For
Russians of the sixteenth century," then, "the title of 'tsar' was firmly connected with the image of the khan, more so than with that of the basileus."
And that image was perhaps "preserved in the idea of the Russian ruler as the
conqueror of Russia and of its people, responsible to no one."[43]

Thus Michael Cherniavsky. But that claim duly acknowledged, it remains
the case that, so far as the specifically sacral characteristics of the Russian tsars
are concerned, the Byzantine legacy was nonetheless the dominant one.
During the reign of Ivan III, in the wake of the Turkish conquest in 1453 of
Constantinople, the concomitant demise of the Byzantine empire, and the
contemporaneous decline of the Mongol overlordship in Russia itself, the

Russian orthodox clergy set out to obliterate the memory of the khan-tsar, to foreground instead the notion of the tsar-basileus as rightful successor to the erstwhile Byzantine emperors, and to position him as obvious claimant to the supreme leadership of the Orthodox world. In the early sixteenth century the notion began to gain currency that just as Constantinople had been the new or second Rome, so now was Moscow "the Third Rome" and rightful bearer of the Roman-Byzantine legacy. Around the same time, moreover, three other links with Byzantium came to be stressed. Having married Sophia Palaeologa, niece of Constantine XI (d. 1453), the last of the Byzantine emperors, Ivan III could well claim to stand in the Roman-Byzantine succession. So, too, could his royal successors. Those successors claimed also that when, centuries earlier, Vladimir I, prince of Kiev, had embraced Orthodox Christianity (c.988), the Byzantine emperor had given him, not only his sister Anna in marriage, but also an imperial crown. And they claimed too that his son Vladimir II – son also, after all, of a Byzantine princess – had received some further pieces of imperial regalia.

While the two latter testimonies to the antiquity and intimacy of the Byzantine connection appear, in fact, to have been no more than legends, they came nevertheless to be incorporated in the Russian coronation ceremony and were to serve across the years to reinforce the widespread Russian belief in the existence of a basic continuity between the second Rome and the third. So far, moreover, as the sacred nature of the tsar's office was concerned, that element of continuity was not entirely dependent on legend or clerical propaganda. It possessed, in fact, some real historical foundations laid back in the early days of the Christian principality of Kiev. Though parts of it may well have been of somewhat later date, the church statute attributed to Vladimir I and issued allegedly in 996 "established an extensive precedent for the acceptance of Greek canon law." It was to provide a model in later times for similar Russian statutes. And it was to be bolstered by the appearance in Russia of collections of canon law that had been translated into Slavonic from the original Greek.[44] The circulation of such collections had a broader significance than the term "canon law" might readily suggest. For they mediated to Russians an acquaintance not only with Byzantine imperial laws concerning ecclesiastical affairs, but also with elements of the Eusebian vision of kingship, with the interdependent relationship between emperor and priesthood, and with the ancient ideal of a *symphonia* or harmony between what we are accustomed to calling church and state.

Certainly, that Byzantine ideal was to become the Russian ideal, too. "Mutual aid linked . . . church and state . . . together irrevocably," both in institutional terms and in the popular mind.[45] If the balance of power was eventually to be tipped in Russia far more towards the power of the monarch than it had ever been in Byzantium, the enduring ideal remained in its essence the same. And enduring it certainly was. Among those who, in the mid-nineteenth century, stood out as defenders of the established official ideology against the corrosive forces of Westernizing rationalism and liberalism, "all approved aspects of the social order were said to be interrelated." Thus for the poet Vasili Zhukovsky the tsarist autocracy was "the final link between the power of man and the power of God." For the novelist Nikolai Gogol – and in this he was reaching down into the deepest layers of the ideological past – the tsar remained "the image of God on earth."[46] However different the trajectory followed by kingship in the modern west, in the Russian east, it seems, what we have called the Eusebian accommodation with the Hellenistic vision of kingship was vital enough in the nineteenth century to be able still to start potent echoes. But the forces of opposition were gathering, religious and intellectual no less than political, and that durable vision was destined in the twentieth century to meet its term.

4
The Carolingian Accommodation
Christian Rulership in the Germanic Successor Kingdoms of Western Europe

By the time of the emperor Constantine's death in 337 Christianity was well on its way to being transformed from a private sect into a civic religion, one that recognized in the person of the emperor its supreme head on earth, and one, indeed, that was increasingly willing to place itself at the service of the imperial ruler cult. In the years that followed the destinies of Church and empire were to become increasingly intertwined, and especially so after 392 when the emperor Theodosius the Great finally proscribed every form of pagan worship throughout the empire.

Theodosius, however, turned out to be the last emperor to be in a position to make quite so ecumenical a gesture, in that he was to be the last emperor whose rule extended to every province of the old empire. After his death the practice, instituted by Diocletian, of dividing up the onerous responsibilities of government between or among two or more imperial colleagues ceased to be an intermittent one. Theodosius's two sons divided the Roman empire into two parts, eastern and western, which were largely independent of one another and whose histories increasingly diverged. If imperial unity survived, it did so increasingly as little more than a beckoning fiction. The eastern Roman empire was to endure for long centuries down to 1453, and, with it, as we have seen, the Eusebian imperial ideology. By the end of the fifth century, however, though its legacy was everywhere apparent, the political structure that we know as the Roman empire of the west had ceased to exist, and its provinces had passed under the control of the several groups of Germanic invaders who had succeeded in breaching its frontiers or gradually infiltrating its territories – Vandals in North Africa, Ostrogoths in Italy, Visigoths and Suevi in Spain, Angles, Jutes, and Saxons in Britain, Burgundians, Alemanni, and Saxons in Gaul and its eastern environs.

The attempt which the eastern emperor Justinian I (527–65) began in

533 to reconquer the western territories which had once belonged to the Romans but had been lost, he said, through "carelessness," succeeded in the course of more than twenty years of bitter fighting in destroying Vandal rule in North Africa and Ostrogothic rule in Italy. It also succeeded in establishing Byzantine control over some territory in south-east Spain. But its long-term results were less impressive. Devastated by the long war of reconquest and groaning anew under a heightened burden of imperial taxation, Italy easily fell prey shortly after Justinian's death to the onslaught of the Lombards, a Germanic people who succeeded in conquering the north of Italy and a good deal of territory further south. Byzantine forces, it is true, retained control of the southernmost part of the peninsula and of a few scattered holdings further to the north – notably Naples, Genoa, Ravenna, Rome, and a strip of land connecting the two last. But despite the presence of the Byzantine exarch in Ravenna, Byzantine rule tended in the course of time to become a reality in the south alone, and Rome, exposed though it was to the constant threat of Lombard attack, was fated to be left increasingly to its own devices. All of these developments, along with the rise of Islam in the seventh century, the concomitant extinction of the Visigothic kingdom, and the passing of Spain into the orbit of the Muslim world, set the context in which the Franks, who (unlike the Goths) had embraced the Nicene Catholic rather than the heterodox Arian form of Christianity, were able to reach out to grasp the future leadership of the west.

Grasp that leadership eventually they did, constructing a universal empire that not only embraced the greater part of Christian Europe but also expanded the boundaries of Christendom eastward into central Europe and into territory that had never been subject to Rome. Under the great king Charlemagne (768–814), indeed, Frankish rule came to extend over the whole of Germanic Europe, except for Scandinavia and England, as well as over the greater part of what had been the western Roman empire, with the exception, again, of England, the southern half of the Italian peninsula, and about two thirds of Spain; it also included some sort of suzerainty over the western reaches of the Slavic world in central Europe. Though some confusion surrounds both the event itself and the precise (and divergent) intentions of the participants, there was a certain appropriateness, then, in the decision of the pope to crown Charlemagne at Rome in 800 as emperor of the Romans, as well as the subsequent (if reluctant) decision of the Byzantine emperor to concede that title to him, thus admitting the reconstitution at least in legal terms of the Roman empire of the west.

One must certainly pay due attention to the importance and governmental creativity of Anglo-Saxon England. But so far as the ideology of kingship is concerned, and the elaborate rituals and performances that gave it enduring expression, it was the Frankish realm, during the years running from the mid-eighth to the late ninth centuries, that came to function as the principal liturgical atelier. It was in that realm, and largely during that era, that the Germanic peoples of the west succeeded finally as Latin Christians in coming to their own distinctive terms with the archaic patterns of sacral kingship once so deeply entrenched among their pagan forebears and capable still, it seems, of generating harmonics in the collective consciousness. They did so (Anglo-Saxons no less than Franks, or Saxons later on), by a process that, by way of parallelism with the Eusebian accommodation, I have again for short-hand purposes termed "the Carolingian accommodation."

"Political Augustinianism" and the Half-life of Sacral Monarchy in the Early Medieval West

The vicissitudes and turbulence of Byzantine and Russian history notwith-standing, the Eusebian apprehension of the Christian Empire as a manifestation of the dawning Kingdom of God, and its insertion, accord-ingly, into the unfolding narrative of salvation history, was destined to cast a long shadow down across the centuries. It did so, however, in the teeth of the New Testament's comparatively negative appraisal of the role and reach of political authority, and that shadow was not destined to fall westwards. Already in the lifetime of Eusebius the Empire's center of gravity had begun to shift to the east, and the subsequent "provincialization" of the territories belonging to the western Empire was accompanied there by the progressive decline in the fortunes of the Greek language. The passage of those territo-ries into barbarian hands, and the subsequent expansion of the Islamic empire at the expense of Byzantine and barbarian alike, accelerated the pro-gressive weakening of the surviving links between east and west. As a result, for its contact with the thinking of Christian antiquity concerning political authority, the early medieval west became dependent largely on the writings of such Latin fathers as Ambrose, Bishop of Milan (d. 397), St Augustine of Hippo (354–430), and Pope Gregory the Great (590–604).

The writings of Gregory the Great helped popularize in the Latin west a packaged and somewhat simplified version of Augustinianism. Certainly, the Augustine whom one encounters in the political thinking of the western (or Latin) Middle Ages is not the Augustine whom one encounters in the pages of the *City of God* (*De civitate dei*), the "huge work" (*ingens opus*) and magister-ial theology of history that he was stimulated to write by the Visigothic capture of Rome in 410, an event which for some contemporaries had seemed to herald the collapse of civilization itself. The political vision embedded in that work was by archaic and classical standards a strikingly negative one, fully in harmony with the desacralizing thrust of the New Testament itself and according, therefore, to the empires and commonwealths of this fallen world a strikingly limited role. They served, Augustine argued, as no more than a "punishment and remedy" for our sinful condition – punishment, because of their dependence on brute domination and the severity of coercive force; remedy, because by the application of that force, however harsh, they contrived to secure a measure of the "earthly peace" or "harmonious agreement of citizens concerning the giving and obeying of orders" that human societies desperately needed if they were to survive at all.[1] That for him, it should be emphasized, was as true of Christian commonwealths as it was for their pagan counterparts. To neither, in effect, and in this unlike Eusebius, did the Augustine of the *City of God* assign any role at all in the order of salvation.

It turns out, however, that the Augustine whom one usually encounters in the Latin Middle Ages is the Augustine of the *City of God* only insofar as that work was reinterpreted in light of the tracts he wrote during the course of his long and bitter struggle against the Donatist heretics in North Africa. In those tracts, written, as it were, in the stress of battle, he was led to assert the principle that Christian rulers were bound to use their power to punish and coerce those whom the ecclesiastical authorities condemned as heterodox. By so doing, he was necessarily according a somewhat loftier dignity, higher authority, and more far-reaching responsibility to Christian rulers than to pagan. As a result, medieval authors who did not fully share his sombre doctrine of grace, who rejected his sternly predestinarian division between the reprobate and the elect, and who saw instead in every member of the visible church a person already touched by grace and potentially capable of citizenship in the City of God (the transtemporal and transpatial congregation of the blessed), broke down the firm distinction between the City of God and the Christian societies of this world that Augustine had drawn so firmly in all but a handful of texts in the *City of God* itself. As a result, they understood him to be asserting that it is the glorious destiny of Christian society – church, empire, Christian commonwealth, call it what you will – to work to inaugurate the Kingdom of God and the reign of true justice in this world. Thus it is on Augustine's glancing portrayal of the ideal Christian emperor, that "happy emperor" who sees his power as ministerial and uses it for the extension of God's worship,[2] that the Carolingian scholar Alcuin builds the vision of the Christian empire with which he associates the reign of Charlemagne. On that same portrayal, Pope Gregory IV (827–44) believed that the emperor Louis the Pious might most profitably focus his attention. In similar vein, Pope Nicholas I (858–67) and other ninth-century authors who deployed Augustine's authority and Augustinian texts contrive unwittingly not to render the precise thinking of Augustine himself, but rather to place those texts at the service of what, in a classic interpretation, H.-X. Arquillière called "political Augustinianism." By that term he meant an essentially theocratic pattern of thought within the modalities of which there is a marked tendency to absorb the natural order into the supernatural, the profane laws of civil society into the sacred laws mediated by the ecclesiastical order (whether under royal/imperial or episcopal/papal leadership), and as a result, to interpret kingship as a divinely ordained and essentially *ministerial* office incorporated within (and at the service of) the Christian church. In effect, and by one of those superb ironies in which the history of ideas abounds, the name and prestige of Augustine became one of the instrumentalities whereby archaic notions of sacral kingship, to all intents and purposes excluded by the New Testament vision of politics, were nevertheless able to survive in Latin Christendom, just as, in the form of the Eusebian vision, they had been able to survive in the Byzantine east. Charlemagne himself, certainly – and Einhard, his biographer, tells us that he was especially fond of Augustine's *City of God* – felt, like Constantine before him, that he had a particular responsibility for the welfare even of those Christians who lived beyond the confines of Christendom. Some scholars, indeed, have been bold enough to assert that "he considered it his mission to build the City of God on earth."[3]

Whether or not that was the case (and the supportive evidence is admittedly slight), the fact remains that even in the thinking of the Augustine of the *City of God* there were some hesitations that rendered that work at least susceptible of being used to support "political Augustinianism." This was especially so if that work was approached in the interpretative light cast by his tracts against the Donatists; still more if its readers were predisposed so to interpret it. It is in vain that one would search the pages of the New Testament or the *City of God* itself for the roots of that predisposition. They must be sought instead elsewhere – in the ideological groundsoil of Western Europe itself and, indeed, in three different layers deposited sequentially across the course of time: first of all, in the religio-political attitudes characteristic of the peoples of Western Europe, Germanic as well as Celtic, during the era prior to their embrace of the Christian faith; second, in the sweeping transformation in status undergone by the Christian Church during the late Roman era, a transformation advanced still further by the socio-political conditions that came to prevail in the Germanic successor kingdoms of the west during the course of the fifth to eighth centuries; third, in the attempt which clerical thinkers made during those centuries to come to terms with that changed status and those conditions via an earnest exploitation of the fragmentary patristic materials handed down to them and of the Old Testament texts that seemed to speak so directly to the conditions of their day. Those three layers we will probe in turn.

King by the Grace of God: Carolingian, Anglo-Saxon, and Ottonian Kingship in the Early Middle Ages

In earlier sections of this book, I have described the striking process whereby the increasingly Christianized late Roman world, with the help of what we have called "the Eusebian accommodation," succeeded in coming to terms with inherited ideas of imperial rulership and with their characteristic emphasis on the exalted and sacred character of the emperor. While acknowledging that the claim could and has been contested, I have also argued that the Germanic peoples were later to bring with them into the conquered provinces of the erstwhile Roman empire of the west, their own particular variant of the worldwide pattern of sacral kingship. The tantalizingly fragmentary nature of the documentary evidence notwithstanding, such deeply rooted inheritances from the past, barbarian no less than Roman, cannot simply be ignored. Nor can their continuing influence be discounted when one attempts to understand the ways in which the Romanized inhabitants of the successor kingdoms as well as their Ostrogothic, Visigothic, Anglo-Saxon, and, above all, Frankish conquerors themselves came to comprehend the status of their kings and the nature of the authority they wielded.

In the early medieval church at large, certainly, the degree of accommodation with the beliefs and practices of pagan society was not only quite striking but also in some measure intentional. On the missionary front the practice of substituting Christian feasts for seasonal pagan celebrations, churches for pagan shrines, and the cult of some Christian saint for that of a local spirit or deity, while viewed it seems as a shrewd and not inappropriate tactic,[4] was destined to have enduring consequences. The African Christians of Augustine's day regarded it as a devout practice "to take meal-cakes and bread and wine to the shrines of the saints on their memorial days," and his mother Monica abandoned the practice only when they went to Milan where St Ambrose, recognizing it for what it was – a survival in barely Christianized guise of the ancient cult of the dead – had forbidden it.[5] In the years after the barbarian invasions, it is doubtful whether bishops even of St Ambrose's stature, confronted by less sophisticated flocks, would have attempted to impose so ambitious a prohibition. By then, popular Christianity had come to embrace too many quasi-pagan practices, and, for long centuries, it was to continue to do so. Noting, for example, that it drew a bitter protest from the great reforming pope, Gregory VII (1073–85), Marc Bloch drew attention (adducing illustrations from thirteenth-century France as well as eleventh-century Denmark) to the propensity of medieval people to view their local priests as a species of magician, to be blamed in the event of illness or pestilence, and even sacrificed in the hope of ending an epidemic.[6] Modern sociologically oriented investigations, indeed, have raised serious doubt about the degree to which some of the more remote rural areas in Catholic western Europe can ever really be said to have been Christianized at all. As one might expect of a society that was overwhelmingly agrarian, the old nature religion, with its sense of the indwelling of the divine in the natural world, its rites for the promotion of fertility, its nostrums for the prevention of natural disasters, proved to be exceedingly robust, so much so that half-understood remnants of such beliefs and practices survived in European legend and folklore right down into the nineteenth century.

That said, and given the degree to which Christian missionary effort was targeted initially on kings rather than their subjects, it is hard to believe that some analogous measure of continuity or religious syncretism was altogether absent from the way in which early medieval Christians in western and northern Europe understood the nature of kingship. Even Alcuin, the great Anglo-Saxon scholarly luminary at Charlemagne's palace school, did not refrain, when writing to the Northumbrian king Aethelred in 793, from associating the king's own goodness with a mild climate, with the fertility of the land, and with the health of his people.[7] It is true that the available evidence is not such as to support the postulation of some sort of *direct* connection between the sacral nature of pagan Germanic kingship and the sanctity that early medieval peoples, from Anglo-Saxon England right across to central and eastern Europe, so often attributed to their monarchs. For centuries, in fact, and as has more than once been pointed out, there was something of a rivalry between the claims made for the Christian saint and those advanced on behalf of the sacral ruler. Even scholars who make a case for continuity between pagan royal sacrality and Christian dynastic sanctity have acknowledged the wariness evinced by the ecclesiastical authorities towards the popular cult of royal saints. But, that wariness may itself attest to the fact that contemporary churchmen detected in that cult the penumbral remnants of pagan commitments, and it has been conceded as probable that in certain instances, at least, that royal cult did indeed incorporate notions stemming from the old pagan vision of sacral kingship.[8]

The tenacious belief in the healing power of the royal touch, advanced already on behalf of the Merovingian king Gunthram (592) and asserted officially on behalf of the French and English kings from the eleventh to the eighteenth centuries, would have been inconceivable apart from some survival into the Middle Ages of pre-Christian notions about the sacred status of kings. It would have been inconceivable, too, without the willingness of the leading clergy to domesticate such notions within the boundaries of ecclesiastical approval, even if, in order to do so, it meant stretching the framework of Christian belief itself. So well domesticated indeed, ecclesiastically speaking, was the royal practice of touching for scrofula that it was to survive the Protestant Reformation and even to find official expression in an order of service incorporated from 1633 to 1715 in the English *Book of Common Prayer.*

The sweeping change of status which the Christian Church underwent during the late Roman and early medieval centuries can only, one must surmise, have eased the way for clerics to make such accommodations with age-old notions concerning the sacrality of kings. As early as the third century, bishops had begun to act as legislators, administrators, and arbitrators in the churches under their supervision. But they had been doing so as leaders of private societies whose membership was no less voluntary than was that of such comparable social organizations in the modern world as colleges, trade unions, and fraternities. Theirs were organizations that directly concerned only one segment of human activity, and their decisions as leaders possessed binding force solely in the degree to which they were able to touch the consciences of the faithful. No more than the leadership of any modern private organization could they claim to wield any public coercive power. By the fifth century, however, Christianity had been transformed from the proscribed religion of a suspect minority into the official religion of the empire, taking the place, therefore, of the civic cult of pagan antiquity. As a result, ecclesiastical authority, supported increasingly by the public force of the imperial administration, was well on the way now to becoming political and coercive in nature. It was also beginning, especially in the beleaguered western provinces, to reach out into areas that we today would regard as pertaining to the state. That is to say, it was beginning to assume (as Pope Gregory the Great was later to do at Rome itself) the burden of public functions in the realm, especially of what we today would call health, education, and welfare. Such developments intensified during the centuries that followed, and as overt paganism died out or was suppressed, membership of the Church and membership of the state gradually moved close, in effect, to being coterminous. The Church ceased to be a voluntary, private organization comparable to other social organizations and became instead a compulsory, all-inclusive, and coercive society comparable to what we call the state and, in its totality, well-nigh indistinguishable from it.

That state of affairs was evident already in the Visigothic kingdom in Spain during the lifetime of Isidore of Seville (c.560–636) who, equating Church and society, portrayed the king as 'servant of God" (*minister dei*), divinely appointed to rule that unitary society, with an authority that extended, accordingly, to matters religious in general and clerical discipline in particular. Of early medieval authors, Isidore may well have been the most widely read (he was certainly one of the most frequently cited) and his apprehension

94

of the facts on the ground and recognition (and approval) of the coalescence into a single society of what we would distinguish as "church" and "state" was doubtless influential. With the extinction of the Visigothic kingdom and the rise of the Frankish people to leadership in Latin Christendom, that process of coalescence was advanced still further. By the time of the emperor Charlemagne in the early ninth century, then, there had emerged in the West a single, public society – Church, empire, Christian commonwealth – a universal commonwealth that was neither voluntary nor private. To that commonwealth all Europeans, even after the collapse of the Carolingian empire, felt they belonged. So far as the Church went, its leadership was by then deeply involved in affairs of state, its laws supported by the coercive power of the civil ruler, and its membership well-nigh indistinguishable from that of civil society itself. And the beckoning vision of a universal commonwealth coterminous with Christendom, sustained in theory by shadowy memories of ancient Rome and guaranteed in practice by the universal and international character of the ecclesiastical structure itself, was to linger on to haunt the purlieus of the European political imagination long after the rise to prominence of an array of de facto national monarchies until, with the advent of the Protestant Reformation, the unity of that ecclesiastical structure was itself finally to be destroyed.

So far as what we are calling "the Carolingian accommodation" goes, attempts to postulate some sort of dramatic ideological revolution dating to 751, when Pepin the Short, the Carolingian mayor of the palace (or de facto shogun-like ruler) deposed Childerich III, the last of the "do nothing" Merovingian kings, and took for himself the title of King of the Franks, do not measure up to the facts. Already by the early eighth century developing Church practice, in its intermingling of the civil and ecclesiastical and especially in the ill-defined authority it was willing to concede to kings in matters religious, clearly reflected a considerable degree of accommodation with the archaic and pagan pattern of sacral kingship. It was left, however, to the (continental) clerical thinkers of the Carolingian era, along with their counterparts in Anglo-Saxon England and their successors in East Frankia under the Ottonian and Salian emperors, to exploit the Bible and the patristic materials available to them in an attempt to make some sort of theological peace with this state of affairs. In that effort they were highly successful. Their legacy was the robust theoretical framework within which the theocratic form of kingship that emerged in the eighth century as the dominant political institution in early medieval Europe was able, for the next three centuries and more, to flourish.

Although the lineaments of that Christianized and theocratic form of monarchy had begun to emerge in the seventh and early eighth centuries under the Merovingian kings, the events of 751 which mark the end of Merovingian and the beginning of Carolingian rule may serve us as a convenient point of departure. What those events involved, it might seem, was nothing more than a forthright recognition of where the realities of power already lay. But that was not the way in which they were viewed at the time. To explain why this should have been so would be difficult without acknowledging the stubbornly sacral character which, despite the Christianization of Frankia and their loss of what we would recognize as real "political" power, had clung to the kings of the Merovingian dynasty. We have seen that their stature as "do-nothing" kings had parallels among sacral monarchies in other parts of the world. Their insistence, unlike the rest of the Franks, in wearing their hair long may well have been of religio-magical significance (an interpretation supported by Vandal and Norwegian parallels), as also the custom whereby they traveled around (like the German fertility goddess Nerthus) in a cart (sacred chariot?) drawn by white oxen.[9] Certainly, the precise way in which Pepin went about the business of disposing of Childerich, and the extreme caution with which he approached that delicate task, does suggest that he viewed it as fraught with some sort of danger.

His moves, therefore, were of a deliberate nature. Only after he had consulted the pope and received his encouragement did Pepin proceed to the deposition. He went about it, moreover, by having both Childerich and his son shorn of their long hair and incarcerated in a monastery. At the same time, he himself, in what for the Frankish kingship was an innovation, was ritually anointed as king, first by St Boniface, functioning as papal legate, then, a little later, by the pope himself. Given the brevity of the sources, it is admittedly hard to be sure about the precise significance attaching to these moves. But the tonsure can plausibly be interpreted as a ritual deprivation of the sacred power inherent, as it were, in the blood of the Merovingian royal family, and the anointing with chrism – the ancient Near Eastern rite for the transference of someone from the sphere of the profane into that of the sacred – as "a piece of church magic"[10] intended to serve as a religious substitute compensating for the Carolingian lack of any such sacral inheritance or *Geblütsheiligkeit*.

If the ancient rite of unction could still be seen to serve such a purpose it was because it had been hallowed by Old Testament example and Christian liturgical practice alike. It had played an important role in Hebraic ceremonial and had been adapted to Christian purposes, especially for baptism and confirmation, for the ordination of priests, and also (though later) for the consecration of bishops. More specifically, as we have seen, the Israelites had adopted it for the initiation of their kings. In an era, then, in which literacy was largely a clerical monopoly, it is comprehensible that biblical parallels should have proved to be so powerfully persuasive. As a result, as Marc Bloch once put it, it was the Bible itself, however ironically, that afforded in the West "the means of reintegrating the sacral royalty of ancient times into the framework of Christian legality."[11] As early as the seventh century unction had become part of the ceremonial initiation of the Visigothic kings of Spain, and, in the early eighth century it *may*, on biblical grounds, have been added for a while to the essentially pagan inaugural rites of the Irish kings. Certainly, after its appearance in Frankia in 751 and England in 786/7 it went on to become the norm in the ninth-century Carolingian kingdoms, spreading thence, eventually, throughout the greater part of western Europe. While some local differences did persist, the usages prevalent in Anglo-Saxon England, West Frankia and East Frankia came to influence one another in intricate and complex ways, contriving in the end to produce liturgical forms that were genuinely international in character.

In the case of Frankia, where the fortunes of the Carolingian monarchs depended in marked degree upon the closeness of their affiliation with the aristocracy, no little importance attached to the fact that the papacy itself linked the anointing of the Frankish kings with the peculiar destiny as a holy and chosen people of the Frankish nation as a whole. Ernst Kantorowicz has argued that, ever since their conclusive victory early in the eighth century over the Arab invaders of Gaul, the Franks "had begun to think of themselves as the new people chosen by God, the 'new sacred people of promise,' as they were styled by the Holy See [itself]." Hence, as the new Israel, "they endeavored, as it were, to wheel into Church history as the continuators of Israel's exploits rather than into Roman history as the heirs of pagan Rome."[12] The rite of royal anointing was suited admirably to promote such views, and along with its introduction into the Frankish realms went an intensification of the clerical habit of comparing the position and attributes of the Frankish monarchs with the sacral position and priestly attributes of the Old Testament kings, as well as with those of Moses and of Melchisedek, king and priest. This development becomes most strikingly evident in the Carolingian era, when contemporaries were prone to portraying the Frankish kingdom as itself "the kingdom of David." During that period, too, the Frankish king, being like his Old Testament forebears the anointed of God, came to regard himself and was in turn so regarded by his people, as a new Moses, a new David, a new Solomon, a truly sacral monarch worthy of being greeted by the assembled clerics of his kingdom as nothing less than "king and priest."

In such an atmosphere, charged as it was with the memory of Davidic kingship and saturated with the language and imagery of the Old Testament (to such a degree, indeed, that contemporary history must sometimes have felt like a replay of biblical history), it is understandable that the desacralizing thrust of the New Testament should have been blunted, and that there should have grown up around the Carolingian rulers and their successors in more than one part of western Europe a version of the archaic ruler cult, though one played out now along the axis of a salvation history that was at once recognizably Christian and distinctively western. Already in the seventh century Visigothic and Lombard kings had been referred to as kings by divine grace (or favor), and in the eighth century Ine, King of Wessex (d. 725) had described himself as king "mid Godes gife." *Rex dei gratia* ("king by the grace of God"), a title still inscribed on British coinage, became with the Carolingian rulers of Frankia a standard formulation of the notion that kings reigned by divine ordination.[13] In the *Laudes regiae*, the liturgical acclamations of the Carolingian kings which date back to the late eighth century, the hierarchy of rulers on earth is portrayed as a reflection or counterpart of the heavenly hierarchy, and the king as triumphant warrior is acclaimed in, with, or through his divine analogy, the supreme, conquering king of heaven.

It is hardly surprising, then, that the modern distinction between ecclesiastical and temporal governance was to remain as alien to these theocratic kings and to their successors in western Europe for the next two centuries as it had been to those Israelite kings in whom, by virtue of their common unction, the clerical ideologists encouraged them to perceive their direct forebears. In the 877 liturgical "order" for the royal consecration, the "holy church" is simply equated with "the Christian people" committed to the king's care. Similarly, in the preface to the *Libri Carolini*, an important piece of court propaganda dating to the late eighth century, Charlemagne is designated as the governor of "the kingdom of the Holy Church."[14] No idle words, these, as the defeated Saxons were to learn when Charlemagne forced them to accept baptism. Whatever his empire was, it was certainly a community of belief and he was the Christian ruler of a Christian people. Religious responsibilities clearly lay at the heart of his royal charge. Of one set of instructions he gave to his *missi dominici* (agents of the central administration) as they made their supervisory rounds visiting those charged with the governance of the various imperial territories, Arquillière (noting their stress on virtuous living and eternal salvation) was moved to declare: "this document . . . is not an administrative text: it is an apostolic act!"[15] As the modalities of his administrative oversight no less than his legislation and court propaganda indicate, Charlemagne clearly regarded himself as charged with the task of leading his subjects to their eternal salvation, to such an extent, indeed, that not even matters of doctrine escaped his scrutiny or failed to reflect his decisive influence.

That being so, it is readily comprehensible that St Augustine's essentially secular understanding of the role and status of civil rulers should be lost sight of during the early medieval centuries, and that the prestige of Augustine's name should come to be attached, not to the sombre and New Testament-oriented Augustinianism of the *City of God*, but to the theocratic pattern of thought now commonly referred to as "political Augustinianism." In this connection, because his work circulated under the name (and authority) of Augustine and, as a result, came to be widely quoted in the early collections of canon law, mention should be made of the anonymous fourth-century writer whom we know as "Ambrosiaster." Often described as something of an ideological counterpart in the west to Eusebius in the east, he draws the traditional Hellenistic parallels between polytheism and anarchy, monotheism and monarchy. He also goes on to conclude that the emperor is the vicar of God and, as such, alone worthy of adoration (*proskynesis*), and, in a curious but influential statement, notes that "the king bears the image of God, just as the bishop bears that of Christ."[16]

But although such ideas and motifs of Hellenistic or Roman provenance gradually clustered around it, it was above all the cultus of biblical kingship that continued to provide the ideological underpinnings for early medieval theocratic kingship. That form of kingship flourished not only in England and the Carolingian empire but also, after the latter's disintegration, became the norm in the successor kingdoms of France, Italy, and Germany which were eventually to pursue their own distinctive destinies. Not least of all did it flourish under the Saxon and Salian rulers of Germany who, from the moment of Otto I's imperial coronation at Rome in 962, were destined to rule that revived "Empire of the Romans" which, in the fullness of time, came to be known as the Holy Roman Empire. To that cultus the sacrament of unction (or rite of anointing) was central. And the notions that clustered around it found broadly influential expression in the great liturgies elaborated for the coronation of European kings, as well as in the iconographical representations of such events.

Flourishing as it did over so wide an area and for so long a time, the ideology which characteristically underpinned this type of theocratic kingship obviously betrayed many a variation – too many, indeed, to dwell on here. A couple of them, however, both reflecting developments across the course of time, are too important to pass over in silence. The first, evident from the late ninth century onwards, is the increasing *clericalization* of the royal office in western Europe. The second, increasingly evident in the tenth and early eleventh centuries, and especially so in Germany, is the degree to which kingship came to be understood in specifically *Christocentric* rather than more generally *theocentric* terms.

The Christocentric or "Liturgical" Kingship of the Tenth and Eleventh Centuries

Of Charlemagne and his dynasty, Pope Stephen III (768–72) had already been willing to affirm that they were "a holy race, royal and sacerdotal," and the bishops assembled in 794 at the Council of Frankfurt had similarly acclaimed him as "king and priest."[17] With unction now firmly established as an integral part of the royal and imperial coronation ceremonies, it was in the period stretching from the late ninth to the eleventh centuries that the clericalization of the royal office was to become increasingly prominent. Anointed like bishops with the holy chrism in a coronation ceremony modeled on and strikingly similar to that for the consecration of a bishop, the king was regarded accordingly as endowed henceforth with a priestly or clerical status. Even a church reformer of the stature of St Peter Damiani (1007–72) shared the widespread view that, like the consecration of a bishop, the anointing of a king constituted a sacrament. The precise nature of the clerical status it conferred was not, admittedly, precisely defined. But that did not preclude its explicit liturgical affirmation. Thus, in the coronation *ordo* of the tenth-century German kings it was stipulated that the Archbishop of Mainz should adjure the king to "receive the crown of the realm at the hands of the bishops . . . and through this thy crown know thyself as partaker in our office." And from the tenth century to the twelfth (when it was quietly dropped) the formula "and here the lord pope makes the emperor-elect into a cleric" was included in the liturgy for the imperial coronation. All of this, as Wido of Osnabrück emphasized in 1084–5, because, "being anointed with the oil of consecration, he participates in the priestly ministry" and is removed from the ranks of the laity.[18]

The second noteworthy development is a related one, namely, the degree to which kingship in the tenth and eleventh centuries became specifically Christocentric in nature, rather than simply theocentric as had been the Davidic kingship of the Carolingians. In the eighth century Cathwulf, an author about whom we know very little but who clearly vibrated to the same ideological frequencies as had Ambrosiaster, could address Charlemagne as the vicegerent of God, whereas he relegates the bishop to "the second place" as "only the vicegerent of Christ."[19] By the tenth century, however, under the influence, perhaps, of the growing clericalization of the royal office and, certainly, of the "uncompromisingly Christocentric" nature of contemporary monastic piety, the kingship of the Ottonian and Salian rulers of Germany and of the rulers of Anglo-Saxon England had become, in effect, "liturgical." That is to say, it had come to be centered not, as in the Carolingian era, on God the Father, but on Christ, the God-man whom they imitated and represented. In the eleventh century Peter Damiani stressed that in the person of the king Christ is to be recognized as truly reigning. In the same century the historian Wipo portrayed the Archbishop of Mainz as having said to the German king Conrad II in 1031: "You are the Vicar of Christ. No one but his imitator is a true ruler."[20] In the previous century, as Ernst Kantorowicz pointed out, in the celebrated miniature produced in the Abbey of Reichenau and incorporated in the Gospel Book of Aachen, the emperor is depicted as elevated to heaven, enthroned in glory, as not merely the Vicar of Christ "but almost like the King of Glory himself." "It is as though," he says, "the God-man had ceded his celestial throne to the glory of the terrestrial emperor for the purpose of allowing the invisible *Christus* in heaven to become manifest in the *christus* [imperial anointed one] on earth."[21]

In arguing thus, Kantorowicz draws insistent parallels with an intriguing set of writings which witness to the clericalization of the royal office, and which reflect in thought no less than language the powerful influence exerted by the contemporary coronation *ordines* and liturgical texts. As a result, they give classic theoretical expression to what may be called the ideology of liturgical kingship.

The writings in question, which date to around 1100, are the *Tractates* of an unknown Norman or Anglo-Norman cleric traditionally referred to as "the Anonymous of York." While it was once common to view them as looking backward to a world of ideas already disintegrating by the time of their composition, that is no longer the case. Scholars now appear more disposed to regard them as expressing, not simply the political ideals of the tenth and early eleventh centuries, but even the *avant garde* views of their own era. Whatever the case, the ideals to which they attest were as current in France and England as they were in Germany. As a group of texts, the *Tractates* expound "the christocentric theory of kingship in its most concentrated, most consistent, and most extreme form."[22] They constitute, in effect, a fitting, peak expression of that complex movement of thought which, out of Germanic, Romano-Hellenistic, patristic and, above all, biblical materials, had fashioned another Christianized but, this time, distinctively western, theory of sacral monarchy and embedded it firmly in the unfolding saga of salvation history. Their somewhat esoteric nature notwithstanding, they warrant, by way of striking illustration of a remarkable phenomenon and as a fitting conclusion to this chapter, a measure of closer scrutiny.

The 33 *Tractates* attributed to the Anonymous, some of them no more than fragments, cover a wide array of topics. But in several minor and two major pieces (notably the *De consecratione pontificum et regum*) the author sets forth his ecclesiastico-political views with a measure of vigor that is not

Figure 6 The German Empire. The Emperor Otto III in majesty. A miniature of the
Reichenau School (c.996) in the Aachen Cathedral Treasury: Gospel Book, fol. 16r.
(© Domkapitel Aachen. photo: Ann Münchow). See note 21

always, it must be conceded, matched by a comparable degree of clarity. Though there is something of a parallel between his general approach and what may be labeled "the Ambrosiaster tradition," his departure from that tradition is an interesting one. Whereas Ambrosiaster in the fourth century, Cathwulf towards the end of the eighth, and Hugh of Fleury in the early twelfth century, all portrayed the king as the image of God and the bishop as (no more than) the image of Christ, the vision of kingship which the Anonymous advanced was quite explicitly Christocentric. If that was so, it was by virtue of the fact that he had elaborated a peculiarly convoluted Christology. For him, Jesus of Nazareth was indeed the true Melchisedek, king and priest. But whereas he was king by virtue of his divine nature and, therefore, through all eternity, he was priest by virtue of his human nature and, as a result, only in time – only, that is, "up to eternity." With this distinction of natures the Anonymous correlated a further distinction which enabled him to speak of Jesus both as a "Christ by nature" by virtue of his divinity, and as a "Christ by grace" by virtue of his "anointed humanity." The "Christ by nature," uncreated eternal king, the Anonymous regarded as equal to God the Father. In Jesus's functioning as Creator of the universe and regenerator of fallen man, the Anonymous represented him, therefore, very much as indistinguishable from the Father. As such he is clearly not to be confused with the "Christ by grace" who, by assuming a created humanity and concealing his royalty, became a priest, and who is, therefore, less than the Father and, indeed, subordinate to him.[23]

As was the case with the imperial Christology that Eusebius of Caesarea had elaborated eight centuries earlier, such formulations are doubtless irritatingly abstruse ones. But they cannot be bypassed because upon them rests the whole structure of the Anonymous's political theology. "On the high Christology of the Eternal Christ," George Williams has said,

> the Anonymous grounds the power of rulers. Thanks to his two Christologies the Anonymous's political theory, while seemingly *Christo*centric, will tend to be *Theo*centric, because the Person of the Humbled Christ has been reduced in significance and may no longer be said to exercise a predominant influence over the conception and image of the God of the Universe. On his "low" Christology of the Humbled Nazarene *sacerdos* [priest] who put off or rather concealed his royal nature the Anonymous bases clerical authority.[24]

The manner in which this political theology is worked out is complex enough to defy any summary incapsulation. It is possible here merely to sketch in two main lines of argument which (at the expense, perhaps, of a little distortion) may be said to control and to dominate the Anonymous's entire pattern of thinking.

According to the first of these, and under the New Testament dispensation no less than that of the Old, king and priest are both "consecrated with the unction of holy oil and sanctified by divine blessing," so that both – themselves now Christs by grace – are "one with God and His Christ . . . very Gods and Christs by the adoption of the Spirit." Thus

> each in his office is the figure and image of Christ and God. The priest, of the Priest; the king, of the King. The priest, of His lower office and nature: that is of His humanity; the king, of the higher: that is of His divinity. For Christ, God and Man, is the true and highest King and Priest.

From this it follows that "as an imitation and emulation of the better and higher nature or power of Christ," the king and the royal power are "greater and higher," too, and that there is nothing unjust about the priestly dignity being "instituted through the regal and subjected to it, because even so it was done in Christ."[25]

If human kingship is thus related to the "Christ by nature" (i.e., the eternal, royal Christ) and, therefore, to God the Father, with the human priesthood related, in contrast, to Jesus of Nazareth (i.e., the human, priestly, and distinctly subordinate "Christ by grace"), and if the appropriate conclusions are drawn therefrom, then the essentially sacred nature of kingship and its concomitant superiority even in matters ecclesiastical are accordingly enhanced. And they are enhanced still further by the second principal line of argument that the Anonymous pursues. According to this the Christian king, by virtue of the sacrament of unction which transforms him into a "Christ by grace" becomes not only an image of the royal God-Christ but also, in common with the bishop and priest, an image of the sacerdotal Christ-Man. As a result, and after the fashion of the biblical Melchizedek, he becomes priest as well as king. And as such, the Anonymous further asserts, he is possessed not only of the responsibility for guiding the church but also of the power to remit sins and to offer the bread and wine in sacrifice.[26]

In advancing these last curious claims the Anonymous appeals (as, indeed, he does elsewhere) to the tenth-century English formulary for the royal coronation that is known to scholars as "the Edgar *ordo*." That being so, it is conceivable that what is intended in the case of the remission of sins may be nothing more than the granting of the usual coronation amnesty. Similarly, in the case of the royal offering, nothing more may be envisaged than the practice whereby the English king after the coronation itself (in this, like the Byzantine and German emperors for that matter) presented to the clergy officiating at the Mass the bread and wine which, after their consecration, he would himself receive at communion. The texts, however, though not fully clear on this point, suggest the possibility, at least, that something more was intended. In the case of the royal offering it may be that the king was being cast in the role of representative communicant making the offering on behalf of the collective Christian people. And by the reference to his remission of sins, it may also be that the consecrated king was being conceived in a fashion redolent of the pagan sacral monarchs as propitiating for the sins of his people, mediating between them and God, serving in fact, and by virtue of the grace divinely bestowed upon him, as in some sense their "savior."[27]

These are, of course, extraordinary claims to make in connection with any Christian political leader. But, then, they serve to confirm that the king was being conceived as something more than a "political" leader in our modern, restricted sense of that term. And they serve also to underline the fact that the society over which he ruled was conceived as something more than a merely civil society. The Anonymous explicitly equates "the Christian people" over which, by virtue of the sacred unction, the king was divinely authorized to rule with "the holy Church of God." When, centuries earlier, Pope Gelasius had spoken of the two powers, sacerdotal and royal, which rule "this world," what he had actually meant by "this world" (*hoc mundum*), or so the Anonymous insists, was in fact nothing other than "the holy Church." The kingdom over which the king is called to exercise the supreme power is, then, to be identified with the Church "which is," we are then told, "the Kingdom of God." It is "the Kingdom of Christ" in which the royal and sacerdotal powers are no longer divided and in which the king reigns "together with Christ."[28] So that, as Williams summarizes the position

> In marked contrast to the Gelasian dictum that Christ had expressly severed the regal and the priestly powers out of recognition of their abuse when united in any but the divine, the Anonymous asserts the divinity of kings by consecration, the fusion of two natures, divine and human, and hence the king's Christlike competence in both the temporal and spiritual realms. The Anonymous holds that the Celestial Christ so far approves of the rejoining of the royal and sacerdotal functions that the king, by virtue of the apotheosis [resulting from the sacred anointing], may be said to co-rule with Him.[29]

That being the case, there should be little to surprise us in the Anonymous's further willingness to portray the coronation feast in Eusebian fashion as a kind of messianic banquet, to designate the king as mediator and shepherd-redeemer, to accord to him the messianic prerogatives, or to apply to him the

105

messianic sayings set forth in Isaiah (22:22; 42:7). Nor should there be much to surprise in the sense persistently conveyed that the Kingdom of God is, at least in part, being "realized within history through the progressive achievement of the royal *christi*."[30]

While in all of this, there is something of Ambrosiaster and more than one harmonic of the Christianized Eusebian version of the Hellenistic philosophy of kingship which was to continue for centuries to dominate Byzantine political thinking, the *Tractates* themselves contain little evidence to suggest any *direct* appropriation of such Hellenistic notions. Instead, the Anonymous grounds his position on biblical precedent, on intimations drawn from the old collections of canon law, and, above all, from what he takes the sacrament of royal anointing to imply. His particular version of "royal messianism," it has been said, "is demonstrably dependent on the Edgar *ordo*" of 973.[31] And that observation is a telling one, especially if one recalls Marc Bloch's warning about the danger of depending too much upon theorists and theologians if one truly aspires to penetrate the mentality that sustained the regal "idolatry" of the era. If, behind the arguments of the Anonymous did not stand the supportive framework provided by the sturdy structure of liturgical practice and symbolic gesture, buttressed also (as Kantorowicz and others have demonstrated) by the royal and imperial iconography of the era, one would be tempted to dismiss them as the stuff of fantasy, as wholly unrepresentative, as the product of anachronistic clerical intellectualizing possessed of no real rootage in the life of the era. In fact, it becomes increasingly clear, these arguments were more representative of the thinking of the Anonymous's own era and of the two centuries preceding than it was usual in the past to concede. Clerical in origin and inspiration such notions may have been, but one would be unwise to conclude from that that even Ottonian and Salian noblemen, however difficult and rambunctious they could often be, were necessarily prone to scoffing at them or brushing them to one side.

If one takes a moment now to stand back a little from the rich complexity of this Western ideology of kingship and to readmit the Byzantine experience into the orbit, at least, of one's peripheral vision, the temptation to align the Anonymous with Eusebius becomes, admittedly, quite strong. That temptation is very much to the point. However different their overall inspiration and the particular materials out of which they construct their respective positions, the general thrust of their argumentation is not dissimilar. It underlines the extraordinary tenacity of the dominion which archaic notions of royal sacrality have exercised over the human psyche. More specifically, it underlines the degree to which messianic notions and Christological concerns opened up a route whereby such pagan notions, linked after all with the cosmic religiosity and inspired by the cyclic rhythms of nature, were still able to enter and colonize a Christian consciousness that was essentially historical in its orientation.

Beyond that, moreover, and insofar as the thrust of their argumentation leads both Eusebius and the Anonymous to assign to kings and emperors a role in the unfolding of the drama of salvation history and to see the kingdoms and empires of this world as standing in close relation to the Kingdom of God, it also leads them both to adopt a stance diametrically opposed to the controlling position which Augustine had hammered out in close accord with New Testament teaching. If the ideas of the Anonymous were doomed to a much less successful career in the west than that enjoyed by the Eusebian ideology in the east, we should attribute that fact less to any comparative lack of cogency or lack of roots in contemporary patterns of thought than to the presence in the west of a whole range of factors differentiating the climate of opinion there from that prevailing in the Byzantine world.

With the recovery of Europe in the late tenth and eleventh centuries from the devastation and confusion caused in religious no less than political life by the last great wave of barbarian invasions (Scandinavian and Magyar) to break upon the west, and with the convergence in the mid-eleventh century of twin reforming movements (royal and monastic) intent upon the restoration of church order, those factors came to the fore. When they did so they precipitated the first great ideological revolution in the religious and political life of the Latin west. To that historic upheaval of the spirit we must now turn.

5
The Sacrality of Kingship in Medieval and Early Modern Europe
Papal, Imperial, National

In the pages preceding, I have been at pains to emphasize the remarkable degree to which archaic and pagan notions of sacral kingship succeeded in acclimatizing themselves to the alien religious conditions prevailing alike in the Byzantine east and the Latin west. The success of that accommodation is not to be gainsaid. Neither should it be taken for granted. Things could easily have turned out otherwise, and it is only, I would suggest, our familiarity with the outcome that has contrived to persuade us of the necessity of the process. Embedded over the course of unimaginable vastnesses of time and space in one or other version of what I have called the cosmic religiosity, notions of sacral kingship, in order to survive the triumph of Christianity, had somehow to be adapted to, or succeed in rooting themselves in, the soil of a vastly different ideological universe. In that transformed world the relationship of the human with the divine was destined henceforth to be played out, not as a comfortably integral part of the predictably cyclic and eternal recurrences of the natural world, but in the open-ended and turbulent arena of the historical, fraught inevitably with a disturbing potential for novelty and instability. So root themselves of course they did, and their success in so doing surely calls for no further elaboration here. It is time, instead, to shift the focus and to dwell now on the concomitants of that success, on the inevitable shallowness and delicacy of the root-systems' archaic notions of sacral monarchy could expect to establish in fundamentally hostile Christian soil, and on the consequent fragility of their continued access to ideological nutrition.

Kingship, it will be recalled, had come late to the ancient Israelites and had arrived as something of a foreign novelty. Its initial reception had been somewhat ambivalent; its subsequent history comparatively brief. In the context of the Yahwist religion it had been dogged persistently by the suspicion that it threatened to derogate from the supreme kingship of the transcendent and omnipotent creator-God. And while, after its demise in the late pre-Christian era, it had lived on in the guise of the messianic hope that Christians were themselves to inherit, that hope, despite its clothing in the vocabulary of sacred monarchy, was destined to be transformed into an adamantly other-worldly set of aspirations. Only in the fourth century, after all, having lived for 300 years as a people set apart, did Christians finally feel moved to grope their way towards some sort of an accommodation with the sacred aura attaching to their imperial rulers. And, even then, they did so uneasily and without unanimity, embedding as a result in what was inevitably to be a conflicted record reservations and qualifications that would return to haunt the would-be imperial dreams of their medieval and early modern successors. These reservations and qualifications, in effect, left open for future generations of Christian (and especially clerical) leadership the possibility of challenging the degree to which their kings had somehow come to be endowed with a sacred aura and charged with a quasi-priestly role in (and over) the Church. That possibility proved to be especially beckoning in the west where there emerged in the early medieval centuries a counter-current of ecclesiastico-political thinking that we have contrived, thus far, to pass over more or less in total silence. Namely, that which, while focusing on the divinely ordained and *ministerial* character of kingship and on the importance of unction in the bestowal of royal authority, did so in such a way as to highlight the crucial nature of the episcopal role in the administration of that sacrament, and to emphasize, accordingly, the subordination of the royal authority to the ecclesiastical.

In terms of the practical politics of the era of Carolingian hegemony, the ecclesiastical establishment, Janet Nelson has properly insisted, "was part of the realm and the king's obligation to safeguard it an essential part of his patrimonial role." At the same time, at least in clerical theory, "the realm, and the king's job were contained within the Church."[1] And for some years in the ninth century, when Carolingian rulers had proved themselves less able to deliver on their obligations, clerical theory had come in fact to bear some practical fruit at the expense of royal authority. Hincmar, Archbishop of Rheims (d. 861), a man who had devoted much effort to the elaboration of rites of royal consecration, had been moved, nonetheless, to argue that no man since the coming of Christ could be both king and priest. He was led, accordingly, to assert the authority of bishops, not simply over the king as individual Christian believer, but over the way in which he was discharging his royal office. Such aspirations to clerical hegemony or assertions of clerical independence proved, in the event, to be evanescent. They serve, nevertheless, to hoist warning signals for any historian so impressed with the sacral aura attaching to the kings of early medieval Europe as to be tempted to lose sight of the formidable barriers which the Yahwist religion of the ancient

Hebrews and the subsequent crystallization of Christian belief had erected against any truly enduring absorption of archaic notions of sacral kingship. Among those barriers it would be difficult to overemphasize the importance of a second factor which, despite its intermittent moments of prominence, we have again contrived thus far largely to ignore. What I have in mind is the persistence across the centuries not merely of a distinct clerical order but, within that order, of a unique locus of divinely-conferred authority and power, namely, the institution of the papacy at Rome.

Just how very important that particular factor could be had become evident already in the lifetime of the Anglo-Norman Anonymous himself. By the mid-eleventh century, the twin efforts of royal and monastic reformers to reestablish a measure of ecclesiastical order had come together under the leadership of a reformed and reinvigorated papacy now delivered from the corrupting tutelage of the Roman aristocracy. Moved by their partial re-appropriation of the New Testament and Augustinian political vision, and adamant in their insistence on the ultimate superiority of the spiritual author-ity to the temporal, the popes had been moved in the latter half of that century to launch a frontal assault upon the supportive ideology of liturgical kingship in particular and of sacral monarchy in general. By so doing, they sponsored the first great ideological revolution in the religious and political life of the west, one less well known to the general reader than the Protestant Reformation of the sixteenth century, but arguably comparable in its dimen-sions and in the wide-ranging nature of its impact. For that great upheaval of the spirit, by evoking Christian roots and denouncing as dangerously com-promising so many of the pragmatic compromises which the Church had made with the social and political conditions prevailing in the late antique and early medieval centuries, called into question the whole, extraordinary set of accommodations which, from the time of Constantine onwards, Chris-tians had contrived to make with the sacred aura attaching to pagan kingship. In the course of that revolutionary upheaval, the supporters of Pope Gregory VII (1073–85) had boldly proclaimed that "the age of priest-kings and emperor-pontiffs" was over. But the tangled skein of history was destined once more to demonstrate its persistently ironic nature, and the obituary thus proclaimed, we shall see now as we come to focus on the papal, imperial, and national monarchies of medieval and early modern Europe, was to prove more than a trifle premature.

The Emergence and Consolidation of the Papal Monarchy

The developmental process whereby the medieval papacy rose to prominence was an uneven one, punctuated by periods of humiliating subordination to the ambitions of the local Roman aristocracy. By the eleventh century, never-theless, the ancient primacy of honor attaching to the popes as bishops of the old imperial capital where the apostles Peter and Paul were both believed to have suffered martyrdom and of which Peter was believed to have been the first bishop, had long since begun to modulate into a primacy that involved claims to jurisdictional or governmental authority over the various provincial churches of the west. Such claims, often couched in an essentially legal and political vocabulary stemming from the traditions of Roman imperial admin-istration had been vigorously advanced by Pope Leo I (440–61), who had attributed monarchical powers to the popes as successors of St Peter and had attached to the papacy the old pagan imperial title of "supreme pontiff" (*pontifex maximus*) not long since abandoned by the emperors themselves. Later on, his example had been followed, notably by Gregory I (590–604) and Nicholas I (858–67). But amid the violence, political confusion, and ecclesiastical disarray spawned in the early medieval centuries by successive waves of barbarian invasions, it had proved impossible, across extended periods of time, to vindicate in practice any such claim to a species of univer-sal jurisdiction. Charlemagne, indeed, if we can believe his biographer Einhard, appears to have viewed the bishopric of Rome as nothing more than the leading metropolitan see in his empire.[2] Similarly, for the German emperor Otto III "the popes were [seen] to be no more than high priests charged with the ministry of prayer,"[3] and it appears to have been the dispo-sition of his Salian successor Henry IV (1056–1106) simply to "consider the pope merely the head of the foremost church in an imperial system of churches."[4] His father Henry III (1039–56) had certainly treated them as such when, taking to Rome itself his persistent effort to restore ecclesiastical order, he had summarily deposed three rival claimants to the papacy and gone on to appoint three others in succession, all of them Germans and the last – Leo IX (1048–54) – his own cousin and a vigorous collaborator in the work of moral reform in the Church.

It was the great irony of this imperial achievement that it succeeded in nudging the disparate efforts on behalf of a renewal of Church life towards a common center at Rome. And it was via its energetic leadership of successful church-wide reform and, from 1095 onwards, its channeling of the martial energies of western Europe into the great crusading effort to recover and hold the Holy Land, that the medieval papacy was to rise to hegemony. The posses-sion of such spiritual titles as bishop, patriarch, pope, successor of St Peter, vicar of Christ, servant of the servants of God notwithstanding, that hege-mony was to be imperial in nature. For the papal office, as it emerged in the high Middle Ages and has persisted down to the present, was, no less in its inner reality than in its self-presentation, to be an essentially monarchical one.

Scattered intimations of that ultimate destiny may be detected during the centuries prior to the revolutionary departures of the late eleventh century. Notable among them was the forged document dating to the mid-eighth century that we know as the "Donation of Constantine." By virtue of its inclusion in the mid-ninth century collection of forgeries exalting the power of pope and bishops and known to historians as the False or Pseudo-Isidorean Decretals, and its transmission thence into the *Decretum* of Gratian (c.1140), the great medieval textbook of canon law, the Donation was readily available for exploitation by later papal propagandists. In that forged document the emperor Constantine is represented as having endowed Pope Sylvester I and his papal successors with the rulership of Rome, Italy, and the western provinces of the empire, and as having transferred to him the use of the imperial regalia – scepter, crimson cloak, crown, and *phrygium*, the last being in fact a piece of white, pointed headgear of Byzantine origin. As a result, and, it seems, by deliberate intent, the Donation depicts the pope as occupying a position equal in status with that of the emperor, as placed at "the centre of the concept of empire," and as clothed "in the splendour which surrounded the earthly *imperator*."[5] As a result, the document was later to lend itself to extensive use by the defenders of a papal sovereignty in matters temporal. It did so, however, only after Innocent IV (1243–54) had reinterpreted it as describing not so much a *conferral* of sovereign power on the popes as a *restitution* to them of a sovereignty, or "royal monarchy in the apostolic see" that Christ himself had conferred on the papal vicar of Christ.[6]

In the earlier emergence, then, and initial development of such claims among the circle of leading reformers whom Leo IX had assembled at Rome, the Donation had played little part. After the deaths of Leo IX and Henry III and under the turbulent conditions attendant upon the minority of Henry IV, those leaders, prominent among them Cardinal Humbert of Silva Candida (d. 1061) and Hildebrand, the future Gregory VII, were moved to extend the reach of their reforming efforts beyond the original focus on moral reform, which had permitted imperial collaboration, and into the matter of the role traditionally played by emperors and kings in the profitable arena of clerical appointments. And there imperial collaboration was understandably not forthcoming. In the centuries preceding, the custom of imperial and royal control over the higher church offices had become as deeply rooted in social custom and ecclesiastical tradition as was the "peculiar institution" of slavery in the southern states of the Union prior to the Civil War. With it went the royal custom of investing bishops with the spiritual symbols of ring and pastoral staff which the reformers now construed as involving the usurpation by a layman of a priestly, sacramental function. That custom came now under attack. And in 1075 a disastrous clash occurred between pope and emperor when the young Henry IV, seeking to vindicate the full range of powers over the Church that his predecessors had wielded, was confronted in Gregory VII by an old and unbending reformer who, with a single-mindedness and intensity of purpose that would have done credit to a New England abolitionist of the nineteenth century, had brushed aside the pleas of the moderates and gradualists among his fellow-reformers with the fateful words: "The Lord hath not said: 'I am Tradition,' but 'I am the Truth'. "

On the detailed history of the great and destructive conflict which ensued we cannot dwell. Nor can we pause to tease apart the shifting points at issue in the subsequent centuries of intermittent strife between empire and papacy that reached its peak in the mid-thirteenth century and was still able to generate a pallid harmonic even in the fourteenth century, when pope and emperor alike had forfeited much of their former prestige and power. Instead, we must content ourselves with noting that the Gregorian reformers advanced two claims, related at their inception but destined in their development for distinct and even countervailing careers.

First, they were moved bluntly to deny the age-old sacrality of kings, the very presupposition, after all, for the extension of imperial and royal control over the highest of ecclesiastical appointments. Second, they were led to claim a crucial measure of jurisdictional superiority for pope over emperor, by so doing setting the papacy itself on the fateful path that was to lead, eventually if ironically, to its own transformation into a form of sacral monarchy.

So far as the former of the two claims went, Gelasius's denial more than half a millennium earlier of the priestly character of emperors was now flourished anew, stripped moreover of the deference which with him had served to soften its original impact. And his celebrated affirmation of the presence in "this world" of a dualism of ruling powers, spiritual and temporal (in itself a recognizable echo of the New Testament vision of things) was interpreted in such a way as to attribute an ultimate superiority even in matters temporal to the priesthood in general and the papacy in particular. "By virtue of the holiness of their conduct and the dignity of their *ordo*" the clergy were to be set apart from the laity and acknowledged to be superior to them.[7] Emperors and kings were no longer to be accorded the priestly attributes to which they had erroneously laid claim and Henry IV himself was to be recognized for what he truly was – "neither monk nor cleric; just a layman, nothing more." No more, indeed, than any other layman, argued Cardinal Humbert, Pope Nicholas II (1059–61) and, finally, Gregory VII himself, could an emperor or king "distribute ecclesiastical sacraments and episcopal or pastoral grace, that is to say crozier staffs and rings, with which all episcopal consecration is principally effected." "A greater power," said Gregory VII, is conferred upon

113

a lowly exorcist "when he is made spiritual emperor for the casting out of devils, than can be conferred upon any layman [however royal] for the purpose of earthly dominion." And no more than a swineherd who fails to discharge his duties, bluntly argued the Gregorian propagandist, Manegold of Lautenbach, should a king who has broken "the bond of mutual fidelity" with his people by ruining and confounding "what he was established to order correctly," be kept in office.[8] Hence the papal effort to reduce in significance the ceremony of anointing emperors, denying to it its old sacramental status, separating it in the coronation ritual from the eucharistic service, removing the clause *a deo coronatus* ("crowned by God") from the affiliated *laudes* or royal acclamations, portraying the pope rather than God as the real source of imperial authority, and representing the papal unction and coronation, therefore, as acts *constitutive* of that authority.[9]

With such theoretical negations and liturgical modifications the formal historical process whereby kingship was to be stripped of its sacral aura was now set in process. Promoted already by the political teachings embedded in the New Testament texts themselves, but lost sight of in the centuries after the triumph of Christianity in the late Roman world, that process, despite the ups and downs and twists and turns of subsequent history, was destined never again to be completely derailed. Instead, it ground on into the nineteenth and twentieth centuries when, having conspired to facilitate nothing less than the de facto demise of the institution of kingship itself, it finally met its term.

Thus far, these were a set of moves consistent enough with the New Testament political vision and, in some measure, with St Augustine's own negative take on the status and reach of political authority even when wielded by rulers who were themselves Christian. Its relation, however, to the sort of "political Augustinianism" regnant in the earlier medieval centuries was somewhat more complex and opened up the route that was eventually, and in the second place, to transform the papacy itself into a species of sacral kingship. By the term "political Augustinianism," it will be recalled, it was Arquillière's intention to denote an essentially theocratic pattern of thought that tended to involve the absorption of the natural order into the supernatural, the profane laws of civil society into the sacred laws mediated by the ecclesiastical order. In the earlier medieval centuries that had meant an ecclesiastical order subject to royal or imperial sway. For the Gregorian reformers, of course, that state of affairs was clearly out of the question. And yet they themselves proved to be so immersed in the traditional understanding of Christian society as a unitary one embracing the political as well as the religious, that when Gregory VII read in the classic statements from the past – that of Pope Gelasius, for example – that the spiritual power was in some fundamental way superior to the temporal, he instinctively took that to mean an explicitly hierarchical, jurisdictional superiority within a single, religio-political governmental order.

No longer was the Church seen as being in the empire. Instead, the empire was in some sense seen as being in the Church. Hence the revolutionary Gregorian claims to the effect that "the priests of Christ are to be considered as fathers and masters of kings and princes and of all believers," that the pope "may absolve subjects of unjust men from their fealty," that "he may [even, indeed,] depose Emperors."[10] And by acting on that last (revolutionary) claim and twice deposing Henry IV, Gregory set the medieval popes on their quest for monarchical supremacy. Supremacy within the hierarchical ecclesiastical order itself, where, in contrast to the rest of the bishops whom they represented as "called only to a [limited] share of the [pastoral] responsibility [*pars sollicitudinis*]," they laid claim to a limitless "fullness of [jurisdictional] power [*plenitudo potestatis*]." And, beyond that, supremacy also in the temporal sphere and in the world at large.

Despite the many ups and downs the papacy has gone through during the subsequent 900 years and more, the former claim to an essentially monarchical supremacy *within* the universal Church it has stubbornly adhered to right down to the present. In his *De regimine christiano* (1301–2), sometimes described as the oldest treatise on the Church, the papalist writer James of Viterbo, for example, treated the universal Church consistently as a kingdom with the pope as its king. Five centuries later, Joseph de Maistre (d. 1821), variously described as "Praetorian of the Vatican" or literary colonel of the papal Zouaves, was to do likewise. The sovereign pontiff he treated as the fixed Copernican point around which the whole vast cosmos of Christendom ceaselessly revolved, and he pushed the same ecclesiastico-political regalism to its logic conclusion by assimilating infallibility to sovereignty and representing it as an attribute of any power that was truly monarchical.[11] Paul VI (1963–78), it is true, set to one side the papal crown and other conspicuous trappings of papal royalty, but in 1983 the revised Code of Canon Law was still to describe the pope as sovereign pontiff, as "Vicar of Christ" possessed "by virtue of his office" of "supreme, full, immediate, and universal ordinary power in the Church which he is always able to exercise freely."[12]

The second claim, however, which involved the possession of monarchical supremacy in the temporal as well as the spiritual realm and in the world at large, was fated to have a more checkered career. The notion, certainly, that the pope possessed a *direct* power to exercise that supremacy over temporal rulers was destined to forfeit its credibility during the century subsequent to Innocent IV's politically driven deposition of the emperor Frederick II in 1245. And if, in the sixteenth and seventeenth centuries, a revived papacy was to assert an *indirect* power to intervene in matters temporal (whereby subjects might lawfully depose princes whom the pope had excommunicated or deprived of their office), by the eighteenth century that claim, too, had ceased to be taken seriously by the Christian world at large.

Nevertheless, during the period stretching from the late eleventh to the early fourteenth century, the papal claim to a direct power in matters temporal was articulated with ever increasing force. In the thirteenth century high papalist canon lawyers like Hostiensis and Alanus Anglicus were particularly bold in their insistence on the derivation of the imperial power from the papacy. Outside the Church, said the latter, "there is no empire." And in this they were to be followed by Pope Boniface VIII (1294–1303) who in 1298, or so the chronicler tells us, received the ambassadors of Albert of Hapsburg, claimant to the imperial throne, in the following fashion:

> Sitting on a throne, wearing on his head the diadem of Constantine, his right hand on the hilt of the sword with which he was girt, he [the pope] cried out: "Am I not the supreme pontiff? Is this throne not the pulpit of Peter? Is it not my duty to watch over the rights of the Empire? It is I who am Caesar, it is I who am emperor."[13]

It is true that his great predecessors Innocent III (1198–1216) and Innocent IV tended in their practical judgments to be a good deal more responsive to the nuance and complexity of the law, but even they appear to have been advocates of what amounted to a papal theocracy. For Christ, or so the latter said, being himself "true king and true priest after the order of Melchisedech . . . [had] . . . established not only a pontifical but a royal monarchy in the apostolic see, committing to Peter and his successors control over both an earthly and a heavenly empire."[14]

It would be improper to dismiss as "mere rhetoric" the language used in that last statement. What it suggests is that while the Gregorian reformers and their successors had certainly intended to deprive of any sacred aura the kingship of the German emperors, we would be unwise to assume that they were totally unresponsive themselves to the lure of the age-old notion of sacral kingship itself. Had that pattern of thinking, indeed, not cast so very long a shadow across their own ambitions for supremacy in Christian society, it would be hard to explain how the popes of the high Middle Ages permitted themselves to emerge as fully-fledged sacral monarchs in their own right. In that period they moved into center stage as the true (or most convincing) successors to the erstwhile Roman emperors, formally claiming many of their attributes (that, for example, of being a *lex animata* or "living law,"), deploying some of their titles ("supreme pontiff," "true emperor," "celestial emperor"), similarly costumed and possessed of the imperial regalia, greeted by comparably imperial acclamations, and ruling with imperial grandeur a highly politicized Church via a centralized bureaucracy and in accordance with a law modeled on (and creatively extended from) that of the Roman empire. We must content ourselves here with the evocation of only a few features illustrative of this new, papal version of sacral kingship – though, if space permitted, such illustrations could easily be multiplied.

Brooding about the ubiquity of sacral kingship and about the close parallel between royal and episcopal unction, A.M. Hocart was once moved to observe that "the king and the priest are branches of the same stem."[15] Certainly, so far as regalia, costume, and ceremonial went, in the mid-eighth century the forged Donation of Constantine took pains to depict the Bishop of Rome as entering into possession of the imperial regalia, namely, the red imperial cloak (or *cappa rubea*) with which popes were later to be formally "enmantled" at their investiture, the imperial diadem itself, and the Byzantine *phrygium*, or tall white hat, which was to evolve, on the one hand, into the mitre worn eventually by all bishops, and, on the other (by the fourteenth century at least), into the triple crown (or *Triregnum*), worn as symbol of their sovereign power by all popes down to the 1960s. That (eighth-century) depiction may have been a little ahead of the actual ceremonial realities, but popes were certainly crowned from the eleventh century onwards, and in the document known as the *Dictatus papae* (1075) it was bluntly stipulated that the pope alone might "use the imperial regalia."[16] Thus was launched the process which was to reach its culmination "in the thirteenth century, when all the symbols of empire were to become attached to the papacy," when Innocent III could say that he wore the mitre as a sign of his pontifical position but the crown as a sign of his imperial power, and when popes like "Gregory IX and Boniface VIII . . . [were] . . . seen to be in every respect successors of Constantine."[17]

In the seventeenth century, when the ideological dust kicked up by centuries of intermittent strife between popes and emperors had begun finally to settle, in a celebrated aside, the great English philosopher Thomas Hobbes was to describe the papacy as "no other than the *ghost* of the deceased *Roman empire* sitting crowned on the grave thereof."[18] It is now time to acknowledge that that observation was no less illuminating in its fundamental perception for being derisive in it conscious intent.

The Fate of Imperial Sacrality

Only with the benefit of historical hindsight, however, can one perceive that empire – or, at least, its Salian successor, the possessor still of a Frankish as well as a Roman heritage – as already in the late eleventh century being destined for the grave. Denouncing as the "Hildebrandine madness" (*Hildebrandica insania*) Gregory VII's arrogation to the papacy of an ultimate jurisdictional superiority over temporal rulers and a concomitant right even to depose emperors, Henry IV fought back along two distinct ideological fronts, both of them destined to be vigorously defended right down to the ultimate papal defeat of the Hohenstaufen dynasty in the late thirteenth century.

The first was explicitly dualistic in nature. It evoked Christ's injunction that we should render to Caesar the things that are Caesar's and to God the things that are God's, and, with it, Gelasius's insistence that by that injunction Christ had "distinguished between the offices of both powers according to their proper activities and separate dignities." Henry accused Gregory accordingly of having "usurped for himself the kingship and the priesthood," thereby holding "in contempt the pious ordination of God" which had separated them. The second front, at once more aggressive and more traditional in nature, invoked the divinely ordained status of the imperial kingship and the fact that the emperor had been "anointed to kingship among the anointed."[19]

That the German emperors, confronted by the pontifical regalism of Gregory VII and his successors, should have opted to dig in along the lines suggested by their own interpretation of Gelasian dualism is not at all surprising. It would be easy enough, indeed, to multiply instances of stubborn adhesion to that essentially defensive position in statements emanating from such later emperors as Frederick Barbarossa (1152–90) or Frederick II (1212–50), from national kings like Philip IV of France (1285–1314), or from a host of later-medieval polemicists. In maintaining that stance they were able to rely on the support, not only of the Civilians (commentators on the Roman or "Civil" law), but also on some of the canon lawyers, too. Thus, among the latter, Huguccio of Pisa (fl. 1180–1210), commenting on the celebrated Gelasian text which Gratian had included in his *Decretum*, endorsed a form of moderate dualism, stating that "the office and rights of the emperor and pontiff were separated by Christ," that neither power was "derived from the other," that having existed prior to the papacy the empire could not draw its power from the latter, and that the emperor had both "the power of the sword and the imperial dignity [instead] from election by the princes and people."[20] The imprint of a similar type of dualistic caution is evident also in the standard commentary (*glossa ordinaria*) to the *Decretum* written by Johannes Teutonicus (fl. 1210–45), of whom it has been said (though with specific reference, admittedly, to Innocent III's views on episcopal authority) that he "objected to Innocent's 'deification' of the papal office."[21]

More surprising, however, and on the second front, is the degree to which, after an initial period of disarray, the traditional emphasis on imperial sacrality – extending sporadically even to the quasi-priestly status of the emperor – survived the Gregorian onslaught on the very notion of sacral kingship. It survived, admittedly, in somewhat attenuated form. But by the mid-twelfth century, and despite clerical attempts to deny sacramental status to the ceremony of royal anointing, a revived emphasis on sacrality was once more becoming evident. In 1152, declaring himself to hold the imperial office "from God alone through the election of the princes," and seated in the great church at Aachen on the throne of the (soon to be canonized) Charlemagne, the emperor Frederick I was crowned by the Archbishop of Mainz and "sacramentally anointed according to the ordinance of the New and Old Testament." The words are those of Otto of Freising, who goes on to insist that Frederick, no less than the bishop-elect of Münster who was consecrated in the same church on the following day, was rightly to be called "the anointed of Christ the Lord." Sacramental lines were eventually to be drawn in such a way as finally to exclude royal unction (once known as "the fifth sacrament"), but it remains the case that as late as 1530 Charles V, the last of the emperors to be anointed (and following in this the example of his imperial predecessors), was to robe and serve as a deacon at the pontifical mass which Pope Clement VII celebrated on the occasion of the imperial coronation.[22]

It is hard to know quite what to make of such facts. By the end of the twelfth century, and reflecting in this the importance of the revived study of the Roman law, the type of sacrality attaching to emperors had begun to lose its Christocentric-liturgical intonation and to take on a somewhat thinner, legally inspired coloration. If the emperor was no longer to be called the "vicar of Christ" (the pope had now come to monopolize that title), under the influence of the old Roman legal vocabulary he was some-times referred to as a "god on earth" or "terrestrial god" and the empire itself came to be known as the *sacrum imperium*. Frederick I did not hesi-tate to proclaim himself to be "following the example" of such "divine [*divi*] predecessors as Constantine, Justinian and Theodosius," and the Hellenistic notion of the king as a "living law" was revived and applied to him. As a result, the emperor came to be portrayed as something of a medi-atorial figure, a "priest of justice," the very "Idea of Justice," or the "Father and Son of Justice" – as Frederick II was described in 1231 in the *Liber Augustalis*, the collected constitutions of his Sicilian kingdom. Emphasiz-ing, then, that "after the Investiture Contest, the prince regained his priestly character through the high pretensions of the Roman legal philosophy," Ernst Kantorowicz not implausibly argued that in the thirteenth century the "hallowing" or "sanctification of the secular state and its institutions" was in some measure to run parallel to the growing "imperialization of the papacy." Frederick II's court was sometimes referred to as "the imperial church," and in his person, certainly, the emperor was to become the focus of quasi-messianic hopes, as his subjects and supporters began to see in him a new Augustus, a new "savior," a providential figure whose destiny it would be to renew the world and "inaugurate the Golden Age."[23]

In the *Divine Comedy*, at the start of the next century Dante, admittedly, was to consign Frederick II to hell – presumably because he understood him to have intruded his power into the spiritual domain. Yet Dante was not himself immune to the providentialist thinking about the empire or the imperial messianism once prevalent among Frederick II's own supporters. Noting in Hellenistic and early Christian fashion the parallelism between monarchy and monotheism, and echoing the Lukan/Eusebian tradition according to which the coincidence of Christ's incarnation with the Augustan peace was to be understood as nothing less than providential, he insisted that it was God who was the immediate source of the emperor's authority. God alone elects rulers. The imperial Electors, accordingly, "should not bear ... [that] ... title, but should [instead] be called heralds of the divine providence." In the euphoria which, in 1311, greeted the descent of the emperor Henry VII (d. 1313) into Italy, Dante was moved, therefore, not only to entitle him as "King of the earth, and minister of God" or "by Divine Providence King of the Romans and ever Augustus," but even to depict him in messianic guise: "Then my spirit rejoiced within me when I said secretly within myself: 'Behold the Lamb of God, which taketh away the sins of the world.'"[24]

Of course, by the time Dante wrote those extraordinary words, the political realities of the day had conspired to ensure that the universalist ideal which he was extending himself to honor was doomed to remain incapable of political realization. Frederick II's disastrous conflict with the papacy along with the subsequent extermination of his Hohenstaufen successors ended the possibility of clothing the dream of universal empire with any truly viable institutional form. The future was to lie, instead, with forces antipathetic to the very idea of universalism. It was to lie, in effect, with the national kingdoms which were now beginning to step out from under the imperial shadow. And those kingdoms, until they themselves entered in the fifteenth century upon their own time of troubles, were destined for a while to take center stage.

Kingship in France and England

As early as the ninth century, taking their cue from Luke 22:38, with its mysterious reference to two swords, papal letters had assumed the text in classic fashion to be referring to "the material sword of secular coercion and the spiritual sword of excommunication." At that time the image was invoked to propose the harmonious ideal of cooperation between the two powers.[25] In the eleventh century, however, the Gregorian reformers had called that ideal into question – or, at least, they had peremptorily changed the ground rules under which such cooperation could take place. In the twelfth century, moreover, St Bernard of Clairvaux (d. 1153) had lent the weight of his formidable authority to the papalist or "hierocratic" interpretation of that classic ideal, whereby "both swords, spiritual and material . . . belong to the church: the one by the hand of the priest, the other by the hand of the soldier, but clearly at the bidding of the priest [*ad nutum sacerdotis*]". By the thirteenth century, that hierocratic interpretation, much debated in the canonist commentaries, had succeeded in entrenching itself in the theology faculties at Oxford and Paris. Early on in the scholastic era, indeed, Robert Grosseteste, the great Bishop of Lincoln (d. 1253), had given it not untypical expression when, acknowledging that Christ himself had "commanded the division of the functions of each of the two swords and of the two laws between temporal and ecclesiastical rulers," he went on to insist that Christ had done so "with the oneness of each sword and each law retained [nonetheless] in the charge of the rulers of the church."[26]

Such hierocratic pretensions, however, which the French baronage dismissed as "outrageous novelties," the French and English monarchs and the legal traditions of their respective kingdoms proved robust enough to keep at bay. As a result, they were able to vindicate in practice the autonomy of the crown within the territorial boundaries of their respective kingdoms and its right to determine, in any given legal case, whether or not jurisdiction should be conceded to the ecclesiastical courts. Great moments of crisis there undoubtedly were – in the case of England the clashes between Henry II and Archbishop Thomas à Becket in the twelfth century, and between King John and Pope Innocent III in the thirteenth; in the case of France, that between Philip IV and Boniface VIII in the early fourteenth. But such moments of outright, protracted confrontation were the exception rather than the rule. So far as the ongoing relationship between the two powers went, the norm in both kingdoms turned out to be a form of dualism tilted in favor of the temporal, what one historian has aptly characterized as "cooperative dualism at the king's command."[27]

Unlike the German emperors, moreover, the kings in question, French and English, were by the fourteenth century well established, hereditary rulers of discrete national territories whose forebears (unlike those of the German emperors) had not had to bear the full brunt of the Gregorian attack on the old tradition of pontifical kingship and all that it had entailed. They retained, as a result, despite the papal effort to deny sacramental status to the ceremony of royal anointing, a recognizably sacred aura. The curative powers which clerics and populace alike believed them to be exercising when they touched those suffering from scrofula (known, significantly enough in both countries, as "the King's Evil"/"*le mal du roi*"), were but one dramatic and continuing manifestation of their sacral status. In France Charles V (1364–80), of whom his court writers employed the most exalted language, promoted that status quite self-consciously. He was at pains to assemble a great collection of books on matters governmental in general and on monarchy and its sacral dimension in particular. Notable among them was the *Traité du sacre* of Jean Golein, a tract which focused on the anointing of the king with a sacred balm believed to have been delivered from heaven during the baptism of Clovis, the first of the Merovingian kings. Golein viewed the royal unction as witnessing to the fact that the king's authority derived from God. It was not only the source of his curative powers. It also functioned in such a way as to "cleanse" (*nettoie*) him from his sins and to transform him into some sort of priestly figure. That priestly status, certainly, is very much on display in the program of miniatures preserved in the *Coronation Book of Charles V* which provides, in effect, a visual record of that king's coronation in 1364. And Charles V's own sincere adhesion to such views is reflected in the fact that he was to wear "a cap throughout his life to preserve the [trace of] oil received at his coronation from any earthly contact."[28]

In his *De officio regis*, written in England at around the same time, John Wycliffe (d. 1384) asserted that the king was the Vicar of God in matters temporal and, as such was owed almost unlimited obedience. He argued further (like Jan Hus in Bohemia) that the king, reflecting the divinity of Christ, was superior in dignity to the priest who reflected only Christ's humanity. In so doing, he was echoing the high regalist point of view embedded in what we have called the Ambrosiaster tradition, in the form imparted to it by the Anglo-Norman Anonymous three centuries earlier. And although there is no evidence to suggest that Richard II (1377–99) himself drew on Wycliffite ideas, that ill-fated king seems to have firmly believed in the divinely conferred nature of his royal office, in the unquestioning obedience owed thereby to him, and in his freedom from those constitutional restraints on the exercise of royal power that Englishmen over the centuries had come to view as customary. Hereditary succession and royal unction (which he clearly viewed as a sacrament) witnessed in his view to his divine right to rule.

The moving speech which Shakespeare puts in his mouth does indeed convey Richard's sincere conviction that

> Not all the water in the rough rude sea
> Can wash the balm from an anointed king;
> The breath of worldly men cannot depose
> The deputy elected by the lord.

(*Richard II*, Act 3, Scene 2, ll. 54–7)

Until his death, then, and despite his deposition in 1399, he continued to view himself, by virtue of his anointment, as the true king of England.

Historians have sometimes been disposed to speak of his deposition as "the revolution of 1399." While that almost certainly exaggerates the dimensions of the change involved in the substitution of Lancastrian for Plantagenet, it remains the case that the better part of the century ensuing did constitute a period of crisis for the English monarchy – and, in fact, for most of the monarchies of Europe. The kingdoms of Portugal and Poland proved to be exceptions to the rule, but kingdoms elsewhere fell into disarray and kingship itself was thrown on the defensive, and for a variety of reasons specific to the individual kingdoms. Disputed succession, dynastic upheaval, factional and religious strife, outright civil war – all played their role. So, too, did the devastating impact of war between nations and rulers: in the east, the remorseless pressure of the Ottoman conqueror; in the west, the destructive continuation of the Hundred Years' War between England and France.

Nor, in the international arena, did the Church itself prove to be immune to the disarray characteristic of this time of troubles. The Great Schism of the west, which for 40 long years had seen, first two, and then three rival lines of claimants compete scandalously for the papal throne, was brought to a definitive end in 1418 with the election of Martin V. But so far as the sweeping claims of the papal monarchy were concerned, that happy outcome had been bought at great price. Where diplomacy, attempts at arbitration, resort, even, to armed coercion had all failed to end the schism, it was left to a general council assembled at Constance (1414–18), the greatest of all medieval representative assemblies, to achieve that goal. And it did so only after embracing in solemn legislation the constitutionalist claim that the general council, in virtue of the fact that it represented the universal Church and wielded the divinely conferred authority that resided ultimately in the entire body of the faithful, possessed a jurisdictional or governmental power superior in certain critical cases to that of the pope alone. By means of that power it could impose constitutional restraints on the pope and could, if need be, go so far as to try, judge, punish, and even depose a recalcitrant papal incumbent.

123

All of those things were in fact done at the Council of Constance, and the pressure on the papacy was continued at the subsequent Council of Basel (1431–49). The essentially constitutionalist challenge which the "conciliarists" at the latter council handed down to Pope Eugenius IV (1431–47) was itself grounded in natural-law assumptions about the ultimate authority residing in political communities, assumptions which had a broad resonance for the late medieval political world at large. Recognizing that fact, and anxious now to marshal support among the kings and princes of Europe, Eugenius IV and his partisans bracketed for the time being the old papal pretensions to some sort of jurisdictional superiority even in matters temporal. Instead, they cast the papacy in more "user-friendly" guise as the beleaguered champion of the monarchical principle itself, which they portrayed now, in its temporal or secular no less than its papal or spiritual form, as being under radical attack at the hands of the allegedly "populist" conciliarists who had seized control of the proceedings at the Council of Basel. If we can take at face value the testimony of the Venetian, Pier da Monte, a staunchly monarchist papal diplomat, the Eugenian claim that Basel did indeed pose a threat to "every kingdom, every province and region, all cities and peoples – the whole world" found responsive echoes in European political circles – even, for example, at the court of Henry VI of England.[29] In the war of propaganda and diplomatic campaign that ensued, the papalists were ultimately to meet with some success, winning over the key temporal rulers, depriving the conciliarists as a result of the political support on which they depended, and putting an end (at least in immediate practical terms) to the conciliar attempt to hem in the glittering papal monarchy with fustian constitutional restraint.

It is true that the conciliarist writers, building notably on the corporatist ideas of the canon lawyers, had brought a heightened measure of theoretical precision to the traditional and essentially practical medieval preoccupation with the role in community and political matters of representation and consent. They had produced (and, during the sixteenth and seventeenth centuries continued to add to) an enormous body of constitutionalist argumentation that served to reinforce in the world of "secular" politics the widespread late medieval sense that the people as a whole, or the "estates" representing them, retained by natural law an ultimate authority over errant monarchs. That conciliarist literature was not to be forgotten in the following centuries. It was destined in the sixteenth century to be exploited by Calvinist advocates of a right of resistance to persecuting or tyrannous rulers, in the seventeenth century by parliamentarian and/or Puritan opponents in England of Charles I's "absolutist" policies, and in eighteenth-century France by those "judicial Jansenists" and "patriot constitutionalists" who found themselves in opposition to royal policies and who were moved to make an oppositional case subordinating the authority of the king to that of the nation as a whole.[30] That notwithstanding, it remains the case that for a century and more after the papal defeat of the conciliarists at Basel, the tide was to flow strongly in favor of the monarchs of Europe, temporal no less than papal.

Out of the fifteenth-century cauldron of conflict and chaos emerged forms of kingship that were more reliably financed, more adequately institutionalized, less subject to limitation by the (decaying) parliaments and representative assemblies of the era, and more prone to confidently advancing quasi-absolutist claims for the reach of their prerogatives. That, certainly, was to be true of the popes in the era of papal "restoration" after Basel. In that era they emerged once more, in theory no less than practice, as monarchs of a distinctly absolutist stamp, despite the limitations of their role as Italian princes, for that, as temporal rulers, was what they had now become. They began, accordingly, to frame their monarchical claims to rulership over the universal Church in such a way as to assert their uniqueness. And they rejected, thereby, the classic conciliarist claim that the Church, being a polity basically akin to polities in general, retained by natural law a residual right to prevent its own ruin even to the point of deposing its ruler. Stressing at the start of the sixteenth century the uniquely divine grounding of papal monarchical power, Cardinal Cajetan insisted that to argue thus in essentially conciliarist fashion was totally unacceptable in that it "perverted" the Church's basic constitutional order, turning it into a democratic or popular one in which all authority resides with the whole community rather than with any single person. One must recognize instead, or so Cardinal Bellarmine added a century later, that given the uniquely *supernatural* grounding of ecclesiastical power, analogies drawn from the profane world of secular politics are altogether irrelevant. "The Holy Church," he wrote in 1606, arguing against the Venetian theologian Paolo Sarpi, "is not like the Republic of Venice which can be said to be . . . above the prince." "Nor is it like a worldly kingdom," where the power of the monarch is derived ultimately from the people. Instead, it is "a most perfect kingdom and an absolute monarchy, which depends not on the people . . . but on the divine will alone."[31]

This was a quintessential formulation, and Bellarmine was to emerge as the doughty defender, not simply of the pope's absolute monarchy within the church itself, but also of a renewed assertion of an indirect papal power in temporal affairs. Nor was this simply a matter of toothless theory, for in 1570 Pope Pius V had exercised that indirect power in classic fashion when, in the bull *Regnans in excelsis*, he excommunicated and declared deposed Queen Elizabeth I of England. The threat that such claims to a papal power, however

125

indirect, over matters temporal posed to the established kingdoms and princi-palities of Europe constitutes one of the two principal circumstances setting the stage for the flowering of the last great body of Christian theorizing arguing for the sacred character of kingship, last, that is, in a series that we have seen stretching back for more than a millennium to what we have called "the Eusebian accommodation" with pre-Christian notions of sacral monar-chy. And that last great body of Christian regal theory, essentially archaizing in nature though occasionally portrayed as something of a novelty, is what histo-rians of political thought have traditionally characterized as the theory of the "Divine Right of Kings."

The second principal circumstance setting the stage for the emergence of that body of theory is of very different provenance. It reflects the failure no less than the success enjoyed by the Lutheran and Calvinist reformers in propagating their beliefs across Europe. The initial impact of the Protestant Reformation, with the almost obsessive insistence of the magisterial reform-ers on St Paul's classic teaching (Romans 13:1–7) on obedience for con-science' sake to the ruling powers, had been to buttress the status and power of kings and princes. That was certainly true of the German states and of the Scandinavian realms of the Lutheran diaspora. It was no less true of England, where the Act in Restraint of Appeals (1533) asserted Henry VIII's govern-mental or jurisdictional omnicompetence within the territorial boundaries of his "realm of England," thereby rejecting any papal claim to exercise jurisdic-tion within that realm. Arrogated to the crown, as a result, was the entire fullness of jurisdictional power in the external or public forum that the pope had previously wielded over the church in England. And any spiritual author-ity possessed by the English priestly hierarchy independently of the crown was henceforth redefined in such a way as to limit it, in effect, to the sacra-mental realm (*potestas ordinis*).[32]

Small wonder, then, that in 1535 a royal propagandist like Stephen Gar-diner, evoking the example of the Old Testament kings and of emperors like Justinian (and with the words "Forsothe, a blynde distinction and [one] full of darkenesse"), could sweep aside the distinction between the Church's spiritual and the prince's temporal government that had formed the very foundation of the typically medieval ecclesiologies and political theories. In so doing, he did not refrain from reminding his readers that the scriptures described the king as "God's lieftenaunt," "as it were the ymage of God upon earthe," upon the subject's obedience to whom they impose also no limits. Small wonder, too, that Richard Taverner, another Henrician apolo-gist, noting that kings "represent to us the parson even of god himself," should assert in 1539 that God "adourneth them whythe the knowable title of his own name callying them Goddes." And thus, following what we have seen earlier to have been a well trodden route from royal theocracy to royal Christology, another author was even moved to refer to King Henry as "the Son of Man."[33]

But if the Reformation did indeed work initially and directly to bolster the dignity and power of kings and to emphasize the religious duty of their sub- jects passively to obey their commands, it ended by undercutting indirectly that dignity, status, and power. It did so because, by a combination of failure and success, it had the effect of creating religious minorities right across Europe: Calvinist minorities where it failed to carry the day (initially in Scotland, permanently in France); Catholic (in parts of Germany but quin- tessentially in England) where it met with greater success. Catholics no less than Calvinists, confronted as they now were with persecuting rulers whom they could only view as heretics, were finally to relinquish any sympathy with notions of passive obedience. Instead, they were led to develop (often in tandem) forms of resistance theory grounded in a reappropriation and even- tual radicalization of the commonplace late medieval insistence that the power of kings and princes stemmed ultimately from community consent and that the community as a whole retained by natural law a residual power which it could wield to curb tyranny and prevent its own ruin.

The continuity with such medieval constitutionalist views is dramatically evident in the writings of such sixteenth-century Protestant resistance tracts as John Ponet's *Shorte Treatise of Politicke Power* (1556) in England, George Buchanan's *De jure regni apud Scotos* (1567) in Scotland, and the Huguenot *Vindiciae contra tyrannos* (1579) in France. It is evident also in many an English parliamentarian and/or Puritan tract written in the next century by way of opposition to the claims of the royalists. Here the degree of familiarity with the precedent of conciliarist constitutionalism and, in many cases, the willingness to cite the works of such fifteenth- and sixteenth-century scholas- tic thinkers as Pierre Ailly, Jean Gerson, John Mair, and Jacques Almain is really quite striking.[34] Aligned as they were with the papal cause, the sup- porters of the Catholic League during the French Religious Wars of the late sixteenth century, and the Jesuit opponents of the Elizabethan and Jacobean religious settlement in England, were understandably more reticent about acknowledging any such theoretical debts. But in their tracts the same intel- lectual affinities are evident and, in that respect at least, King James I was very much on target when he dubbed Jesuits as being "nothing other than *Puritan-papists.*" James, of course, was a leading advocate of the theory of the divine right of kings. His words may serve to remind us that that theory came to the fore in late sixteenth-century France and England in the context of two interrelated contemporary developments, first, the revived papal claim to possess an indirect power in matters temporal and second, the alarming circulation in both Catholic and Calvinist circles of arguments affirming the ultimately popular origins of political authority and the retention of a concomitant right by the community as a whole to resist, even by force, an heretical or tyrannous monarch, Catholic no less than Protestant.

The Divine Right of Kings

Almost a century ago now, in a classic formulation, John Neville Figgis encapsulated what he called "the completest form" of divine right theory in four succinct propositions. First, that the institution of kingship is divinely ordained. Second, that to God alone are kings held to be accountable. Third, that on pain of eternal punishment God enjoins on subjects the twin duties of passive obedience and non-resistance. Fourth, that the hereditary right of succession to the throne stemming from birth into the legitimate royal line is under no circumstances subject to forfeiture. As a right, that is to say, heredity regulated by primogeniture is "indefeasible."[35]

The formulation is a helpful one, though it should be added that of the four propositions the two first were the more ancient, with roots well engaged in the rich soil of medieval imperial and regal ideology. The latter two were of more recent provenance. The solemn emphasis on passive obedience and non-resistance would have seemed odd to most medievals. It reflected, in fact, the revolutionary changes introduced by the Reformation, both the obsessive emphasis of the magisterial reformers on Romans 13:1–7, and the subsequent shattering of the religious unity of Christendom, the emergence, accordingly, of dissident religious minorities, and the concomitant threat to public order and political stability which the long-drawn-out agony of the French Religious Wars had brought home so devastatingly in the closing decades of the sixteenth century. Similarly, the stress on indefeasible hereditary right reflected the dynastic turbulence of the century and more preceding. It was in virtue, after all, of their royal birthright alone that Henry IV of France and James I of England had come to occupy their respective thrones – the former despite his unacceptable religious allegiance, the latter in the teeth of two acts of parliament formally excluding the Stuart succession.

While, in Figgis's "complete" form, divine-right theory began to rise to prominence in the closing years of the sixteenth century and the early years of the seventeenth, it was to enjoy its heyday in England probably only in the era of the Restoration, after the trauma and uncertainties of civil war and interregnum (1642–60), and in France, after the turbulence of the Fronde (1648–53), an uprising of nobility directed against the royal government then presided over by the regent, Cardinal Mazarin. The theory itself was not lacking in variation and complexity. Sir Robert Filmer's celebrated "patriarchal" understanding of kingship, for example, in which kings were to be viewed as (or, at least, *as if* they were) rightful successors to the type of patriarchal authority exercised over his children by Adam, the first father, represents a very important, if distinct and subsidiary, strand in divine-right thinking, though one evident already in the *De imperandi authoritate et Christiana obedientia* (1593) of the Elizabethan divine, Hadrian Saravia. But prescinding here from such variations, we will content ourselves with two brief illustrations of the theory. The first is drawn from several writings of James VI of Scotland/James I of England and dates to the turn of the sixteenth/seventeenth centuries. The second is taken from the pertinent sections of the *Politique tirée des propres paroles de l'Écriture Sainte* written by the great French churchman Jacques-Bénigne Bossuet (later bishop of Meaux) during the 1670s when he was serving as tutor to the dauphin.

Although the *Trew Law of Free Monarchies* which James wrote in 1598 as King of Scotland, with its blunt denial of any right of resistance against a king who is "heritable overlord," represents the most complete statement of his divine-right views, his notorious *Speech to the Lords and Commons of the Parliament at White-Hall* (1610) is adequately representative of those views and has the added advantage of being no less helpfully succinct than forcefully compelling. The context in which the king was speaking was one set by the unhappy conjunction between a royal request for additional and substantial financial supply and an outburst of parliamentary irritation over the extravagant claims which Dr John Cowell, professor of civil law at Cambridge, had made in a recently published book concerning the reach of the royal prerogative. It was a context to which the king seems to have been less sensitive than he might have been.

Having warmed up his audience with an outline of the topics he intended to address, James launched into his discourse with the following words. "The state of MONARCHIE," he said,

> is the supremest thing on earth. For Kings are not only GODS Lieutenants upon earth, and sit upon GODS throne, but even by GOD himselfe they are called Gods.

And if they "are justly called Gods," it is because "they exercise a manner or resemblance of Divine power upon earth." For just as "God hath power to create, or destroy, make, or unmake at his pleasure, to give life, or send death, to judge all and to be judged nor accomptable to none," so, too, do kings. "[A]ccomptable to none but God onely," they have the power to "make and unmake their subjects," to "exalt low things, and abase high things, and make of their subjects like men at the Chesse."

These were hardly sentiments designed to warm the hearts of the restive parliamentarians, many of them practitioners at the common law; nor can James's (doubtless well-meaning) attempt to assuage their worries have been of much help. For it involved the invocation, not only of further general correspondences between king and God, but also, in particular, the application to the royal power of the old scholastic distinction between the absolute and ordained (or ordinary) power of God (*potentia absoluta et ordinata seu ordinaria*) which the canonist Hostiensis had borrowed from the theologians over two centuries earlier in order to elucidate the ineffable reach of papal power. So that if "it is Atheism and blasphemie to dispute what God *can* do [*de potentia absoluta*]: good Christians content themselves with his will revealed in his word [*potentia ordinaria*]." Similarly, while "the mysticall reverence, that belongs unto them that sit in the Throne of God" entails that the "absolute Prerogative of the Crowne is not lawfully to be disputed," that is not the case when it comes to his ordinary power, that is "the Kings revealed will in his Law."[36]

James's discourse was learned enough, certainly, as also was that of Bishop Bossuet a half-century and more later. If the learning of which Bossuet disposed was less scholastic and more self-consciously biblical and patristic in nature, and the tone of his work (much of it written for the instruction of the dauphin) more relentlessly didactic even than that of James I, nevertheless the basic stance he adopts towards the institution of kingship is not dissimilar. His point of departure is the insistence that "there was never a finer state constitution than that under which" the subjects of the Old Testament kings lived, and no finer exemplars of monarchy than David and Solomon themselves (1–2).[37] For "royalty has its origin in divinity itself" (58). "It is God who makes kings and who establishes reigning houses"; "the royal throne is not the throne of a man" but nothing less than "the throne of God" (244).

Royal judgments, then, are to be "attributed to God himself." No coercive force runs against kings, nor do they have to account to any but God himself for what in the height of their majesty they choose to do (82–3; 162). That majesty is to be recognized for what it truly is: "the image and greatness of God in a prince." Just as "the power of God can be felt in a moment from one end of the world to the other," so, too, "the royal power acts simultaneously throughout the kingdom," holding "the whole kingdom in position just as God holds the whole world." And just as the world, were God to withdraw his providential hand, would lapse back into the nothingness from which he had drawn it, so, too, were the royal authority to be withdrawn, would the kingdom itself lapse into its own primordial chaos (160). If, then, there is "something religious in the respect one gives to the prince," it is properly so. For God has, indeed, "put something divine" into kings. To them, says the psalmist (Psalm 81:6), "[y]ou are Gods, and all of you the sons of the most High" (60). Everywhere kings are "called Christs or the Lord's anointed." "Under this venerable name the prophets themselves revered them, and viewed them as associates in the sovereign empire of God, whose authority" it is, after all, that they exercise "over the people" (58).

Regal divinity, it seems, was as alive in the France of the 1670s as it had been in England at the start of the century. Alive, it may be, but not necessarily all that well. In hindsight it is clear that the days of that sort of thinking were already numbered, and that the storm clouds, so far as the institution of kingship was concerned, were now beginning to gather. And perhaps not only in hindsight. Scattered straws in the wind signaling the disasters that lay ahead were already beginning to appear. If the resistance theories spawned by the persecution of Protestant and Catholic minorities alike were by no means republican in inspiration, considerable significance attaches nonetheless to the degree to which they insisted on the role of the popular will in the institution of kingship, as well as to their conviction that in the people still resided the power to curb the tyrannical abuse of the royal office. Similarly significant was the degree to which the author of the *Vindiciae contra tyrannos* (in this, certainly, unlike Bossuet later on) resonated to the ambivalence toward the very institution of monarchy evident in the Book of Samuel's discussion of the institution of the Israelite kingships, the sense there conveyed, indeed, that God himself felt rejected when the Israelites expressed their wish to have a king "like all the nations."[38] Even more significant were the events on the ground. The successive assassinations by Catholic fanatics of Henry III and Henry IV of France had ushered in an era in which the sacrosanctity of kings could no longer be taken for granted, an era which, in mid-century, was to be shaken to its very foundations by the trial, condemnation, and execution of Charles I and the subsequent attempt to terminate the English monarchy altogether.

Towards the end of the Preface to his *Philosophy of Right*, and reflecting (famously) on the business of "giving instruction as to what the world ought to be," the German philosopher Hegel was later to concede that "philosophy . . . always comes on the scene too late to give" such instruction. "When philosophy paints its grey in grey," he added, "then has a shape of life grown old. The owl of Minerva spreads its wings only with the falling of the dusk."[39] Something similar, I would suggest, may properly be said about the body of thought we know as the divine-right theory of kingship. When finally it came to flower in seventeenth-century Europe, the shadows were already beginning to lengthen for the age-old institution to which it accorded so very lofty a status.

6
The Fading Nimbus
Modern Kingship and its Fate in a Disenchanted World

Change being the very lifeblood of the historical endeavor, it would be churl-
ish for any historian to complain about it. But the long, twilight struggle to
identify, chart, and assess the enduring processes that have driven millennial
change can still be, if not the stuff of nightmare, at least the trigger of insom-
nia. To recognize in the ancient and ubiquitous pattern of sacral kingship a
politics of enchantment is, I believe, unexceptionable enough. Nor, at least
since Max Weber's great studies in comparative, historical sociology, should
the identification of a *religious* source – Old Testament Yahwism and New
Testament Christianity, perhaps especially in its Calvinist variant – as the wellspring of the "disenchantment of the world" be the occasion of much
surprise. To disentangle, however, across the long centuries of largely unwit-
ting compromise, the intricate and intermittent working of the factors that
gradually destabilized the archaic way of comprehending what we (instinctively if anachronistically) categorize as the *political* is another story
altogether. The more so if one is called upon somehow to convey in brief
compass at least an approximate sense of what actually happened. And that,
alas, in this brief essay in interpretation, is our unforgiving fate.

What, then, can be said that can at least claim to be, on balance, less misleading than illuminating? Two basic claims, I believe, neither of them
altogether counter-intuitive. First, that so far, at least, as the institution of
kingship in Europe is concerned, the period stretching from the seventeenth
century to the nineteenth was, indeed, one of marked, and in some measure,
cumulative desacralization. If here I risk belaboring the obvious, it is because
we cannot simply ignore the fact that those centuries were also punctuated
by flickers of *re*sacralization – France at the start of Louis XVI's reign in
1774,[1] for example, or England in the closing years of the nineteenth
century. The latter, however, as David Cannadine has insisted, involved a

rather self-conscious effort by court "liturgists" and publicists that, by the mid-twentieth century, had met with such success that some commentators were moved, in the wake of Elizabeth II's coronation in 1953, to complain about a worrying *over*emphasis on the sacred dimension of the royal office and about the unfortunate degree to which the Queen had "continued to appear more sacerdotal than secular."[2] Second, that the marked acceleration in the process of desacralization occurring in the modern centuries is not simply to be taken for granted as a matter of "commonsense." It is, after all, without historical precedent, and it has ended by delegitimating the very institution of monarchy itself. Nor will we be able fully to comprehend it unless we are willing to push back beyond such obvious and salient features of modernity as the collapse of religious unity, the concomitant pluralization of "life-worlds" and the strain on plausibility that goes with it, the markedly secularizing thrust of scientific reason and technological progress, the institutionally demystifying impact of commercial, industrial, and bureaucratic rationalization, and, in particular, the impersonal governmental routines and this-worldly disciplines of what is sometimes called "the rational state." Instead, we must probe deeper and seek the ultimate wellsprings of change in the complex intersection in the late medieval and early modern world of an array of long-term developments, the most fundamental among them stemming from the destabilizing novelty of the Hebraic religious vision itself. To those two fundamental claims, we must now in sequence turn.

The De-mystification of the European Monarchy and the Crisis of Legitimacy

When, in the late 1860s, Walter Bagehot sat down to write his celebrated essay on *The English Constitution* and came to address the role of the monarchy, he identified it as "the solitary transcendent element" in that constitution. In earlier times, indeed, and in comparison with "the parliament, the law, the press" – human institutions all – it had been viewed as nothing less than "a Divine institution." Even now, the hostility of time and the erosion of religious loyalties notwithstanding, the monarchy still "strengthens our government with the strength of religion," and by "its religious sanction" still "confirms all our political order."[3] In 1953, almost a century later, the coronation of Elizabeth II took place. It was the first such event to be mediated by television to the world at large. Contemplating its tone, one might easily be tempted to detect in it a measure of deference to Bagehot's sentiments, did not the liturgy involved correspond so closely (despite subsequent accretions) to the oldest of the coronation rites for Anglo-Saxon kings of which we have a complete record – namely the Edgar *ordo* of 973, from which, as we have seen, the Anglo-Norman Anonymous in the late eleventh century drew so much of his inspiration. It was linked closely with a eucharistic service and involved not only the actual coronation of the monarch but also, before that and more centrally, her anointing by the Archbishop of Canterbury and subsequent vesting in the distinctively sacerdotal garb of alb, dalmatic, and stole – all in a manner evocative of the consecration of a bishop. In a subsequent and celebrated article, the sociologists Edward Shils and Michael Young succeeded in raising a few academic eyebrows by declaring that "the monarchy has its roots in man's beliefs and sentiments about what he regards as sacred," and that the coronation ceremony "provided at one time and for practically the entire society such an intensive contact with the sacred that we believe we are justified in interpreting it . . . as a great act of national communion."[4] As such, we have seen, it was later to draw negative commentary from critics opposed to the "sacerdotalization" of the monarchy. But it was also to be commended as an "act of sacralisation" by more recent British commentators who have come to the unexpected conclusion that the monarchy is "an essentially sacred institution," have criticized, accordingly, the currently fashionable advocacy of secularizing reform, and have urged, instead, the wisdom of "*re*sacralization."[5]

The current debate about the future of the British monarchy has been punctuated unhelpfully by the familial scandals and elephantine gaffes to which the Windsors have of late fallen prone. It is destined, accordingly, to be played out in the harsh glare of media attention. But whatever its outcome, we would be well advised not to lose sight of the fact that the sentiments Bagehot expressed about the monarchy in 1867 were in many ways *pre*scriptive rather than *de*scriptive. What he wrote, that is to say, was far from being valid as a depiction of the state of the monarchy at that specific time – or indeed, as he himself obliquely suggested, of its state at any time since the accession of George I in 1714. "During the whole reigns of George I and George II," he noted, "the sentiment of religious loyalty altogether ceased to support the Crown."[6] If it began to make something of a comeback during the trials and tribulations of George III's reign, the process of recovery was to prove slow and halting. That king's royal successors, George IV and William IV, the former womanizing and extravagant, the latter ignorant and prejudiced, were to do much to discredit the monarchy. Nor did Queen Victoria, however upright she was in her personal life, emerge as anything that could be called a popular figure. In her early years the butt of ribald cartoonists, in her middle years she came to be the target of editorial criticism in the pages of a press that wavered between lack of sympathy and outright hostility. And to "this dowdy and unpopular crown," the inept and slapdash way in

Figure 7 Great Britain. The Archbishop of Canterbury crowning Queen Elizabeth II, June, 1953. (TopFoto)

which the various royal ceremonies and rituals were performed did nothing at all to add any luster. "For the majority of the great royal pageants staged during the first three-quarters of the nineteenth century oscillated between farce and fiasco."[7]

All of that was to change, of course, in the last quarter of the century and the years running up to the outbreak of the Great War in 1914. That was a period marked right across Europe (and in Japan, too) by the invention, "mass production," and refining of a good deal of ceremonial tradition. But so far as royal ceremonial went, while it doubtless succeeded (and not only in England) in evoking a pleasing sense of imperial grandeur and regal mystery, it did so via a novel and highly self-conscious exploitation of the royal or imperial person with the object of manipulating mass psychology. This was novel – "unlike traditional [and more court-oriented] royal ceremonials designed to symbolize the rulers' relation to the divinity" – in that it was in large measure "directed at the public," at the masses of subjects with whom even the most autocratic of rulers now felt called upon, if they wished to retain their thrones, to establish some sort of direct relationship.[8] That was quintessentially true of the great imperial assemblage and subsequent *durbars* which successive viceroys and governors-general of India mounted in 1877, 1903, and 1911. At the last of those extraordinary assemblies, indeed, George V made what can only be described as an imperial epiphany when he crowned himself before a vast assemblage as Emperor of India.

For English people, of course, at least since the death of Queen Anne in 1714, the function of royal ritual could scarcely have been other than public-oriented. Or, more accurately, the meaning attaching to it could no longer be that which had still attached to it during the Stuart heyday of divine right theory and revived regal sacrality. Charles II had made a point of exercising his curative powers by touching for scrofula no fewer than 20,000 times in his first four years as king. Queen Anne, however, was to be the last English monarch to do so (memorably, at least, in the case of Dr Johnson), and the Cardinal of York, last of the Stuart pretenders, appears also to have been the last (in 1802) to work that particular piece of royal magic. After the great upheaval of 1688 and the abrogation, with James II's flight and the accession of William III, of the fundamental divine-right principle of indefeasible hereditary succession, the leading Anglican prelates proved able to rescue a shred of royal sacrality by interpreting that revolutionary transition as a work of divine providence in favor of the Protestant cause.[9] But that option was hardly available after the Act of Settlement of 1701, when the parliament boldly skipped over the more direct and impressive hereditary credentials of some 52 (regrettably Catholic) claimants in order to lodge the succession in the safely Protestant progeny of the distant Sophia, Electress of Hanover. If the Glorious Revolution of 1688 was at least susceptible of being interpreted in terms other than the Whig affirmation of parliamentary supremacy, Lock-eian social contract, and the indefeasible right of a sovereign people to choose its own rulers, the bleakly demystifying provisions of the Act of Settlement surely were not. Despite subsequent, understandably self-conscious, and no more than intermittently successful, attempts at *re*mystification, the English monarch, as Bagehot put it, was henceforth to be viewed as no more than "a useful public functionary who [might] be changed, and in whose place you [might] make another."[10]

In comparative context there was, no doubt, something a bit precocious about the demystified drabness of the monarchical state of affairs in England after the accession of George I in 1714. But if the process of desacralization had been moving more slowly and unevenly in relation to the other monarchies of Europe – more tentatively, it may be, in the Habsburg states, more obviously in Scandinavia and France – that it was in motion, Paul Kléber Monod has recently argued, was unquestionable. Taking as his point of departure the assassination by a Dominican friar of Henry III of France and bringing his analysis to a close with the death of Louis XIV in 1715, he has constructed a rich and subtly nuanced account of the complex way in which that process had been unfolding right across Europe. In the sixteenth century, he argues, kings had still conceived of themselves and been viewed by others, not as beings "dependent on popular approval," but "as a reflection of God, an ideal mirror of human identity," a mediating "link between the sacred and the self." By 1715, however, a "momentous change" had occurred, one which ushered in the beginning of Weber's "disenchantment of the world." What had taken place, in effect, was "a marked decline in the effectiveness of political explanations that rested on the assumption of sacredness or divine grace." These had come to be supplemented, not so much as yet by outright secularism as by "a religiously based [if quite external] obedience to an abstract, unitary human authority, combined with a deepened sense of individual moral responsibility" on the part of the subject or citizen – in effect, "sovereignty plus self-discipline," the very foundation of "the rational state."[11]

In the years intervening, two great upheavals had helped lubricate and accelerate this complex process of change. First, the continued miseries of the French Religious Wars, during the course of which, and in succession, the Huguenots on the Protestant side and the supporters of the Catholic League on the Catholic "right" came to threaten the kingship itself in terms that were at once both religious and constitutionalist. Second, the riots, disorders, and outright rebellions of the 1640s and 1650s, which reached well beyond England and France and extended to Scotland, Ireland, Spain, Portugal, Naples, Poland, the Ukraine, and Russia, and have led some historians to speak, accordingly, of "the general crisis of the seventeenth century."[12] Thus the assassination by Catholic fanatics in 1589 and 1610 respectively of Henry III and Henry IV of France were straws in the wind, signs of "the continuing fragility of French monarchy" (77), sailor's "telltales" signaling shifting winds and the portent of heavy weather to come. The first case, certainly, inspired as it was by the propaganda of the Catholic League with its insistence that the king was responsible to the people, Monod describes as "an unmistakable sign of the waning of the sacral monarchy throughout Europe, the outcome of seven decades of religious reformation"(6). Similarly, the dramatic trial, judgment, and execution in 1649 of Charles I of England had Europe-wide repercussions, and, while for some it fueled a lively cult of "Charles the Martyr," for others it "marked a decisive rejection of royal mediation between God and the self" (146).

While conceding that the contemporaneous mid-century upheavals elsewhere in Europe were doubtless responsive to a broad array of differing, localized discontents and cannot properly be understood without attention paid to the political, religious, economic, and institutional specificities of time and place, Monod is bold enough to insist that they still had "certain religious and intellectual features in common." Notable among them was "a tendency to appeal to an authority that was vested by God in . . . the body of the people rather than that of the monarch," in "a distinct national community" rather than in the king (150–1). That was true, if fleetingly, of Catalonia, where those rebelling in 1641 against the Spanish king, before throwing their allegiance to Louis XIII of France, toyed with the establishment of a republican state. It was true later on of Naples where, in 1647–8, a republic was actually established. It was true, again, of the United Provinces in 1650. There, in the attempt to pre-empt what was taken to be the wish of William II, Prince of Orange, to transform into a monarchical one his office of stadtholder, an effort led by the provincial estates of Holland came close to eliminating that position altogether in favor of an oligarchically controlled republican form of government. It was true, quintessentially of course, of England, where the kingship was in fact abruptly abolished and the country ruled for 11 years in a republican mode represented (at least) as being more responsive to the fundamental principle that political power is inherent in the people itself. It was even in some measure true of the more radical among the Frondeurs in France where, in 1652–3, the rebels at Bordeaux (the *Ormistes*), rallying under the motto "Vox Populi, Vox Dei," claimed to have established nothing less than "a Democratic Government" (179).

None of these anti-monarchical moves ultimately succeeded. By the end of 1650, William II had brought Amsterdam and Holland to heel. By 1652, the Spanish king had crushed the rebellions in both Catalonia and Naples, and Louis XIV's troops had stamped out the Fronde. Eight years later, the English experiment with republican institutions ended with a whimper rather than a bang, and the principle of hereditary kingship by divine right was asserted once more in practice and lauded fulsomely in theory. Things, however, were never to be quite the same again. The very foundations of kingship had sustained a great shock and measures had to be taken to respond to the potential for aftershocks. In order to avoid being sent away once more on his travels, Charles II had to maneuver deftly, accede to policies he did not like, and be flexible enough to bend before more than one storm. His brother and successor, James II, proved unable or unwilling to do likewise, and he paid the price in 1688 by forfeiting his throne – an event the Whigs, at least, came eventually to represent in Lockeian terms as the vindication of individual rights, social contract, and popular sovereignty. Even the seeming counter-case of Frederick II of Denmark, who succeeded in 1660 in breaking free from high noble control and transforming his title to the throne from an elective into an hereditary one, involved, in fact, a species of pact with his subjects, codified in explicitly contractarian forms in the Royal Law of 1665, which Monod describes (207) as "one of the earliest founding documents of the rational state." In France, too, Bossuet's essentially religious vision of kingship to the contrary, Louis XIV came to view "the state in rationalist terms as a collective entity separate from his body, rather than a mystical dignity within him" (214). He himself appears to have lacked any real inward or personal piety; the complex and much-analyzed rules of etiquette (*civilité*) on which the palace of Versailles operated were "entirely external and had nothing to do with inner piety." "However reverential its ceremonies, French [palace] etiquette 'embodied' a rational pact between the self and the state, not a mystical community with the deity" (218–19).

France was, of course, the most powerful state in Europe, and the trajectory followed by its monarchy down to the time of its abolition in 1793 and the execution of Louis XVI was to serve as exemplar or reference point for the subsequent transformation of kingship elsewhere. Already in the seventeenth century, Monod argues, that trajectory had come in observable measure to be a desacralizing one. Disagree with one another though they may about the pace and timing of change, perhaps also about the precise nature of the corrosive agents at work, other historians of France would not call that basic claim into question. And in the eighteenth century the pace of secularization was to quicken.

During that century the progressive ebbing of the credence given to the "royal religion" was, of course, most dramatically evident in the derisive incredulity of Enlightenment intellectuals like Montesquieu, whose *Persian Letters* obliquely mock the French king as a "great magician" who had succeeded in conning his subjects into the foolish belief that he could "cure them of all kinds of diseases by touching them."[13] In the shaping of public opinion the *philosophes* had some success in substituting themselves for king, magistracy, and clergy as the true spokesmen for the public interest. They stripped "the king of his religious character," they "scoffed at the coronation ceremony, and declared that the king ruled not 'by the grace of God' but 'by the grace of his subjects.'" Further than that, indeed, "they parted company with most of their contemporaries by repudiating the traditional conjunction of religion and politics outright."[14]

These were dramatic developments enough, but for most of those contemporaries in fact – or so historians now incline to suggest – factors of a specifically religious nature may have done more than the *philosophes* to sponsor a growing alienation from the regal pieties of yesteryear. Such factors, certainly, may properly be numbered among the corrosive forces destined to converge by the end of the century in such a way as to delegitimate the very institution of kingship itself. Of the working of such factors two illustrations must suffice.

Across the course of the seventeenth century, as age-old modes of royal sacrality came to be transposed into a less magical and more transparent key, they may be said to have taken on a less mediatorial and more representative tone. No longer, that is to say, did it suffice for the king to claim somehow to *incorporate* the sacred. Instead, he was now called upon to exemplify in his personal life the confessional values and spiritual aspirations of his subjects, and, in what Monod has dubbed felicitously as "the theatre of royal virtue," to make public display of his commitment to "the constant religious and moral principles that bound together the Christian community."[15] This public role as "first of believers," if played with conviction and skill, could serve to bolster and strengthen the monarchy. It did so, certainly, in the case of the emperor Ferdinand II (1617–37), a man of unaffected and disciplined personal piety in the reformed Catholic mode. But it could just as easily damage the cause if the royal actor who was called upon to play the role was obviously lacking in that sort of spiritual and moral commitment. Despite (or because of) a surfeit of spiritual counsel and his own (concomitant?) religious scruples, that proved somewhat disastrously to be the case with Louis XV of France (1715–74). His long string of well-known and undiscriminating adulterous relationships got in the way of his confessing and receiving communion, and that, in turn, or so he concluded on the advice of his rigorist confessors, precluded for some 34 years his performing the royal miracle of touching for the *mal du roi*. Coupled with his unpopularity and the arbitrariness and indirection that marked the royal government during his latter years, this provoked a degree of revulsion, vilification, and popular demythologization that the piety and moral uprightness of his grandson and successor, Louis XVI (1774–93), was to prove powerless to efface.

But even had Louis XV's deportment in his private life not been so damagingly compromising, there is little reason to believe, that the sacral status of the monarchy could have survived the bitter religious divisions occasioned in France by the clash between Jansenist and Jesuit. That great clash was radicalized by attempts to implement the sweeping condemnations voiced in the controversial papal bull *Unigenitus* (1714), which had cut so undiscriminating a swathe through the thickets of Jansenist and supposedly Jansenist views, and it was further exacerbated in the 1750s and 1760s by the unfortunate vacillations evident in royal religious policy. What ensued, Dale Van Kley has said, was

the formation or reformation of a Jesuitical and episcopal *parti dévot* ("devout" or "pious" party) on the monarchy's right in some respects

reminiscent of the Catholic League, while some Jansenist energies chan-
neled themselves into a political *parti janséniste* and developed a closer
resemblance to Protestantism. The result was that the mid-eighteenth
century replayed, albeit in a minor key, the religious-political conflicts of
the sixteenth century.

Such "Jansenist-related controversies," he adds, which "quite apart from the
French Enlightenment" had done much to undercut regal sacrality,

> brought Bourbon absolutism to its knees, undermining its last and best
> justification, which was to have imposed religious peace and to have suc-
> cessfully transcended the confessional fray. By the mid-eighteenth century,
> all the legislative and religious symbols of Louis Quatorzian divine-right
> absolutism . . . were all but dead letters.[16]

Disagree though they may about the generality, provenance, or pace of change
in public opinion earlier in the century, historians appear generally to agree
that the latter half of the eighteenth century was, for France at least, a period
of quickening secularization.[17] "Disenchantment," the "crash" of "a system
of belief," "desacralization of the monarchical person," "dissolution of the
affective ties that had lent meaning to the symbolism of the royal body,"
"breakdown" of the royal political mission, "besmirching" or "dysfunctional-
ity" of divine right, "transformation of criticism of the monarch into a more
structural critique of the monarchy" itself, "privatization of religious sentiment", and desacralization of "everything between God and the 'individual'
religious conscience, divine right monarchy not excepted" – this by now
almost liturgical litany of historiographic gloom could readily be extended.
The kingship of which we catch a glimpse in the forbidden or underground
literature that Robert Darnton has analyzed emerges not only as discredited
but also as so desacralized by the behavior of its incumbents as finally to have
"lost its legitimacy."[18] Citing the *cahiers de doléances* (or nationwide memo-
randa of concerns and grievances submitted in 1789), Chartier has noted "a
shrinkage in the sacred nature and person of the king," with whatever "sacrality" still attached to him being "no longer necessarily held to be divinely
instituted," but "often conceived as having been conferred by the nation."
And it was this "symbolic disenchantment," he adds, "that by separating the
king from divinity made possible (because conceivable) the revolutionary
holding him up to ridicule and finally executing him."[19] By the winter of 1792
the principle of royal inviolability was being dismissed as nothing more than a
"stupid dogma" or "political superstition." Louis XVI had been transmuted
from gold into dross, from His Most Christian Majesty into mere Louis

Capet. He was but a man, proclaimed Robespierre, and a guilty man at that, a man "deserving of death," whose condemnation was nothing other than "a measure of public safety" or an "act of national salvation."[20]

The Deeper Wellsprings of Change

That "act of national salvation" took place on January 21, 1793. Reporting on that same day to the Commune of Paris, one of the commissioners appointed to attend the event said:

> we did not take our eyes off Capet until he reached the guillotine. He arrived at ten hours ten minutes; it took him three minutes to descend from the conveyance. He wanted to speak to the people. Santerre denied this; his head fell. The citizens dipped their pikes and their handkerchiefs in his blood.

Citing that report and noting that "the same acts of devotion were repeated as had occurred after the decapitation of Charles I [of England]" in the previous century, Sergio Bertelli has commented, nonetheless, that "in the three minutes that it took Louis Capet to descend the steps of his carriage, a thousand years of the *religio regis* [religion of the king] ended."[21]

That the event marked the culmination of the process of desacralization that had quickened in France two centuries earlier with the assassinations of Henry III and Henry IV and accelerated in England with the execution of Charles I is not in doubt. However electrifying, the brutal elimination in 1918 of Nicholas II, Tsar of Russia, and his entire immediate family, constituted no more than a belated coda to the history of a process that had already reached its term. In that respect, Bertelli's comment is very much to the point. In one form or another, however, the *religio regis* of which he speaks reached much further back into the distant past than a mere thousand years. And so, too, it must once more be insisted, did the process of desacralization itself.

In the chapters immediately preceding we focused on the complex accommodations which, in the teeth of the secularizing thrust of biblical and Qur'ānic revelations alike, all three of the Abrahamic religions were led to make with archaic notions of sacral kingship. Those accommodations, however, proved ultimately to be unstable, and in the first part of the present chapter we went on to focus on the concluding phase of the desacralizing process during which they finally lost their cohesion and effectiveness. In so doing, we have been subjecting such developments to comparatively close scrutiny under a species, as it were, of historiographic microscope. It is time now, I would suggest, and as we close in on a conclusion, to stand well back from those accommodations and that culminating phase, substituting tele-scope, if you wish, for microscope, and allowing the full course of millennial change to enter, distantly at least, within the ambit of our vision. Once we do that, a whole concatenation of pertinent and complexly interacting ideologi-cal factors come gradually into focus. Of these, we will have to content ourselves here with selecting for brief discussion no more than a handful.

For those convinced that the religious tradition of the Christian west, faithful in this to its desacralizing biblical roots and in "an ongoing dialectical relationship with the 'practical' infrastructure of social life," has "carried the seeds of secularization within itself," the big question has always been why the whole process took so very long to reach critical mass, why, in effect, we have to wait until the seventeenth and eighteenth centuries before its disen-chanting impact begins to become altogether transparent. And to that question the standard response, since Hegel at least, has been to distinguish between what have been called the *normative* and *historical* forms of Chris-tianity, and to emphasize the degree to which "those biblical norms about human nature and human destiny that give to Christianity whatever identity it may possess" were muffled – for centuries, even, lost – in that *historical* Christianity which, "though much of it is not specifically Christian," still "reflects the composite of those cultural impulses that make up what is com-monly thought of as Christian civilization." Or, with Peter Berger, putting it somewhat more bluntly, to emphasize the degree to which *Catholic* Chris-tianity, with its numinous sense of the world as a sacramental one, suffused with the sacred and punctuated by miracles, constituted "an arresting and retrogressing step in the unfolding of the drama of secularization," though in the Latin west, at least, it still retained a "secularizing potential." Thus, only with the Protestant Reformation do we see "a powerful re-emergence of pre-cisely those secularizing forces that had been 'contained' by Catholicism not only replicating the Old Testament in this, but going decisively beyond it."[22]

Recognizing with Berger the degree to which Protestantism, when com-pared with Catholicism, did indeed involve "an immense shrinkage in the scope of the sacred in reality,"[23] one must concede the force of that response. At the same time, one must insist that it comes a little too easily. For without recognizing also the prior impact on European intellectual sensibilities (and long before the Reformation) of demystifying factors that owe nothing to Protestantism, it will be impossible to make adequate sense of the whole, extraordinary process of desacralization that has so profoundly shaped our modern Western consciousness.

Of these factors I select here for discussion only three. They pertain to ways in which people have striven for an understanding, respectively, of nature, man, and society. While acutely conscious of the danger of imposing an undue measure of schematization on a formidably complex array of historical developments, I narrow down attention to these three because I believe them to be the most fundamental drivers of desacralizing change. I choose them, too, because however theoretical in nature they may have been they all intersected with other developments – social, political, technological – of more gritty, practical import. They did not, in effect, function in grand isolation but stood (in Berger's sociological terms) "in an ongoing dialectical relationship with the 'practical' infrastructure of social life."[24] I choose them, finally, because present among them and at the deepest level of all, is a certain interconnectedness stemming either from intellectual affinity or direct logical entailment, and reflective of the sinuous continuities that exist in any coherent intellectual system between the seemingly disparate realms of natural theology, natural philosophy, and moral, legal, and political philosophy.

The first of these factors is the most straightforward one and is widely recognized to have been revolutionary in its implications – so much so, indeed, that it is unnecessary to belabor its importance here. What I have in mind is the firm distinction which the New Testament draws between religious and political loyalties. Again and again across the centuries, we have seen the force of that distinction blunted by imperial and papal aspirations to establish a unitary Christian commonwealth under the leadership of either pontifical kings or monarchical pontiffs. Its importance might well have been lost sight of had it not linked with, found expression in, and, in return, been reinforced by, the gradual emergence in western Europe of rival governmental structures, temporal and ecclesiastical, both of them serving to limit each other's effective power. And that was to be true, not only of Catholic Christendom, but also, after the Reformation, in those parts of Europe where Calvinism held sway.

If, then, the great upheaval engendered in the eleventh century by the Gregorian reform marked the onset of several centuries of intermittent but widespread tension between the ecclesiastical and temporal authorities in Latin Christendom, it was a tension not simply between competing ideals but between rival governmental structures. That institutional dualism served increasingly to give teeth to the fundamental distinction which Christ had originally drawn. And there was something altogether novel about the state of affairs thus engendered. "[T]here is really nothing unusual," Brian Tierney has said, "in one ruler aspiring to exercise supreme spiritual and temporal power. That . . . is a normal pattern of human government." What was unusual about the Middle Ages "was not that certain emperors and popes aspired to a theocratic role but that such ambitions were never wholly fulfilled."[25] No doubt the dualism of governments that sponsored this novel state of affairs was also the cause of an immense amount of wasteful and destructive conflict. But it was a conflict that marked, nevertheless, the birth pangs of something new in the history of humankind, a society in which the state was eventually to be stripped of its age-old religious aura and in which its overriding claims on the loyalties of men were balanced and curtailed by a rival authority – which was in turn, reciprocally, and in no less significant fashion, to find its own imperial ambitions thwarted by the power of the state. A society distinguished therefore, by an established institutional dualism and racked by the internal instability resulting therefrom.

It was, then, between the hammer and the anvil of conflicting authorities, ecclesiastical and temporal, that political freedoms were to be forged in the west and monarchical ambitions (both secular and spiritual) eventually to be chastened. Medieval constitutionalism may have been the product of many mutually supportive factors, by no means all of them religious; but whatever the strength of those factors, without the Christian insertion of the critical distinction between the religious and political spheres and without the instability engendered as a result by the clash of rival authorities, it is extremely unlikely that the Middle Ages would have bequeathed to the modern world any legacy at all of limited government.

From the thirteenth century onwards, popes and temporal monarchs alike had begun to develop representative instrumentalities and techniques in their effort to marshal the cooperation of their subjects and to secure for their policies and the mounting taxes necessary to finance them the consent, not simply of the baronage but of the other (increasingly powerful) propertied groups among their subjects. The consent involved was initially consultative or procedural in nature, in some ways akin, if you wish, to that involved today in cases where the public authorities exercise their power to take possession of property by eminent domain (compulsory purchase). If anything one might choose to call self-government was involved, it was, what one historian labeled as "self-government at the king's command."

In the course of time, however, that type of consent was destined to modulate into the type that can truly be called "political" or "democratic" – in effect, the sort of consent that expresses the sovereign will of the people and implies some sort of limitation on the ruler's prerogative. In the centuries before the Protestant Reformation the persistent tension between kings and popes helped sponsor that change, with kings turning to parliaments and representative estates in order to rally national opposition to papal pretensions, and, for similar reasons, at least from the time of Philip IV of France (1285–1314) onwards, mounting appeals from the authority of the papal monarch to the superior authority seen to reside in the entire body of the faithful and given expression by the general council representing it. Again, in the century and a half after the onset of the Reformation, religious minorities, Calvinist and Catholic, anxious to be able to render to God the things that were God's, were likewise to appeal from the authority of the kings who were persecuting them to the superior authority they believed to reside in the entire community of the realm and in the parliaments or estates representing it.

The New Testament distinction between religious and political loyalties, along with the form of governmental dualism that in the Latin Middle Ages gave it teeth, served also, then, to nudge to the forefront the historic principle that it was popular consent that ultimately legitimated governmental authority. Originally very much a gritty practicality of effective government, consent came to be understood in the later Middle Ages as something more than that, as a fundamental constitutional principle and one grounded in the mandates of the natural law itself. By the early modern era it had modulated accordingly into the fundamental legitimating principle to which even royal authority was in some measure subordinate. But it is important to be clear about what consent actually meant for even the most "advanced" of medieval consent theorists, or for the Protestant constitutionalists and resistance theorists of the sixteenth and seventeenth centuries (French, Scottish, English, Dutch), as also for their counterparts among the ideologists of the Catholic League in France, and for the Spanish writers on matters political, Jesuit as well as Dominican. Namely, it was the consent of free communities possessed at a minimum of the original right to choose their rulers, perhaps also to choose the form of government under which they were to live, maybe even to participate on some sort of continuing basis in the governmental process and to serve as a counterweight to the abuse of monarchical power. Absent from it, however, was the crucial feature that serves truly to distinguish the whole modern contractarian tradition of political thinking running from Hobbes, via Locke, to Kant – that is, the ascription to the autonomous individual will of an unprecedented importance, a real choice as to whether or not to implicate itself in politics at all. Consent, in effect, and despite some formulations seemingly "modern" in their intonation, was not yet quite understood as the assent of a concatenation of free and equal individuals imposing on themselves an obligation which of their ultimate autonomy they could well avoid. It came to be understood in that novel way only when traditional notions of community or corporate consent had come to be impregnated by Christian notions of moral autonomy, by an individualism and a voluntarism that were ultimately of biblical provenance. And the rise to prominence of that species of individualism and voluntarism was the second fundamental factor advancing the process of desacralization that can be seen to have been at work long before the coming of the Reformation.

In one of those lucid shafts of historical insight that pierce the gloom of his philosophical discourse, Hegel made a series of interrelated claims directly pertinent to this issue. First, that "the principle of the self-subsistent inherently infinite personality of the individual, the principle of subjective freedom . . . is historically subsequent to the Greek World," that it is "the pivot and the center of the difference between antiquity and modern times." Second, that it was Christianity that gave it full expression, making it "the universal effective principle of a new form of civilization." Third, that that principle arose first in religion and was introduced into the secular world only "by a long and severe effort of civilization." Fourth, that during the Middle Ages, the authoritarianism and externalism of the hierarchical church had the effect of blunting that effort, taking itself the place of man's conscience, laying its stress on "outward actions" that were not "the promptings of his own good will" but were performed at *its* command, and succeeding in obscuring the fundamental principle of subjective freedom until that principle was finally thrown into bold relief by "the all-enlightening *Sun*" of the Protestant Reformation.[26]

Hegel distorted the picture somewhat, I would judge, when in his fourth claim he confined the process almost entirely to the period after the Reformation. But with that caveat duly noted, I would affirm the rectitude of his general claim. The deepest roots of what he calls "the principle of subjective freedom," along with the related emphasis on will and responsibility, are indeed engaged, not in Hellenic soil, but in the biblical doctrine of divine omnipotence and the historically singular doctrine of creation that goes with it.[27] That principle and its related emphases were indeed felt first in matters religious and it was centuries before they touched the secular sensibilities and began to revolutionize the modalities of western political thinking. During the patristic period, even in matters religious, the form of individualism that we think of as quintessentially Christian was able to make its way but slowly in the teeth of such alien notions as the cyclicity of time or that of the divine soul and its primordial fall into matter. With the collapse of the Roman world, moreover, and the transformation of Latin Christianity through its encounter with religious sensibilities shaped in the mould of Celtic and German paganism, the characteristically Christian concern with the relationship of the individual soul to God was to a remarkable degree submerged in the rhythms of a devotional life that was communal rather than personal, external rather than internal, public rather than private – one very much at home, in fact, with societies in which kings were seen to play a sacred, mediatorial role between their subjects and the divine.

Only in the late eleventh century did that form of Christian individualism begin once more to surface in the spiritual literature. Linked now with a

marked emotionalism and a firm stress on the role of the individual will in
the encounter with the divine, and borne far and wide by the proponents first
of the Cistercian spirituality and then of the Franciscan, it came to reside at
the very heart of late medieval religion. During the fourteenth and fifteenth
centuries, moreover, its voluntarism was paralleled in moral philosophy and
theology by the heightened emphasis which the scholastic thinkers of the
Franciscan school came to place on the role of will, duty, and intention in
matters ethical. Notwithstanding the prominence, however, of the role
ascribed to the individual will in religious and moral living, one would search
the medieval world in vain for any parallel insistence that the political life, like
the life of moral virtue, requires moral assent, personal choice, the expressed
willingness of the individual to implicate himself in that life. That insistence
was to come only much later, long after the inception of the Reformation
and after some of the Puritans of Elizabethan England had finally abandoned
their earlier scruples about separating from the Anglican church establishment and had come to think in terms of reform "without tarrying for any."[28]
Only then did the sectarianism of the "Radical Reformation" begin to make
truly significant inroads upon one of the established strongholds of Protestantism, bringing with it the concept of the Church as a sect or voluntary
society based on a covenanted group of true believers who had entered it "on
the basis of conscious conversion."[29] As the seventeenth century wore on,
those separatists appear to have gone on "to interpret bodies politic as if they
were sectarian congregations," attributing "to citizens, as natural rights, the
rights of moral autonomy and self-government that they had demanded for
themselves as members of the congregation."[30]

Thus, by 1645–6, in the wake of the First Civil War in England, John Lilburne, the Leveler leader, and his colleagues Richard Overton and William
Walwyn were clearly applying to secular political society the same voluntaris-
tic, consensual, and implicitly contractarian model they had long since been
accustomed to applying to the visible church. "God," Lilburne argued, "the
absolute Soveraigne Lord and King of all things," having endowed man his
creature "with a rationall soule or understanding, and thereby created him
after his own image," made him Lord over the rest of his creatures, but not
"over the individuals of Mankind, no further than by free consent or agreement, by giving up their power, each to the other, for their better being."
Similarly, in the classic invocation of natural rights with which he opens his
pamphlet *An Arrow against all Tyrants*, Overton states that "To every Indi-
viduall in nature, is given an individual property by nature, not to be invaded
or usurped by any: for every one as he is in himselfe, so he hath a selfe propri-
ety, else could he not be himselfe." All being naturally equal and free,

from this foundation or root, all just humaine powers take their original; not immediately from God (as kings usually plead their prerogatives) but mediately by the hand of nature . . ., for originally God hath implanted them in the creature, and from the creature those powers immediately proceed; . . . Every man by nature being a King, Priest and Prophet in his owne naturall circuite and compasse, whereof no second may partake, but by deputation, commission, and free consent from him, whose naturall right and freedom it is.[31]

Lilburne, Overton, and the other Levelers were, of course, extremists. So, too, though in a different fashion, was Thomas Hobbes. During the same decade, if via a somewhat different route, he, too, broke through to a similarly individualistic and voluntarist conception of the foundations of political legitimacy – though in his case placing it in service to the cause of governmental absolutism and in opposition to the traditional constitutionalism which Lilburne had sought to radicalize, simplify, and purify. Writing nearly half a century later, John Locke was to share the voluntarism and radical individualism that was central to the political thinking of Hobbes and the Levelers alike. Unlike Hobbes, it is true, he contrived to wed it to the older constitutionalist tradition. At the same time, and in this unlike the Levelers, he clearly did not feel unduly compelled to radicalize that tradition or to develop it in a more democratic direction. What he did do, however, and most influentially, was to project forward into the eighteenth century, and to help naturalize in the new political "common sense" that was now crystallizing in that era, a secularized vision of politics. That new vision was destined to undercut the very foundations of divine-right theory and to consign to ideological redundancy any notion of sacred royal mediation between God and the individual subject or citizen.

That it did so, moreover, owed something to the fundamental congruence between Locke's moral and political thinking and his new, "scientific" understanding of the nature and operations of the natural world. And that reflects, in turn, the complex workings across time of the third, and most abstract, of the three factors sponsoring the process of desacralization that I have identified as fundamental. That factor falls into the realms of natural theology and natural philosophy and concerns the changing ways in which human beings have understood the *nature* of the natural world at large. In the first chapter of this book, making the case that the "cosmic religiosity" was the very foundation for the archaic pattern of divine or sacral kingship, I emphasized how very fundamental was the archaic sense that there existed a consubstantiality between God, nature, and man, a divine continuum, as it were, linking humankind with nature and the state with the cosmos. In the second chapter, discussing the Hebraic kingship, I argued further that the biblical idea of creation and the understanding of God as one, transcendent, and omnipotent which it presupposed, logically entailed the denial of that consubstantiality and the de-divinization or desacralization of nature – or put differently, the drainage of the divine from a natural world, created, as it was, out of nothing by the omnipotent *fiat* of a divine will external to it. Hence the destruction of the metaphysical underpinnings for any understanding, archaic style, of the state as "the embodiment of the cosmic totality."

The trouble is, of course, that despite the periodic pangs of what I have called "Abrahamic unease" evident in the attitude of the Hebrew prophets towards the status of their kings, the sort of "logical entailment" of which I have so casually spoken necessarily presupposes the existence of an essentially *philosophical* consciousness about what the nature and attributes ascribed in the biblical texts to Yahweh might in themselves mean, as also what they might entail for one's understanding of the nature of nature and the nature of humankind. It was to take centuries for such a consciousness to crystallize. It emerged, in fact, only in late antiquity, not long before the dawn of the Common Era when Jerusalem finally encountered Athens, and Jewish intellectuals in the great Alexandrian community as well as their Hellenizing successors among the Christian church fathers (men like Philo, Clement of Alexandria and Origen) began to exploit the modalities of Greek philosophical thinking in order to penetrate and elucidate the meaning of the biblical message. When they did that, as we saw in chapter 3, with Philo being the great pace-setter, they opened up the way for the historic Eusebian absorption of the Hellenistic philosophy of kingship and for the elaboration of a Christianized version of the archaic pattern of sacral kingship that lay behind it.

Their engagement with Greek thought, however, took place along a much broader intellectual front than that of political philosophy alone. It was to lead not only to the deep penetration of Christian modes of theologizing by philosophic notions of Greek provenance, but also to the elaboration by the great medieval philosopher-theologians of a variety of metaphysical systems, most of them Neoplatonic or Aristotelian in their inspiration. And if that extraordinary achievement was to leave a legacy that has been compared in its architectonic grandeur to the contemporaneous splendor of the great Gothic cathedrals (Panofsky), it was not an achievement bereft of structural flaws.[32]

Both Plato and Aristotle had elaborated distinctive and highly sophisticated conceptions of God. Behind those conceptions, however, lay a pre-philosophical understanding of the divine which, in its broad characteristics, the Greeks shared with the other peoples of the archaic world. It is the point of view that we have seen to underpin notions of sacral kingship, one that failed to differentiate the divine from the world of nature, or, to the extent to which it did achieve such a differentiation, did so by regarding the natural world in general, and natural things and processes in particular, as in some sense a manifestation of the divine. Though Plato and Aristotle both advanced beyond that point of view, they did so without wholly abandoning it. Thus Plato could speak of the universe as "a blessed god" and Aristotle could characterize as "inspired" the old myth that the first substances "are gods and that the divine encloses the whole of nature."[33]

Translated onto the philosophic plane, however, the archaic point of view found more characteristic expression in the notion of the divine as being immanent in nature, related to it as an indwelling and organizing principle, the source at once of the order of its movements and of the unity of its disparate parts. The analogy involved was the relation of mind to body in man, and the universe was conceived as a great organism permeated by mind or soul; but if the Greeks saw in the orderliness of natural processes the working of an intelligence, eternal and divine, it was not a divine intelligence that transcended nature, nor was it any more eternal than was the material world itself. When Plato sought to vindicate the presence of mind in the universe, he did so without questioning the eternity of the matter out of which the universe had been fashioned. Thus in the *Timaeus* (an extremely problematic work but the Platonic dialogue that Philo, the early Christian fathers, and the medieval theologians all knew best) he depicts the Demiurge or World Maker as a sort of cosmic artisan fashioning an intelligible universe out of preexistent matter in accordance with the eternally subsistent "Forms," essences, archetypes, or "Ideas" that serve him as the exemplars, patterns, blueprints, or templates for all things.

As we have seen Mircea Eliade to suggest, the *Timaeus*, therefore, has something in common with such archaic creation myths as the Babylonian *Enûma Elish*. Like those myths it is concerned, not with creation in the sense that Jews, Christians, and Muslims usually ascribe to that word, but rather with the emergence of *cosmos*, or ordered, harmonious system, out of some sort of preexisting chaos. The Demiurge, certainly, is no omnipotent creator-God. Neither the Ideas nor matter owe their existence to him; far from it, indeed, for both by their existence impose limits on his creative activity. Nowhere is it suggested that he should be an object of worship, and Plato may well have intended him not to be understood literally but rather as a mythical symbol standing for the presence in the universe of a divine reason analogous to man's and "working for ends that are good." Something similar may be said of Aristotle's *Metaphysics*, in which he presents no creation story, it is true (his universe is eternal), but the notion of a *First Principle* which, while it transcends the universe is also immanent in it "as the order of its parts." Aristotle calls this first principle "God," but it is neither a personal

God, nor a creator-God, nor an object of worship. Instead, it is an Unmoved Mover, the final and highest good that, because all things aspire and ceaselessly strive to emulate its perfection, serves as the cause of motion or change in the universe. Thus, as Dante tells us in the profoundly Aristotelian words with which he concludes the *Divine Comedy*, it is "love that moves the sun and the other stars."

Put in this way, both Plato's and Aristotle's understanding of the nature of the divine, of the universe, and of the relationship between them would appear to be wholly incompatible with the parallel Judaic and Christian views; but then neither Plato nor Aristotle put these things quite so simply. Their writings were fraught with ambiguities and problems of interpretation that were to leave room for subsequent Christian philosophers to mould Platonic and Aristotelian views in such a way as to render them less difficult to harmonize with biblical notions. That was to be the fate of Plato in the Mediterranean world during the first centuries of the Common Era (or, at least, the fate of the "Neoplatonic" extension of his ideas). Later on, in the European scholastic world of the late twelfth and thirteenth centuries, it was also to be the fate of the newly rediscovered Aristotelian system.

So far as the fate of the Platonic inheritance goes, there can be few developments in the history of philosophy more tangled, more complex, more dramatic than the movement of ideas in late antiquity that culminated in the fourth century in the Neoplatonic patterns of thought which St Augustine encountered in what he was wont to call "the books of the Platonists." Reflecting, among other things, a persistent tendency to understand the mysterious Demiurge of Plato's *Timaeus*, not as some sort of mythic symbol, but, literally, as a World Maker, it went on to conflate him with the transcendent Unmoved Mover of Aristotle's *Metaphysics* – the final and highest good which he himself called "God," and then to interpret the Forms, essences, or Ideas no longer as independent entities but rather as thoughts or ideas or archetypes in the *mind* of the supreme God produced by that macrocosmic conflation. Thus emerged the notion of a transcendent God, at once the Highest Good to which all things aspire, the First Cause from which all things derive their being, the Supreme Reason to which all things owe their order and intelligibility, and, increasingly (Neoplatonism being a path of salvation as well as a philosophy) the object of a real devotional sentiment.

Given this development, it is not too hard to understand how St Augustine, following in the fifth century the trail first blazed at Alexandria by Philo Judaeus and later broadened by the Greek church fathers, was able, via an extraordinary achievement of philosophico-theological bridge-building and in a fashion that proved to be definitive for Western Christian philosophy, to engineer a further and really quite stunning conflation: the identification of the Neoplatonic God – the God of the philosophers, as it were, in its final, most complex, and most developed form – with the biblical God of Abraham, Isaac, and Jacob, the personal God of power and might who not only transcends the universe but also, of his omnipotence, created it, not out of Platonic or Aristotelian pre-existent matter, but out of nothing. The providential God, moreover, from whose omniscient purview not even the fall of a sparrow escapes (Matthew 10:29) and against whose miraculous intervention not even the might of a Nebuchadnezzar was proof (Daniel 3). In so doing, Augustine attempted to close the way to any further Christian flirtation with the Greek notion of the eternity of the world such as that indulged by the Alexandrian theologian Origen two centuries earlier. At the same time, by agreeing with Philo, the Neoplatonists, and many of his Christian predecessors that the creative act was indeed an intelligent one guided by Forms, Ideas, or archetypes in the Platonic mould, but Ideas now situated in the divine mind itself as a sort of creative blueprint, he responded to the Greek concern to vindicate philosophically the order and intelligibility of the universe.

This was clearly a quite extraordinary accommodation. I would suggest, however, that what it reflected was a victory for delicate philosophical and theological diplomacy rather than the achievement of any truly stable synthesis. In the historic encounter between Athens and Jerusalem, between the Greek philosophical tradition and religious views of biblical provenance, the great stumbling block had been (and was to remain) the sheer difficulty of reconciling the personal and transcendent God of power and might, upon whose will the very existence of the world was radically contingent, with the archaic and characteristically Greek intuition of the divine as limited and innerworldly and of the universe as necessary and eternal, or, to put it differently, with the persistent tendency of the Greek philosophers to identify the divine with the immanent and necessary order of an eternal cosmos.

The retention of the Platonic ideas witnesses to the impact of that enduring tension. The denial of their independent existence and their location in the mind of God reflects the desire to make room for the biblical conception of the divine as almighty power and unimpeded will. But the nagging question of course remained: Was it room enough? If the universe was truly rational and ultimately intelligible, could God ever be willful? And if God could really be willful, could the universe be fully rational and intelligible? What had guaranteed the bedrock rationality of Plato's universe, after all, had been the subordination of the Demiurge's craftsmanlike creative activity to the patterns, blueprints, or archetypes presented to him in the independent and co-eternal Forms or Ideas. But when the biblical Job had sought some justification comprehensible in terms of human reason, for the disasters his

Hebraic God had visited upon him, God's reply was not a reassuring vindication of the rationality and stability of his justice, but rather a disdainful and terrifying evocation of his omnipotence. "Where were you when I laid the foundations of the earth? . . . Have you commanded the morning since your days began? . . . Can you bind the chains of the Pleiades or loose the cords of Orion? . . . Shall a faultfinder contend with the Almighty?" (Job 38:4, 12, 31; 40:2).

Much has been written over the years about the dramatic impact of Athens upon Jerusalem, about the enrichment of the primitive Christian vision resulting from the penetration of biblical modes of thought by philosophic ideas of Greek provenance. Without it, certainly, and the type of specifically *Catholic* Christianity it helped shape, the desacralizing thrust of the biblical vision would not have been blunted to the extent it was, nor for so very long. Without it, too, the Eusebian and other complex patterns of Christological thinking which eased the way for the survival into the Middle Ages and beyond of Christianized versions of the archaic notion of royal sacrality would scarcely have been possible. Without it, again, the subsequent erection in the thirteenth and fourteenth centuries of those grand, architectonic scholastic structures of thought – of which Thomas Aquinas's *Summa theologiae* is the most celebrated – would have been altogether inconceivable.

But while it has been much less common to do so, we need to acknowledge also, if we are to penetrate to the heart of the Western intellectual tradition, the less obvious but no less profound impact of Jerusalem upon Athens. That impact, which made itself felt quite slowly and largely in the course of the late medieval and early modern centuries, was the necessary precondition for the emergence of the natural philosophy presupposed by the emergent physical science of the seventeenth century, as also for the secularist character of the subsequent Enlightenment project. We need to acknowledge, that is to say, the internal tensions built into the very fabric of the Christian accommodation with Greek philosophical patterns of thought, and the concomitant instability of those grand scholastic structures which, in the great effort to render compatible the contradictory and harmonious the dissonant, depended upon the employment of an array of exceedingly refined but weight-bearing and supportive distinctions. Or, substituting for the architectural a terrestrial image to which I have become attached, we need to recognize the fact that a profound geologic fault runs right across the conflicted landscape of our Western intellectual tradition. Along that fault seismic activity is inevitably to be expected – the bumping, the grinding, the subduction, if you wish, of those great tectonic plates of disparate Greek and biblical provenance which collided in late antiquity to form the unstable continent of our *mentalité*.

Two particular episodes of such seismic activity may be identified as having been powerful enough to affect a significant reshaping of the intellectual landscape. The first of these occurred in European university circles of the late thirteenth and fourteenth centuries and thrust up into prominence the quasi-empiricist mode of thinking pioneered by William of Ockham (d. 1349) and those who followed him in the "nominalist" tradition of thinking or what came to be known as "the modern way" (*via moderna*). The second occurred in the seventeenth century and, having pushed to one side the Neoplatonic modes of thought dear to the so-called Cambridge Platonists and shaken to its very foundations the regnant Aristotelianism of the day, eventuated in the atomistic and mechanistic natural philosophy pioneered by such thinkers as Pierre Gassendi, Walter Charleton, and Robert Boyle, given classic and enormously influential expression by Sir Isaac Newton, and leaving as its residue the forms of deistic thinking common among the *philosophes* of the eighteenth-century Enlightenment.

It is impossible here to dwell at any length on either of those episodes. Suffice it to say that both involved a theologically driven reaction to the danger that Aristotelian rationalism was seen to pose to the freedom and omnipotence of the Christian God. That that was the case with William of Ockham – whose thinking has been described as dominated by the first words of the Christian creed: "I believe in one God, the Father Almighty"[34] – is generally conceded. And that it was almost equally the case with those who hammered out the tradition of natural philosophizing culminating in what it was once fashionable to call "the Scientific Revolution" is coming increasingly to be recognized. After all, it was Boyle himself who, having cited the Aristotelian denial to God of both the creation and providential governance of the world, confessed that he took "divers of Aristotle's opinions relating to religion to be more unfriendly, not to say pernicious to it, than those of several other heathen philosophers" – prominent among them, it seems clear, the atomistic views of those he called the "Epicurean and other corpuscularian infidels."[35] In their intense preoccupation with the divine omnipotence, fourteenth-century nominalists and seventeenth-century scientists were alike led to set God over against the world he had created, to view that world as composed of a concatenation of singular existents radically dependent on the divine decision, and to regard the order of that world, accordingly, as deriving not from any sort of participation (Thomistic or Cambridge Platonist fashion) in the divine reason, but rather from the peremptory mandates of the divine will. The uniformities observable in nature, to which the seventeenth-century scientists applied the term "laws of nature," they viewed, not in Greek fashion as the manifestation of an immanent divine reason, but as being, rather, of external divine imposition (in

Ockham's terms, "the laws ordained and instituted by God"), and the world itself, not as a "living" organism possessed of its own intelligibility, but as an inanimate machine operating in accordance with the norms of behavior thus imposed upon it.

The dominion which the Aristotelian physics continued to exercise over the minds even of the late medieval nominalists was such that they failed to work through or realize the full implications of their own fundamental philosophical commitments for the realm of what we would call natural science. That was to be the achievement, instead, of the great physical scientists of the seventeenth century who finally broke with the classical Greek understanding of nature as an intelligible organism, an understanding based ultimately on an analogy between the world of nature and the individual human being. Instead, and reflecting in this the historic confluence between the biblical idea of a creative and omnipotent God and the rich late medieval and early modern experience of designing and constructing machines (thus R.G. Collingwood),[36] the seventeenth-century physical scientists came to view the world as being devoid of intelligence and life, bereft of numinosity, drained of the last vestiges of the sacred or divine, a great and wondrous machine grinding on its inexorable course in accord with those laws or uniformities which God at the creation had imposed upon it.

As, in the course of the late seventeenth and eighteenth centuries, the new physical science grew in power and prestige, and as its simplified popularizations grew in influence, the thoroughly disenchanted picture of the universe which it projected served understandably to deprive already enfeebled notions of royal sacrality of whatever lingering measure of sustenance they may still have been able to derive from the memories of more congenial and traditional modes of natural theology and philosophy. Already in the mid-seventeenth century the philosophical writings of Thomas Hobbes gave a clear (if precocious) signal about what the new way of viewing nature might entail for political philosophy. For characteristic of the Hobbesian system of "Will and Artifice," as Michael Oakeshott has pointed out, the thought as it were that pervades its parts, is the understanding of the universe as the contingent creation of an omnipotent divine will; of the "civil order," accordingly, as an artificial creation of a concatenation of individual acts of autonomous human willing; the understanding of philosophical knowledge as "conditional not absolute," for "there is no effect which the power of [the omnipotent] God cannot produce in many several ways"; the definition of law, divine and natural no less than human, as the mandate of a sovereign will; the understanding of the civil order no less than the world at large "on the analogy of a machine, where to explain an effect we go to its immediate [efficient] cause; and to seek the result of the cause we go to its immediate

156

effect"; and the concomitant banishment from the realm of law and politics no less than from the natural world at large of those age-old teleological pre-occupations which ill-accorded with so mechanistic an understanding of reality.[37]

Nor was that the only signal that Hobbes gave. In the *Leviathan*, speaking of the compromising accommodations which "the doctors of the Roman Church" had made with pagan religious practices, and describing them as having "filled up again" those "old empty bottles of Gentilism . . . with the new wine of Christianity," Hobbes also predicted that in the end that heady new wine could not fail to break them.[38] Of that process, the fate of the Christianized version of archaic regal sacrality may be said to be a case in point. It may have taken an unconscionable amount of time to do so, but, as the very tenor of Hobbes's own philosophical system makes clear, that new wine was indeed destined finally to burst those age-old bottles. On that, if not necessarily on everything, Hobbes in effect was right.

Epilogue
Survivals and Revivals

The assumption that the nineteenth, twentieth, and twenty-first centuries are to be lumped together as constituting no more than an epilogue to the millennial career of kingship may well seem questionable. The defeat of Napoleon I in 1815 ushered in, after all, a conservative era of monarchical restoration. The ancient Bourbon dynasty was returned to the French throne, and the popes, whose monarchical office had seemed destined for extinction along with that of the Holy Roman Emperors, regained their poise and something more than that. As the century wore on, they were able in fact to ride a gathering wave of grass-roots support to a dramatic triumph at the First Vatican Council (1870) over the tradition of conciliarist constitutionalism which had in the past so often threatened to hem in with legal restraints the free exercise of their high prerogatives. The latter decades of the century, moreover, were also to see the formal establishment of a British Indian empire, the dramatic return of the Japanese imperial office from centuries of provincial obscurity to the very center of national government, and the advent in Europe of a new German empire and a unified national kingdom in Italy. In mid-century, it is true, the British had put an end to the Moghul empire in India. Later on, evanescent spin-off monarchies had risen and fallen in Mexico and Brazil, and in 1913, though Pu Yi, its last incumbent, was to live on until 1967, the age-old office of Chinese emperor ceased, in effect, to exist. But in 1914, on the eve of the First World War, the great majority of European states, certainly, remained stolidly monarchical.

Stolidly, it may be, but not necessarily solidly. The regal realities were no longer what they once had been. For reasons other than those Shakespeare may have had in mind, it was indeed the case in the nineteenth century that uneasy lay the head that wore a crown. In 1830, a revolution of liberal inspiration led in France to the abdication of the Bourbon king Charles X and the

158

installation in the person of Louis-Philippe of the quasi-constitutionalist July monarchy. It had the effect also of setting off revolutionary reverberations in Belgium, Poland, and some of the German and Italian states. Again, in 1848, a citizen-uprising in Paris, eventuating rapidly in the collapse of the July monarchy and the establishment of a republic, set the example for revolutionary upheavals right across Europe – from Sicily and the papal states in the south to Saxony and Hanover in the north, Hungary and Austria in the east to Württenberg and Baden in the west. By 1850, order had everywhere been restored, republican institutions and liberal constitutions had been dismantled, and kings were once more in command. But the institution of monarchy had sustained a massive onslaught and the fragility of its rootage in popular esteem had been exposed. So, too, had the need for kings to connect more effectively with their subjects and to find some way to bolster their legitimacy with at least a simulacrum of popular consent. When Louis-Philippe, who was sometimes to be referred to as the "Citizen King," was proclaimed successor to the erstwhile Charles X on the French throne, he was dubbed "King of the French by the Grace of God *and the Will of the People.*" And the later Bonapartist penchant for the plebiscite reflects the growing sense that without some solicitation of popular consent royal legitimacy could hardly be vindicated. If hypocrisy is indeed the tribute that vice pays to virtue, the device of the plebiscite was henceforth to be the tribute that modern authoritarian rulers felt it necessary to pay to the ideal of popular sovereignty.

That notwithstanding, for kings, emperors, and their families, the nineteenth and twentieth centuries were to be punctuated and shadowed by abdications, depositions, assassination, and the fear of assassination. Despite tightening security and the creation of secret police agencies, such attempts sometimes succeeded. Such was the case with Tsar Alexander III of Russia in 1881, with the Empress of Austria in 1898, with the king of Portugal and his heir in 1908 (followed in 1910 by the deposition of their successor), with the king of Greece in 1913, and in 1914, with the Archduke Franz Ferdinand, heir-apparent to the Austrian throne – the event that was to precipitate the onset of the Great War.

Any doubt about the increasing fragility of the royal purchase on power and the progressive weakening of the affective ties binding subjects to their kings was to be dissipated by the veritable clean-out of emperors and kings that was to occur in Europe and elsewhere in the wake of the two world wars. The German, Russian, Austro-Hungarian and Ottoman empires all ceased to exist in the immediate aftermath of the Great War. Spain (though the monarchy there was later to be restored) became a republic in 1931, Yugoslavia in 1945, Albania, Bulgaria, and Italy in 1946, Romania in 1947, Egypt in 1952,

Iraq in 1958, Yemen in 1962, Libya in 1969, Cambodia in 1970 (though the monarchy there was later to be restored), Afghanistan and Greece in 1973, Ethiopia and Laos in 1974–75, Iran in 1979 – the list is impressive enough for one writer to refer to it as a veritable "culling" of the royal ranks.

Recent years have witnessed scattered talk about the possible restoration of kingship in Afghanistan, Bulgaria, and Iraq, and in 1975 it made a decisive and successful return to Spain, where in 1981 the new king, Juan Carlos, won the hearts of his people by standing firm against the threat of a military coup and, in a dramatic television address, rallying the nation in support of the democratic constitution. For those of staunchly monarchist sympathies, however, the established trend can hardly seem encouraging. Of the handful of monarchies that have survived into the twenty-first century, those of Nepal and Cambodia are clearly beleaguered, and only an inveterate gambler, I suspect, would put much money on the long-term survival of kingship in Bhutan, Jordan, Morocco, Saudi Arabia, or Swaziland. Other royal figures elsewhere in Africa, especially anglophone West Africa, continue to play important ritual and informal political roles as arbiters of status and wielders of influence in public life, but they have long since been "moved to a position of governmental marginality" and, however significant as social and religious figures, function "outside the realm of the official structures of the state."[1] The well established constitutional monarchies of Japan, Thailand, Great Britain, Holland, Belgium, Denmark, Norway, and Sweden still possess, of course, an official and much more secure political status. But even in such comparatively safe harbors for monarchy, royal families have found their institutional moorings occasionally strained by the outbreak of storms of adverse public opinion. Edward VIII of Great Britain was nudged into abdication in 1936, popular hostility forced Leopold of Belgium to abdicate in favor of his son Baudouin in 1951, and in the years since then the Dutch, Norwegian, and British monarchies have all been rattled by the negative reverberations of what their irritated subjects clearly viewed as scandalous or inappropriate royal behavior. In the case of the British royal family, indeed, it has led to their becoming once more the object of intermittent derision, rather than of the persistent adulation heaped upon them during the greater part of the twentieth century.

If, then, one stands well back and views the royal scene from afar, the one case where a monarchy can be seen to have gained from the nineteenth century to the present in both power and prestige would appear to be that of the papacy. Its specifically temporal power, confined now to the narrow compass of Vatican City, may have been reduced to the status of little more than symbolic remnant. But in the degree to which, via effective centralized governmental agencies, mechanisms, procedures, and instrumentalities of communication, it is actually able on a day-to-day basis to impose its sovereign will on the provincial churches of Roman Catholic Christendom, the papal monarchy stands today at the very apex of its effective power within the Church and, after the long, high-profile pontificate of John Paul II, close to the apex of its prestige worldwide. The Second Vatican Council (1962–5) made much of the collective or "collegial" responsibility of the corps of bishops for the mission and wellbeing of the universal Church. But it should not be forgotten that at every point in *Lumen gentium* (its "constitution" or decree on the Church) it assigned the explicitly governmental or jurisdictional power to the episcopal college's papal head alone. Only in "hierarchical communion with the head of the college and its members" can bishops exercise their various offices, governance included. Only through papal convocation and confirmation can a council be ecumenical. Only with papal approbation can the acts of such a council become valid. Further than that, as head of the episcopal college the pope "alone can perform certain acts which are no way within the competence of the bishops," can proceed, taking "into account the good of the Church" and "according to his own discretion," in "setting up, encouraging, and approving collegial activity," and, "as supreme pastor of the Church, can exercise his power at all times *as he thinks best*" (*suam potestatem omni tempore ad placitum exercere potest*).[2]

In the 1960s, Pope Paul VI conspicuously retired to museum status the papal crown and other traditional trappings of papal regality. But he relinquished none of the prerogatives and powers pertaining to his ancient high office. Though it would doubtless try to shrug off the designation, it remains the case that the papacy, which a thousand years ago launched a frontal assault on the sacral pretensions of the German emperors, stands out in solitary splendor today as itself the last of the truly great sacral monarchies.

It is not inappropriate, then, to view the nineteenth and twentieth centuries as constituting no more than an epilogue to the long career of kingship. The claims commonly made for the French Revolution as being the decisive turning point in the desacralization of kingship and the delegitimation of the monarchical office would appear to be warranted. Time, then, to return, by way of conclusion to that great historical watershed. In *The Rebel* (*L'Homme Revolté*) Albert Camus wrote that "1789 is the starting point of modern times, because men of that period wished, among other things, to overthrow the principle of divine right." "To traditional tyrannicide," therefore, they added "the concept of calculated deicide." The attempt on the person of Louis XVI in 1793 was "aimed at the King-Christ, the incarnation of the divinity, and not at the craven flesh of a mere man." The regicide was, in effect, "the murder of the King-priest" and it stands, he went on,

Figure 8 The Papacy. Cardinal Alfredo Ottaviani places the triple crown on Pope Paul VI's head during an outdoor coronation ceremony in St Peter's Square, June 30, 1963. The beehive-shaped tiara, 15 inches high and weighing close to 10 pounds, is made of cloth-of-silver; three gold coronets studded with jewels ring it and a small cross rises from the top. (TopFoto)

at the crux of our contemporary history. It symbolizes the secularization of our history and the disincarnation of the Christian God. Up to now God played a part in history through the medium of kings. But His representative in history has been killed, for there is no longer a king. Therefore there is nothing but a semblance of God, relegated to the heaven of principle.

Deploring the regicide, then, as the removal from the scene of "the divine emissary in charge of human affairs," and mourning the concomitant loss of a universal norm of justice linked with the divine, Camus was led to conclude that with that murderous act "the revolutionaries dealt a terrible blow to Christianity."[3]

The claim is an arresting one, almost as arresting as the event itself. That event, it should be conceded, is one of great singularity and complexity, and one that has not readily yielded its meaning to those who have attempted to construe it. But if any rectitude attaches to the case I have been making for the ultimately biblical wellspring of the desacralizing process, then a fundamental irony attends upon that regicidal event. And it is an irony that appears wholly to have eluded Camus. Louis XVI's execution and the events that unfolded in its train did indeed deal a great blow to the "throne and altar" Catholicism of the French *ancien régime*. But the more devastating blow, surely, was the *coup de grâce* that the slow seepage of Christian belief into the popular consciousness had finally succeeded in delivering to the "anthropological and historical truism" that "kings are sacred" and to humankind's millennial yearning for a kingship anchored in the divine.

Notes

Prologue

1 Michael Oakeshott ed., *The Leviathan of Thomas Hobbes* (Oxford: Basil Blackwell, 1946), Introduction, p. x.

2 Thus, Michelle Gilbert, "The Person of the King: Ritual and Power in a Ghanaian State," in *Rituals of Royalty: Power and Ceremonial in Traditional Societies*, eds. David Cannadine and Simon Price (Cambridge: Cambridge University Press, 1987), pp. 298–330 (at p. 298).

3 Roger Mousnier, *Monarchies et royautés de la préhistoire à nos jours* (Paris: Librairie Académique Perrin, 1989), pp. 10–11.

4 John Neville Figgis, *The Divine Right of Kings* (New York and London: Harper Torchbooks, [1896] 1965), p. 1.

5 Thus one could read George H. Sabine's influential textbook, *A History of Political Thought*, 3rd edn. (New York: Henry Holt and Company, 1953) – which went through multiple editions and reprintings in subsequent decades, and which was widely read by generations of students in the anglophone world – without realizing that Aristotle thought that "the cult of the gods should be a matter for citizens," and that "the directors of the state include priests as well as magistrates." See *Politics*, VII, ix, §9 and xii, §6; trans. Ernest Barker, *The Politics of Aristotle* (Oxford: Clarendon Press, 1946), pp. 303 and 310.

6 The words quoted are those of Frank M. Turner, *The Greek Heritage in Victorian Britain* (New York and London: Yale University Press, 1981), pp. 7–8. "Across the Western world," he adds, "Victorian authors and readers were determined to find the Greeks as much as possible like themselves and to rationalize away fundamental differences."

7 For Ullmann's position and the numerous works in which he developed it, along with a critical appraisal of what it involves, see Francis Oakley, "Celestial Hierarchies Revisited: Walter Ullmann's Vision of Medieval Politics," in Oakley, *Politics and Eternity: Studies in the History of Medieval and Early Modern Political Thought* (Leiden, Boston, Cologne: E.J. Brill, 1999), pp. 25–72.

8 Thus, in order of citation (all italics mine), Sabine, *History of Political Thought*, p. 159; Francis Dvornik, *Early Christian and Byzantine Political Philosophy: Origins and Background*, 2 vols. (Washington, DC: Dumbarton Oaks Center for Byzantine Studies, 1966), vol. 2, p. 488; Christopher Morris, *Western Political Thought: I Plato to Aristotle* (New York: Basic Books, 1967), p. 166; C.H. McIlwain, *Growth of Political Thought in the West* (New York: Macmillan, 1932), p. 146; John B. Morrall, *Political Thought in Medieval Times* (New York: Harper and Row, 1962), pp. 10–11. Cf. among more recent works, Joseph Canning, *A History of Medieval Political Thought 300–1450* (London and New York: Routledge, 1996), pp. 127–8.

9 Numa Denis Fustel de Coulanges, *The Ancient City*, trans. Willard Small (Garden City, NY: Doubleday Anchor Books, 1955), first published in 1864. Cf. W.K.C. Guthrie, *The Greek Philosophers: From Thales to Aristotle* (New York: Harper and Row, 1960), pp. 3–4, where, acknowledging the indebtedness of modern classicists to anthropological studies, he remarks of the Greeks that they remain "in many respects a remarkably *foreign* people, and to get inside their minds . . . means unthinking much that has become part and parcel of our mental equipment so that we carry it about with us unquestioningly and for the most part unconsciously."

10 Christopher Dawson, *Religion and Culture* (New York: AMS Press, 1981), p. 116.

11 Peter Berger, *The Sacred Canopy: Elements of a Sociological Theory of Religion* (Garden City, NY: Doubleday Anchor Books, 1969); Marcel Gauchet, *The Disenchantment of the World*, trans. Oscar Burge (Princeton, NJ: Princeton University Press, 1997); Gianni Vattimo, *After Christianity*, trans. Luca d'Isanto (New York: Columbia University Press, 2002).

1 Gate of the Gods

1 For these examples, see Harold Nicolson, *Kings, Courts and Monarchy* (New York: Simon and Schuster, 1962), p. 55; Henri J.M. Claessen and Peter Skalnik eds., *The Early State* (The Hague, Paris, New York: Mouton Publishers, 1978), p. 165; A.M. Hocart, *Kings and Councillors: An Essay in the Comparative Anatomy of Human Society*, ed. Rodney Needham (Chicago and London: University of Chicago Press, 1970), p. 165; C.M. Frähn, *Ibn Fozhans und anderer Araber Berichte über die Russen Alterer Zeit: Text und Übersetzung* (St Petersburg, 1823), pp. 21–2; H. Munro Chadwick, *The Heroic Age* (Cambridge: Cambridge University Press, 1926), p. 367.

2 Clifford Geertz, *Negara: The Theatre State in Nineteenth-Century Bali* (Princeton, NJ: Princeton University Press, 1988), p. 13.

3 Thus H.P. L'Orange, "Expressions of Cosmic Kingship in the Ancient World," in *The Sacral Kingship: Contributions to the Central Theme of the VIIIth International Congress for the History of Religions (Rome, April, 1955)* (Leiden: E.J. Brill, 1959), pp. 481–92; idem, *Studies in the Iconography of Cosmic Kingship in the Ancient World* (New York: Caratzas Brothers, 1982), esp. pp. 103–9; Chadwick, *The Heroic Age*, p. 368; Walter Schlesinger, "Über germanisches

Heerkönigtum," in *Das Königtum: Seine geistigen und rechtlichen Grundlagen,*
ed. T. Mayer (Lindau u. Konstanz: J. Thorbeke, 1956), pp. 105–41 (at p. 134);
J.M. Wallace-Hadrill, *The Long-Haired Kings and Other Studies in Frankish
History* (London: Methuen, 1962), p. 158: idem, *Early Germanic Kingship in
England and on the Continent* (Oxford: Clarendon Press, 1971), pp. 6–7, 19.

4 As, for example, the situation in ancient India, where the sacral character of the
king was not in doubt, nor his responsibility for rainfall and the general wellbeing of his people – see John H. Spellman, *Political Theory of Ancient India: A
Study of Kingship from the Earliest Times to circa AD 300* (Oxford: Oxford University Press, 1964). Speaking, however, of "the ambiguity of the king–brahmin
relationship," Heesterman has insisted upon the lack in the Vedic ritual texts of
any "unified view of kingship" or "consistent overall scheme that would give
substance to a consolidated theory of sacral kingship" – J.C. Heesterman, *The
Inner Conflict of Tradition: Essays in Indian Ritual, Kingship, and Society*
(Chicago and London: University of Chicago Press, 1985), pp. 111 and 142.

5 Insofar, that is, as causality is taken to function in a mechanical, impersonal
fashion.

6 Henri Frankfort, John A. Wilson and Thorkild Jacobsen, *Before Philosophy: The
Intellectual Adventure of Ancient Man* (Baltimore, MD: Penguin, 1949),
p. 237.

7 Ibid., p. 238.

8 Mircea Eliade, *Cosmos and History: The Myth of the Eternal Return* (New York:
Harper and Row, 1959), p. 36.

9 Henri Frankfort, *Kingship and the Gods: A Study of Near Eastern Religion as the
Integration of Society and Nature* (Chicago: University of Chicago Press, 1948),
p. 3.

10 Arend T. Van Leeuwen, *Christianity in World History: The Meeting of the Faiths
of East and West*, trans. H.H. Hoskins (New York: Charles Scribner's Sons,
1965), pp. 168–70.

11 Max Weber, *The Religion of China: Confucianism and Taoism*, trans. H.H. Gerth
(Glencoe, IL: Free Press of Glencoe, 1959), pp. 261–2, n. 63. No isolated inci-
dent. Weber comments also that "as late as 1832 rain . . . [had] . . . followed the
public confession of the emperor."

12 Van Leeuwen, *Christianity in World History*, p. 170.

13 Thus John W. Perry, *Lord of the Four Quarters: Myths of the Royal Father* (New
York: George Braziller, 1966), pp. 5, 26. Cf. Edmond Rochedieu, "Le Caractère
sacré de souveraineté à la lumière de la psychologie collective," in *The Sacral
Kingship*, 48–53.

14 D.C. Holtom, *The Japanese Enthronement Ceremonies, with an Account of the
Imperial Regalia*, 2nd edn. (Tokyo: Sophia University, 1972), pp. 2–3.

15 The words are those of T. Fujitani, *Splendid Monarchy: Power and Pageantry in
Modern Japan* (Berkeley, Los Angeles, London: University of California Press,
1996), p. 248, n. 7.

16 For the Victorian "reinvention" of the British monarchy, see David Cannadine,
"The Context, Performance and Meaning of Ritual: The British Monarchy and
the 'Invention of Tradition,' c.1820–1977," in *The Invention of Tradition*, eds.

Eric Hobsbawm and Terence Ranger (Cambridge: Cambridge University Press, 1983), pp. 101–64. For the Meiji parallel in Japan, Fujitani, *Splendid Monarchy*, esp. pp. 1–28, 230–45.

17 I depend here on the detailed account in Holtom, *The Japanese Enthronement Ceremonies*.

18 See Steven R. Weisman, "Akihito Performs his Solitary Rite," *New York Times*, November 23, 1990, A7.

19 Thus Holtom's interpretation, *The Japanese Enthronement Ceremony*, pp. 114–16. He also notes, however, that "the fact that the food offering is placed on a mat that is turned in the direction of Ise [where the Sacred Regalian Mirror is enshrined] may be legitimately interpreted as a special expression of thanksgiving to Amaterasu-ō-mikami," and in 1990, certainly, some Japanese speculated that the ceremony involved a sort of symbolic sexual coupling with the sun-goddess – for which, see Weisman, "Akihito performs his solitary rite," A7.

20 Certainly, it was not to the people but "to the first ancestors of the imperial line" that the Meiji emperor pledged to uphold the constitution of 1889, and that oath he repeated to his imperial ancestors and followed up by an act of worship to the national deities. Thus Fujitani, *Splendid Monarchy*, pp. 107–8. He also notes (pp. 237–8) that in 1946 the emperor followed up his proclamation of the new constitution by reporting that fact "to the national gods in the palace's Inner Sanctuary."

21 Jan Vansina, *The Children of Woot: A History of the Kuba Peoples* (Madison, WI: University of Wisconsin Press, 1978), p. 242; idem, "The Kuba State," in *The Early State*, eds. Henri J.M. Claessen and Peter Skalnik (The Hague, Paris, New York: Mouton Publishers, 1978), 359–79 (at 378). I base my remarks on these two works of Vansina as well as on Joseph Cornet, *Art royal Kuba* (Milan: Edizioni Sipiel, 1982).

22 "Surplus did not make the state. Rather the reverse" – thus Vansina, "The Kuba State," 378; cf. idem, *The Children of Woot*, ch. 10, and esp. pp. 194–6.

23 Vansina, *The Children of Woot*, p. 207.

24 Vansina, "The Kuba State," p. 365.

25 Michael D. Coe, *The Maya*, 5th edn. (London: Thames and Hudson, 1993), p. 190. I base what I have to say in this section largely on Coe's standard work, as well as on Linda Schele and David Freidel, *A Forest of Kings: The Untold Story of the Ancient Maya* (New York: William Morrow, 1990) and David Carrasco, *Religions of Mesoamerica: Cosmovision and Ceremonial Centers* (Prospect Heights, IL: Waveland Pres, 1990).

26 Schele and Freidel, *A Forest of Kings*, p. 98; cf. pp. 57, 120; Carrasco, *Religions of Mesoamerica*, p. 40. I would note that the use of the word "supernatural," however understandable, is both anachronistic and inappropriate in relation to a people to whom the biblically inspired distinction between "nature" and "supernature" would probably have been utterly incomprehensible.

27 Schele and Freidel, *A Forest of Kings*, p. 129.

28 Carrasco, *Religions of Mesoamerica*, pp. 29, 35–6.

29 Schele and Freidel, *A Forest of Kings*, p. 90.

30 Though Carrasco, *Religions of Mesoamerica*, ch. 4 ("Maya Religion: Cosmic

Trees, Sacred Kings, and the Underworld"), pp. 92–123, gives an admirably succinct and coherent description.

31 Schele and Freidel, *A Forest of Kings*, pp. 103–16 (at p. 116).
32 Ibid., pp. 217–19.
33 Ibid., pp. 225–6.
34 D.A. Binchy, *Celtic and Anglo-Saxon Kingship* (Oxford: Clarendon Press, 1970), p. 14. In what follows I rely on Binchy as well as Maartje Draak, "Some Aspects of Kingship in Pagan Ireland," in *The Sacral Kingship*, pp. 651–63; Prionsias MacCana, *Celtic Mythology*, rev. edn. (New York: Peter Bendrick Books, 1983); J.A. MacCulloch, *The Religion of the Ancient Celts* (Edinburgh: T. and T. Clark, 1911).
35 MacCana, *Celtic Mythology*, p. 117.
36 Similarly, the failure of his powers in any of these areas, or the impairment of his body, might necessitate his abdication or deposition – thus Draak, "Some Aspects of Kingship in Pagan Ireland," pp. 660–3.
37 Thus, according to Binchy (p. 24), "we are entitled to speak of a 'Common Celtic' type of kingship." Cf. MacCulloch, *The Religion of the Ancient Celts*, pp. 159–60.
38 Ake V. Ström, "The King God and His Connection with Sacrifice in the Old Norse Religion," in *The Sacral Kingship*, p. 702; cf. E.O.G. Turville-Petrie, *Myth and Religion of the North: The Religion of Ancient Scandinavia* (New York: Holt, Rinehart and Winston, 1964), esp. ch. 9, pp. 190–5. In light of the critical views since expressed by Walter Baetke, *Yngvi und die Ynglinger: Eine quellenkritische Untersuchung über das nordische "Sakralkönigtum"* (Berlin: Akademie-Verlag, 1964), the confidence evident in Ström's judgment now seems to have been a little premature.
39 Ström, "The King God and His Connection with Sacrifice," pp. 714–15.
40 Otto Höfler, "Der Sakralcharakter des germanischen Königtums," in *The Sacral Kingship*, p. 681.
41 A.M. Hocart, *Kings and Councillors: An Essay in the Comparative Anatomy of Human Society*, ed. Rodney Needham (Chicago and London: University of Chicago Press, 1970), p. 12.
42 William Stubbs, *The Constitutional History of England*, 3rd edn. (3 vols., Oxford: Clarendon Press, 1880), vol. 1, pp. 2, 231, 233.
43 See Baetke, *Yngvi und dei Ynglinger*, pp. 8–10, 171ff., for a particularly blunt statement of this position.
44 H.G. Güterbock, "Authority and Law in the Hittite Kingdom," *Supplement to the Journal of the American Oriental Society*, no. 17 (July–Sept., 1956), 19; O.R. Gurney, "Hittite Kingship," in S.H. Hooke ed., *Myth, Ritual and Kingship* (Oxford: Clarendon Press, 1958), pp. 115, 121.
45 Chadwick, *The Heroic Age*, p. 368; Höfler, "Der Sakralcharakter des germanischen Königtums," pp. 694–6; Schlesinger, "Über germanisches Heerkönigtum," pp. 105–41 (at p. 140).
46 Ammianus Marcellinus, *Res gestae*, xxviii, 5, 14; ed. and trans. John C. Rolfe, *Ammianus Marcellinus*, 3 vols. (Cambridge, MA: Harvard University Press, 1935), 3:168–9; cf. Schlesinger, "Über germanisches Heerkönigtum," p. 135.

47 Höfler, "Der Sakralcharakter des germanischen Königtums," pp. 700–1.
48 Procopius, *De bello gothico*, II, 14:34–42, and 15:27–36, in Procopius, *The History of the Wars*, ed. and trans. H.B. Dewing, 3 vols. (London: Loeb Classical Library, 1919), vol. 3, pp. 413, 420, 424.
49 Thus Frankfort, *Kingship and the Gods*, p. 251.
50 Henri Frankfort, *Egyptian Religion* (New York: Harper and Row, 1948), pp. 42–3. idem, *Kingship and the Gods*, p. 5.
51 Frankfort, *Kingship and the Gods*, p. 51; Frankfort et al., *Before Philosophy*, p. 89.
52 Frankfort et al., *Before Philosophy*, pp. 214–15.
53 Frankfort, *Kingship and the Gods*, pp. 150–1.

2 Royal Saviors and Shepherds

1 Mircea Eliade, *Cosmos and History: The Myth of the Eternal Return* (New York: Harper and Row, 1959), p. 34.
2 E.O. James, *The Ancient Gods: The History and Diffusion of Religion in the Ancient Near East and the Eastern Mediterranean* (London: Weidenfeld and Nicolson, 1960), pp. 129–33; Arne Furnmark, "Was there a Sacred Kingship in Minoan Crete?," in *The Sacral Kingship: Contributions to the Central Theme of the VIIIth International Congress for the History of Religions, Rome, April, 1955* (Leiden: E.J. Brill, 1959), pp. 369–70. Partial dissent in H.S. Rose, "The Evidence for Divine Kings in Greece," ibid., pp. 372–8, though it should be noted that Rose is concerned to reject the presence in the Greek world not of sacred or sacerdotal monarchs but only of *divine* kings "of the kind made famous by [Frazer's] *The Golden Bough*."
3 Francis Dvornik, *Early Christian and Byzantine Political Philosophy: Origins and Background*, 2 vols. (Washington, DC: Dumbarton Oaks Center for Byzantine Studies, 1966), vol. 1, p. 155.
4 The words cited are from Plato, *The Statesman*, §290E; in *The Collected Dialogues of Plato*, eds. Edith Hamilton and Huntington Cairns (Princeton, NJ: Princeton University Press, 1961), p. 1059, and from Dvornik, *Early Christian and Byzantine Political Philosophy*, vol. 1, p. 155.
5 *Aristotle on the Constitution of Athens*, §§57 and 3; trans. E. Poste (London: Macmillan, 1891), pp. 92 and 4; James, *The Ancient Gods*, p. 133.
6 James, *The Ancient Gods*, p. 133.
7 Such is the case made with extensive documentation by Dvornik, *Early Christian and Byzantine Political Philosophy*, vol. 1, pp. 207–21.
8 Citing the translation given by E.B. Goodenough, "The Political Philosophy of Hellenistic Kingship," *Yale Classical Studies*, 1 (1928), 55–102 (at 68 and 91).
9 Ibid., esp. pp. 91 and 100–2; Dvornik, *Early Christian and Byzantine Political Philosophy*, vol. 1, pp. 205–77.
10 Cicero, *Ad Quintum fratrem*, 1:9, 26; in *Letters to his Friends*, ed. W.G. Williams, 3 vols. (London: Heinemann, 1927–9), vol. 3, pp. 414ff.
11 Charles N. Cochrane, *Christianity and Classical Culture* (New York: Galaxy Books, 1957), pp. 110–13 (first published in 1940).
12 Dvornik, *Early Christian and Byzantine Political Philosophy*, vol. 2, p. 484;

M. Hammond, "Hellenistic Influences on the Structure of the Augustan Princi-
pate," *Memoirs of the American Academy in Rome*, 17 (1940), 1–25 (esp.
pp. 3–13).

13 Thus Simon Price, "From Noble Funerals to Divine Cult: The Consecration of
the Roman Emperors," in David Cannadine and Simon Price eds., *Rituals of
Royalty: Power and Ceremonial in Traditional Societies* (Cambridge: Cambridge
University Press, 1987), pp. 56–105 (at 57 and 103); also Simon Price, *Rituals
and Power: The Roman Imperial Cult in Asia Minor* (Cambridge: Cambridge
University Press, 1984), especially his helpful concluding reflections on "Rituals,
Politics and Power" (pp. 234–48). Cf. Sabine G. MacCormack, *Art and Cere-
mony in Late Antiquity* (Berkeley, Los Angeles, London: University of California
Press, 1981), pp. 93–115. Cf. Robert Graves, *I, Claudius* (London: Penguin,
1953), p. 164.

14 H.W. Pleket, "An Aspect of the Emperor Cult: Imperial Mysteries," *Harvard
Theological Review*, 58 (Dec., 1965), 331–47; similarly Price, "From Noble
Funerals to Divine Cult," pp. 56–105.

15 E.g. S.H. Hooke, A.R. Johnson, M. Engnell, G. Widengren. For a useful account
of the development and unfolding of the "myth and ritual" approach, Hooke's
earlier volumes – *Myth and Ritual* (1933) and *The Labyrinth* (1935), as well as
affinities with the work of scholars like A.M. Hocart and Sigmund Mowinckel, see
his, "Myth and Ritual: Past and Present," in *Myth, Ritual and Kingship: Essays on
the Theory and Practice of Kingship in the Ancient Near East and in Israel*, ed.
S.H. Hooke (Oxford: Clarendon Press, 1958), 1–21. For a critical appraisal of the
school, see S.G.F. Brandon, "The Myth and Ritual Position Critically Considered," ibid., 261–91.

16 Isaiah 9:6–7, 11:3–5, 42:1–7; cf. Jeremiah 23:5–6, 33:15–16; see the discussion
of these texts in Dvornik, *Early Christian and Byzantine Political Philosophy*,
vol. 1, pp. 335–9.

17 Isaiah 42:1–7, 49:1–9, 50:4–9, 52:13–15, 53:1–12; cf. the discussion in
Dvornik, *Early Christian and Byzantine Political Philosophy*, vol. 1, pp. 339–47,
and the literature referred to therein, especially C.J. Gadd, "Babylonian Myth
and Ritual," in *Myth and Ritual*, ed. Hooke, pp. 40–67, which summarizes the
unfolding of the New Year Festival's ritual of atonement.

18 Thus Eric Voegelin, *Order and History: I Israel and Revelation* (Baton Rouge,
LA: Louisiana State University Press, 1956), p. 282. The discovery is associated
especially with the names of Hermann Gunkel and Sigmund Mowinckel. For a
helpful account of the development of Old Testament scholarship on this whole
matter, see A.R. Johnson, "Hebrew Conceptions of Kingship," in *Myth, Ritual
and Kingship*, ed. Hooke, pp. 204–35.

19 The words quoted are those of Johnson, "Hebrew Conceptions of Kingship,"
p. 222, and Sigmund Mowinckel, *Psalmenstudien*, 6 vols. (Kristiania: J. Dybwad,
1922), vol. 2, p. 301.

20 As long ago as 1932 C.R. North pointed out that in the Hebrew it need mean
no more than "Thy throne is [everlasting] like that of God" – "The Religious
Aspects of Hebrew Kingship," *Zeitschrift für die alttestamentisch Wissenschaft*, 1
(1932), 8–38 (at pp. 29–30).

21 The words cited are drawn from North, "The Religious Aspects of Hebrew Kingship," p. 35, and Sigmund Mowinckel, "General Oriental and Specific Israelite Elements in the Israelite Conception of the Sacral Kingdom," in *The Sacral Kingship*, pp. 283–93 (at p. 286).

22 The words are those of G. von Rad and E.A. Speiser, cited from *Creation: The Impact of an Idea*, eds. Daniel O'Connor and Francis Oakley (New York: Scribner's Sons, 1969), p. 6. The essays gathered together in the book provide an introductory discussion of the philosophical significance of the biblical doctrine of creation, of the underlying conception of God that it presupposes, and of its impact upon later thinking about man and nature.

23 Mowinckel, "General Oriental and Specific Israelite Elements," p. 290.

24 "It is true that the explicit term 'the kingdom of God,' is not found in the Old Testament or in Jewish literature outside the New Testament. . . . But the *idea* is there, nevertheless, at least in its major aspects" – thus F.C. Grant, "The Idea of the Kingdom of God in the New Testament," in *The Sacral Kingship*, pp. 439–46 (at pp. 440–1). Cf. the discussion in Dvornik, *Early Christian and Byzantine Political Philosophy*, vol. 1, pp. 311–402.

25 See Dvornik, *Early Christian and Byzantine Political Philosophy*, vol. 1, pp. 396–402.

26 I follow here Dvornik, *Early Christian and Byzantine Political Philosophy*, vol. 1, pp. 278–402, cf. Voegelin, *Order and History*, vol. 1, pp. 488–515.

27 Grant, "The Idea of the Kingdom of God in the New Testament," p. 445.

28 Hans Küng, *The Church*, trans. Ray and Rosaleen Ockenden (New York: Sheed and Ward, 1967), p. 87.

29 E.g., in relation to the royal title of "savior," Paul's epistles to Timothy and Titus may be read as a direct attack on the Hellenistic divinization of kings. For Christ alone is the Savior, the "one mediator . . . between God and men," (1 Timothy 2:1–6; Titus 3:1–8). Per Beskow, *Rex Gloriae: The Kingship of Christ in the Early Church*, trans. Eric J. Sharpe (Stockholm: Almquist and Wiksell, 1962), pp. 71–3, suggests, however, that what is involved in these texts is less a polemic directed against Hellenistic royal claims than simply "a case of borrowing" through contact with the Hellenistic Judaism of the Diaspora.

30 Jean-Jacques Rousseau, *The Social Contract*, 4:8; in Jean-Jacques Rousseau, *The Social Contract and Discourses* (London: J.M. Dent and Sons, 1947), pp. 106–15 (at p. 108). Numa D. Fustel de Coulanges, *The Ancient City*, trans. Willard Small, 12th edn. (Garden City, NY: Doubleday Anchor Books, 1955), pp. 393–4.

31 John 12:31, 14:30, 16:11; 1 John 5:18–19; and esp. Revelation 13, where Rome is represented as a beast deriving its authority from Satan and demanding worship from its subjects under penalty of death. See L. Cerfaux, "Le Conflit entre Dieu et le Souverain divinisé dans l'Apocalypse de Jean," *The Sacral Kingship*, pp. 459–70.

32 For the importance of the Persian inheritance, see Aziz Al-Azmeh, *Muslim Kingship: Power and the Sacred in Muslim, Christian and Pagan Polities* (London and New York: I.B. Tauris, 1997); Patricia Crone, *God's Rule: Six Centuries of Islamic Political Thought* (New York: Columbia University Press, 2004), pp. 148–64.

33 Cited from Gavin R.G. Hambly, "The Pahlavī Autocracy: Muhammad Rizā Shāh," in *The Cambridge History of Iran*, eds. Peter Avery, Gavin Hambly, Charles Melville, et al., 7 vols. (Cambridge: Cambridge University Press, 1968–91), vol. 7, p. 285. Such reservations had not prevented the rulers of the Ottoman empire (c.1290–1922) from adopting the Persian title of "emperor," portraying themselves as the heirs of Darius and Alexander, or styling themselves "king of kings" (*malik-al-muluk*). See Antony Black, *The History of Islamic Political Thought: From the Prophet to the Present* (New York: Routledge, 2001), p. 205. For the early antipathy towards kingship, see Crone, *God's Rule*, pp. 7, 148–64.

34 In their attempt to condemn the rule of the Umayyad caliphs, their Abbāsid rivals had condemned the use of the title *malik* (king) and the term *mulk* (kingship). But *malik* had earlier been viewed as perfectly acceptable and used as a synonym for caliph. See H. Ringgren, "Some Religious Aspects of the Caliphate," in *The Sacral Kingship*, pp. 737–48 (at p. 738).

35 Al-Azmeh, *Muslim Kingship*, pp. 63–5. Al-Azmeh adds (p. 63): "It is now anachronistic to presume that the Rightly-Guided caliphate (632–61), the primitive proto-Muslim polity at Medina and later briefly at Kūfa, had produced statutes and forms of state and of kingship of any determinative or definitive character that informed the later crystallization of Muslim politics. The Muslim religion and the texts and exemplary geneaologies that are ascribed to the formative period of Islam were later elaborations created over many generations in the light of conditions prevailing in polities the Arabs set up from Iraq and Syria. Elements derived from the slight Arab tradition of kingship, heavily impregnated by Byzantine and Iranian paradigms, were combined with the enduring heritage of Semitic religion, priesthood, and kingship."

36 Cited from Black, *The History of Islamic Political Thought*, p. 162.

37 On the *Sharī'a*, Erwin I.J. Rosenthal, *Political Thought in Medieval Islam: An Introductory Outline* (Cambridge: Cambridge University Press, 1958), p. 8, comments: "A Muslim's life – ideally at least – is ruled in its entirety by the *Sharī'a*, which lays down precise rules and regulations governing his relations with God as well as with his fellow-Muslims and non-Muslims. We are used to term the former 'religious' and the latter 'secular.' But where a religious law is all-comprehensive this distinction falls to the ground."

38 Rosenthal, *Political Thought in Medieval Islam*, pp. 26, 8–9. Cf. Crone, *God's Rule*, pp. 10–16, 389–90, 393–8; Black, *The History of Islamic Political Thought*, pp. 11–14; cf. Al-Azmeh, *Muslim Kingship*, p. 15. It should be noted, however, that under the de facto rule of sultans, an essentially secular title (sultan = power), there developed in practice a quasi-separation between the secular and the religious. For the periodic emergence in Islam (theoretical formulations to the contrary) of such a de facto institutional separation of the "political" and the "religious," see Ira M. Lapidus, "State and Religion in Islamic Societies," *Past and Present* 151 (1996), 3–27.

39 Ringgren, "Some Religious Aspects of the Caliphate," pp. 738, 740, 746; cf. Al-Azmeh, *Muslim Kingship*, pp. 78–9, 156–7.

40 Black, *The History of Islamic Political Thought*, pp. 39–48 (at pp. 40–1).

41 Ibid., pp. 222–37.
42 Al-Azmeh, *Muslim Kingship*, pp. 158–62.
43 Thomas Hobbes, *The Leviathan*, Part 4, ch. 45; ed. Michael Oakeshott (Oxford: Blackwell, 1946), pp. 430–1 and 435.

3 The Eusebian Accommodation

1 Francis Dvornik, *Early Christian and Byzantine Political Philosophy: Origins and Background*, 2 vols. (Washington, DC: Dumbarton Oaks Center for Byzantine Studies, 1966), vol. 2. pp. 558–65 (at 565). Cf. Erwin R. Goodenough, *The Politics of Philo Judaeus: Practice and Theory* (New Haven, CT: Yale University Press, 1938), pp. 1–120, and Per Beskow, *Rex Gloriae: The Kingship of Christ in the Early Church*, trans. Eric J. Sharpe (Stockholm: Almquist and Wiksell, 1962), esp. pp. 187–211.
2 Beskow, *Rex Gloriae*, p. 188.
3 This statement occurs in a fragment from one of Philo's last works that is quoted in a twelfth-century source. I cite it from Dvornik, *Early Christian and Byzantine Political Philosophy*, vol. 2, p. 563.
4 Beskow, *Rex Gloriae*, p. 188.
5 Dvornik, *Early Christian and Byzantine Political Philosophy*, vol. 2, pp. 594–615 (at p. 597).
6 Thus Norman H. Baynes, "Eusebius and the Christian Empire," in *Mélanges Bidez, Annuaire de l'Institute de Philologie et d'Histoire Orientale*, 2 (Brussels: 1934), pp. 13–18.
7 George H. Williams, "Christology and Church–State Relations in the Fourth Century," *Church History* 20, 3 (1951), 3–33 (at p. 14), 4 (1951), 3–26. Cf. F. Edward Cranz, "Kingdom and Polity in Eusebius of Caesarea," *Harvard Theological Review* 45, 1, 1952), 47–65. My references will be given to the English translations of the *Oration* and *Life* printed in Philip Schaff ed., *Select Library of Nicene and Post Nicene Fathers*, 2nd series 14 vols. (New York: The Christian Literature Co., 1886–90), vol. 1, pp. 481–559 (*Life*), pp. 581–610 (*Oration*); and W.J. Ferrar, *The Proof of the Gospel: Being the* Demonstratio Evangelica *of Eusebius of Caesarea*, 2 vols. (London: Society for Promoting Christian Knowledge, 1920). The problem of the alleged non-Eusebian interpolations in the *Life* need not concern us here.
8 *Oration*, ch. 16, p. 606.
9 Ibid., ch. 13, pp. 602–3; ch. 16, pp. 606–7; *Proof of the Gospel*, Bk. 3, ch. 7, in Ferrar, vol. 1, p. 161.
10 *Oration*, ch. 16, pp. 606–7.
11 *Proof of the Gospel*, Bk. 8, ch. 3, in Ferrar, vol. 2, pp. 140–1.
12 *Life*, Bk. 1, ch. 44, p. 494.
13 What is involved here is more than Constantine's vision before the battle of the Milvian bridge, the account of which in the *Life*, Bk. 1, chs. 28–9, p. 490, some have maintained, is not the work of Eusebius. See also *Oration*, ch. 11, p. 595, and ch. 18, p. 610.
14 *Life*, Bk. 1, ch. 12, p. 485, ch. 20, p. 488, chs. 38 and 39, pp. 492–3.

15 *Life*, Bk. 3, ch. 15, pp. 523–4; cf. the comment of Williams, "Christology and Church–State Relations (i)," 5.

16 *Oration*, ch. 6, p. 591; cf. the comment of H. Berkhof cited in Cranz, "Kingdom and Polity," 56 n. 46.

17 *Oration*, ch. 11, pp. 596–7; cf. ch. 12, p. 598. For pertinent commentary on Eusebius's use of Philo's "political metaphysics," see Dvornik, *Early Christian and Byzantine Political Philosophy*, vol. 2, p. 621; Beskow, *Rex Gloriae*, esp. pp. 261–7, 318–19.

18 *Oration*, chs. 13–15, pp. 603–6.

19 Ibid., chs. 1, p. 583, 3, p. 585, 11, pp. 595–8, 12, p. 600.

20 Ibid., ch. 1, p. 583, chs. 4–5, pp. 585–6.

21 Ibid., ch. 2, pp. 583–4; cf. *Life*, Bk. 4, ch. 65, p. 557.

22 Williams, "Christology and Church–State Relations (i)," 4.

23 Beskow, *Rex Gloriae*, p. 319; cf. Williams, "Christology and Church–State Relations (ii)," 15–16.

24 *Life*, Bk. 3, ch. 15, pp. 523–4.

25 Dvornik, *Early Christian and Byzantine Political Philosophy*, vol. 2, pp. 672–99, 731–95.

26 Ibid., pp. 772–8.

27 I cite the translation reprinted in Brian Tierney, *The Crisis of Church and State: 1050–1300* (Englewood Cliffs, NJ: Prentice-Hall, 1964), pp. 14–15; cf. Dvornik, *Early Christian and Byzantine Political Philosophy*, vol. 2, pp. 804–9.

28 Translation in Tierney, *The Crisis of Church and State*, p. 13.

29 Francis Dvornik, "Pope Gelasius and Emperor Anastasius I," *Byzantinische Zeitschrift* 44 (1951), 111–16.

30 Dvornik, *Early Christian and Byzantine Political Philosophy*, vol. 2, pp. 809ff.

31 Cited from D.M. Nichols, "Byzantine Political Thought," in *The Cambridge History of Medieval Political Thought* c. 310–c.1450, ed. J.H. Burns (Cambridge: Cambridge University Press, 1988), pp. 51–72 (at p. 71).

32 For this distinction between the *potestas ordinis* and *potestas jurisdictionis* as well as its history and the literature pertaining to it, see *Dictionnaire de droit canonique*, 7 vols. (Paris: Letourzey et Ané, 1935–65), vol. 8, pp. 98–100, s.v. "Pouvoirs de l'église."

33 I draw this descriptive phrase from Ernest Barker, *Social and Political Thought in Byzantium: From Justinian I to the last Palaeologus* (Oxford: Clarendon Press, 1957), p. 12.

34 Baynes, "Eusebius and the Christian Empire," 13; cf. Nichols, "Byzantine Political Thought."

35 *Corpus Juris Civilis*, eds. W. Kroll, P. Krueger, T. Mommsen and R. Schoell, 3 vols. (Berlin: Weidman, 1899–1902), vol. 3, p. 53 (*Novellae*, 7, 2, 1); I cite the English translation in Dvornik, *Early Christian and Byzantine Political Philosophy*, vol. 2, p. 816.

36 Dvornik, *Early Christian and Byzantine Political Philosophy*, vol. 2, pp. 640ff.; André Grabar, *L'Empéreur dans l'art byzantin* (London: Variorums Reprints, 1971), pp. 90–6.

37 Dvornik, *Early Christian and Byzantine Political Philosophy*, vol. 2, p. 643; Euse-
    bius, *Life of Constantine*, Bk. 4, chs. 8–13, pp. 542–4.
38 I cite the translation in Barker, *Social and Political Thought in Byzantium*,
    pp. 194–5.
39 I cite the article from Thornton Anderson, *Russian Political Thought: An Intro-
    duction* (Ithaca, NY: Cornell University Press, 1967), p. 129.
40 Ibid., p. 82.
41 Arnold J. Toynbee, "Russia's Byzantine Heritage," in Toynbee, *Civilization on
    Trial* (New York: Oxford University Press, 1948), pp. 182–3.
42 Dmitri Obolensky, "Russia's Byzantine Heritage," in *Oxford Slavonic Papers*, 1
    (1950), 37–63 (at 59); cf. B.H. Summers, *Peter the Great* (New York: Collier
    Books, 1962), pp. 129–31.
43 Michael Cherniavsky, "Khan or Basileus: An Aspect of Russian Medieval Political
    Theory," *Journal of the History of Ideas* 20, 4 (1959), 456–76 (at 462–6, 468,
    471, 473, 476).
44 Anderson, *Russian Political Thought*, pp. 28–9; cf. Francis Dvornik, "Byzantine
    Political Ideas in Kievan Russia," *Dumbarton Oaks Papers*, 9 and 10 (Cam-
    bridge, MA: Harvard University Press, 1956), pp. 71–121.
45 Anderson, *Russian Political Thought*, pp. 36–7.
46 Ibid., pp. 173–88 (quotations from p. 174).

4 The Carolingian Accommodation

1 St Augustine, *De civitate dei*, 19:17; trans. Henry Bettenson, as Augustine, *Con-
   cerning the City of God against the Pagans*, ed. David Knowles (Harmondsworth,
   Middlesex: Penguin Books, 1972), p. 877.
2 Augustine, *De civitate dei*, 5:24 in Bettenson, pp. 219–20.
3 Thus Francis Dvornik, *Early Christian and Byzantine Political Philosophy:
   Origins and Background*, 2 vols. (Washington, DC: Dumbarton Oaks Center for
   Byzantine Studies, 1966), vol. 2, p. 849; Walter Ullmann, *The Carolingian
   Renaissance and the Idea of Kingship* (London: Methuen and Co., 1969), p. 3.
4 In this connection the instructions sent in 601 by Pope Gregory to the Benedic-
   tine missionaries in England are revealing: "[W]hen by God's help you reach our
   most revered brother, Bishop Augustine, we wish you to inform him that we
   have been giving careful thought to the affairs of the English, and have come to
   the conclusion that the temples of the idols in that country should on no account
   be destroyed. He is to destroy the idols, but the temples themselves are to be
   aspersed with holy water, altars set up, and relics enclosed in them. For if these
   temples are well built, they are to be purified from devil-worship, and dedicated
   to the service of the true God. In this way, we hope that the people, seeing that
   its temples are not destroyed, may abandon idolatry and resort to these places as
   before, and may come to know and adore the true God. And since they have a
   custom of sacrificing many oxen to devils, let some other solemnity be substi-
   tuted in its place, such as a day of Dedication or the Festivals of the holy martyrs
   whose relics are enshrined there. . . . For it is certainly impossible to eradicate all
   errors from obstinate minds at one stroke, and whoever wishes to climb to a

mountain top climbs gradually step by step, and not in one leap. It was in this way that God revealed himself to the Israelite people in Egypt, permitting the sacrifices formerly offered to the Devil to be offered thenceforward to Himself instead." (Bede, *Historia ecclesiastica gentis Anglorum*, 1:30: trans. Leo Shirley-Price as *A History of the English Church and People* (Baltimore, MD: Penguin Books, 1965), pp. 85–7.

5 *Confessions, 6:2*; trans. R.S. Pine-Coffin (Baltimore, MD: Penguin Books, 1961), pp. 112–13.

6 Marc Bloch, *Les Rois thaumaturges: Étude sur le caractère surnaturel attribué à la puissance royale particulièrement en France et en Angleterre* (Strasburg: Librairie Istra, 1924), pp. 76–7.

7 Cited in K.J. Leyser, *Rule and Conflict in an Early Medieval Society: Ottonian Saxony* (Oxford: Basil Blackwell, 1989), p. 80 and n. 23.

8 See the excellent analysis of the state of scholarly play on the matter in Gábor Klaniczay, *Holy Rulers and Blessed Princesses: Dynastic Cults in Medieval Central Europe* (Cambridge: Cambridge University Press, 2002), esp. pp. 1–113; and for a powerful version of the case to be made for pagan–Christian continuity in one (perhaps exceptional) region, see William A. Chaney, *The Cult of Kingship in Anglo-Saxon England: The Transition from Paganism to Christianity* (Manchester: Manchester University Press, 1970).

9 Bloch, *Les Rois thaumaturges*, pp. 60–1, n. 1; cf. Tacitus, *Germania*, ch. 40; in *Tacitus on Britain and Germany*, trans. H. Mattingly (West Drayton, Middlesex: Penguin Books, 1948), pp. 133–4.

10 The term used by J.M. Wallace-Hadrill, "The *Via Regia* of the Carolingian Age," in *Trends in Medieval Political Thought*, ed. Beryl Smalley (Oxford: Basil Blackwell, 1965), p. 28, where he adds that Charles the Bald, later on, "believed, by having his queen Irmintrud crowned and anointed in 866, she would again become fruitful and give him better children than the bad lot he already had."

11 Bloch, *Les Rois thaumaturges*, p. 66.

12 Ernst Kantorowicz, *Laudes Regiae: A Study in Liturgical Acclamations and Medieval Ruler Worship* (Berkeley and Los Angeles: University of California Press, 1946), p. 56.

13 P.D. King, "The Barbarian Kingdoms," in *The Cambridge History of Medieval Political Thought c.350–c.1450*, J.H. Burns ed. (Cambridge: Cambridge University Press, 1988), pp. 123–53 (at p. 128).

14 Ullmann, *The Carolingian Renaissance*, pp. 98–9, 135.

15 H.-X. Arquillière, *L'Augustinisme politique*, 2nd edn. (Paris: J. Vrin, 1955), p. 166.

16 Ambrosiaster/Pseudo Augustine, *Quaestiones Veteris et Novi Testament*, 35; the text is conveniently reproduced in R.W. and A.J. Carlyle, *A History of Mediaeval Political Theory in the West*, 6 vols. (Edinburgh and London: William Blackwood and Sons, 1903–36), vol. 1, p. 149 n. 2.

17 Bloch, *Les Rois thaumaturges*, pp. 74–5; Kantorowicz, *Laudes regiae*, p. 57.

18 Cited from Fritz Kern, *Kingship and Law in the Middle Ages*, trans. S.B. Chrimes (Oxford: Basil Blackwell, 1939), p. 38; Wido's words are cited from Bloch, *Les Rois thaumaturges*, p. 189.

19 The text is reproduced in Carlyle and Carlyle, *History of Mediaeval Political Theory*, vol. 1, p. 215 n. 3.

20 English translation of the text in Theodor E. Mommsen and Karl F. Morrison, *Imperial Lives and Letters of the Eleventh Century* (New York and London: Columbia University Press, 1962), p. 67.

21 Ernst Kantorowicz, *The King's Two Bodies: A Study in Medieval Political Theology* (Princeton, NJ: Princeton University Press, 1957), pp. 61–78 (at pp. 64–5). Kantorowicz dates the miniature to c.975 and identifies the emperor in question as Otto II; Domkapitel Aachen, however, which supplied the image for Figure 6, dates the Gospel Book to c.996 and identifies the emperor depicted, pace Kantorowicz, as Otto III.

22 Ibid., p. 61.

23 Following here George H. Williams, *The Norman Anonymous of 1100 AD Toward the Identification and Evaluation of the So-Called Anonymous of York* (Cambridge, MA: Harvard University Press, 1951), pp. 128–32.

24 Ibid., p. 132; cf. p. 190.

25 *De consecratione pontificum et regum*; printed in *Monumenta Germaniae Historica, Libelli de lite imperatorum et pontificum*, 3 vols. (Hanover, 1891–7), vol. 3, 662–79 (at 662–8); I cite the English translation in Ewart Lewis, *Medieval Political Ideas*, 2 vols. (London: Routledge and Kegan Paul, 1954), vol. 2, pp. 562–6.

26 *De consecratione*; in *MGH*, *Libelli de lite*, vol. 3, pp. 664–7, 678.

27 Williams, *The Norman Anonymous of 1100 AD*, pp. 169–74.

28 *De consecratione*; in *MGH*, *Libelli de lite*, vol. 3, pp. 663–8; much of this crucial section is translated in Lewis, *Medieval Political Ideas*, vol. 2, pp. 563–6.

29 Williams, *The Norman Anonymous of 1100 A.D.*, pp. 187–8.

30 Ibid., pp. 170–3, 192–5, 156–7, where the pertinent texts are cited.

31 Ibid., pp. 77 and 10.

5 The Sacrality of Kingship in Medieval and Early Modern Europe

1 Janet Nelson, "Kingship and Empire," in *The Cambridge History of Medieval Political Thought* c. *310–c.1450*, J.H. Burns ed. (Cambridge: Cambridge University Press, 1988), pp. 211–51 (at p. 220).

2 Thus Einhard, *Vita Karoli Magni*, §33; in *Einhard and Notker the Stammerer: Two Lives of Charlemagne*, trans. Lewis Thorpe (Harmondsworth, Middlessex: Penguin Books, 1969), p. 88.

3 Robert Folz, *The Concept of Empire in Western Europe from the Fifth to the Fourteenth Century*, trans. Sheila Ann Ogilvie (New York and Evanston, IL: Harper and Row, 1969), p. 64.

4 Karl F. Morrison, "Introduction" to *Imperial Lives and Letters of the Eleventh Century*, trans. and ed. Theodor E. Mommsen and Karl F. Morrison (New York: Columbia University Press, 1962), p. 26.

5 Thus Folz, *Concept of Empire*, p. 11.

6 In the encyclical letter *Eger Cui Levia* (c.1246); English translation in Brian Tierney, *The Crisis of Church and State: 1050–1300* (Englewood Cliffs, NJ: Prentice-Hall, 1964), pp. 147–9.

7 I.S. Robinson, "Church and Papacy," in *Cambridge History of Medieval Political Thought*, pp. 252–305 (at pp. 265–6).

8 Humbert, *Libri III Adversus Simoniacos* (1054–8); Letter of Gregory to Bishop Hermann of Metz (March, 1081); *Manegoldi ad Gebehardum Liber* (1080–5) – I cite the translations printed in Tierney, *Crisis of Church and State*, pp. 40–1, 66–73, 78–80.

9 All such modifications embedded in the *ordo* for imperial unction used from the time of Otto IV (1198–1215) to that of Charles V (1519–56), the last emperor to be anointed. See Folz, *Concept of Empire*, pp. 87–9 and 199.

10 Letter of Gregory to Bishop Hermann of Metz (March, 1081); *Dictatus papae* (1075), §§27 and 12; both cited from Tierney, *Crisis of Church and State*, pp. 69, 50, 49.

11 H.-X. Arquillière, *Le Plus ancien traité de l'église: Jacques de Viterbe, De regimine christiano (1301–1302)* (Paris: G. Beauchesne, 1926); Joseph de Maistre, *Du Pape* (1819), eds. Jacques Lovie and Joannes Chétail (Geneva: Librairie Droz, 1966); idem, *L'Église gallicane dans sa rapport avec le saint-siège* (Lyons: Librairie Catholique E. Vitte, 1931).

12 See the pertinent text and extended commentary in *New Commentary on the Code of Canon Law*, John P. Beal, James A. Coriden, Thomas J. Green eds. (New York: The Paulist Press, 2000), Art. I, canon 331; pp. 431–6.

13 *Summa Domini Henrici Cardinalis Hostiensis* (1250–3), cited from Tierney, *Crisis of Church and State*, pp. 156–7; Chronicle of Francesco Pipino, cited from Folz, *Concept of Empire*, p. 207.

14 The words are drawn from Innocent's encyclical letter *Eger Cui Levia* (c. 1246), cited from Tierney, *Crisis of Church and State*, p. 148.

15 A.M. Hocart, *Kingship* (London: Oxford University Press, 1927), p. 128.

16 *Dictatus papae*, §8; in Tierney, *Crisis of Church and State*, p. 49.

17 Folz, *Concept of Empire*, p. 79; cf. pp. 201–3.

18 Hobbes, *Leviathan*, Pt. 4, ch. 47; ed. Michael Oakeshott (Oxford: Basil Blackwell, 1946), p. 457.

19 Words drawn from the imperialist tract *De Unitate Ecclesiae Conservanda* (1090–3), the Letter of Henry to the German bishops (1076), and the Letter of Henry to Gregory refusing to recognize him as pope (1076) – all cited from Tierney, *Crisis of Church and State*, pp. 81, 61–2, 59–60.

20 Huguccio, Commentary on Dist. 96, c. 6 (1189–91), cited from Tierney, *Crisis of Church and State*, pp. 122–3.

21 Thus Kenneth Pennington, *Pope and Bishops: A Study of the Papal Monarchy in the Twelfth and Thirteenth Centuries* (Philadelphia, PA: Pennsylvania University Press, 1984), p. 41.

22 Otto of Freising, *Deeds of Frederick Barbarossa*, Bk. II, ch. 3; ed. and trans. Charles Christopher Mierow (New York: Columbia University Press, 1953), pp. 116–17. For Charles V as deacon, see Sergio Bertelli, *The King's Body: Sacred Rituals of Power in Medieval and Early Modern Europe*, trans. R. Burr Litchfield (University Park, PA: Pennsylvania State University Press, 2001), p. 14.

23 Ernst Kantorowicz, *The King's Two Bodies: A Study in Medieval Political Theology* (Princeton, NJ: Princeton University Press, 1957) – the whole of ch. 4 "Law-

Centered Kingship" is pertinent to this process. The words cited occur at pp. 185 and 192; also Folz, *Concept of Empire*, pp. 103, 117–18.

24 Dante, *De monarchia*, 1:8, 16; 2:8, 12; 3:16; trans. Herbert W. Schneider as Dante, *On World Government* (Indianapolis, IN: Bobbs-Merrill, 1957), pp. 10–11, 22–3, 44, 49–51, 79. Also *Dante Alighierii Epistolae*, ed. Paget Toynbee, 2nd edn. (Oxford: Oxford University Press, 1966), chs. 6 and 7; pp. 67–8, 77, 87, 90–1, 100–1.

25 Robinson, "Church and Papacy," p. 303.

26 I cite St Bernard's words and those of Grosseteste from J.A. Watt, "Spiritual and Temporal Powers," in *Cambridge History of Medieval Political Thought*, pp. 367–423 (at pp. 373 and 388).

27 Ibid., p. 399.

28 So claims Bertelli, *The King's Body*, p. 26. Extracts from Golein's treatise are printed in Appendix 4 to Marc Bloch, *Les Rois thaumaturges: Étude sur le caractère surnaturel attribué à la puissance royale particulièrement en France et en Angleterre* (Strasburg: Librairie Istra, 1924), pp. 478–89. Claire Richter Sherman, *The Portraits of Charles V of France 1338–1380* (New York: New York University Press, 1969), pp. 13–14 and 35, discusses Golein and the pertinent miniatures.

29 See J.H. Burns, *Lordship, Kingship, and Empire: The Idea of Monarchy 1400–1525* (Oxford: Clarendon Press, 1992), pp. 109–14.

30 Francis Oakley, *The Conciliarist Tradition: Constitutionalism in the Catholic Church 1300–1870* (Oxford: Oxford University Press, 2003), pp. 215–49.

31 Thomas de Vio, Cardinal Cajetan, *De comparatione auctoritate papae et concilii, cum Apologia ejusdem Tractatus*, cap. 6; ed. V.M. Pollet (Rome, 1936), pp. 46–7; English translation in J.H. Burns and Thomas M. Izbicki eds., *Conciliarism and Papalism* (Cambridge: Cambridge University Press, 1997), pp. 25–6. Robert, Cardinal Bellarmine, *Risposta ad un libretto intitulato Trattato e resolutione sopra la validità de la scommuniche di Gio Gersono* (Rome, 1606), p. 76.

32 See Francis Oakley, "Edward Foxe, Matthew Paris, and the Royal *potestas ordinis*," *Sixteenth Century Journal*, 18 (1987), 347–53.

33 Stephen Gardiner, *De vera obedientia/The Oration of True Obedience*, in *Obedience in Church and State*, Pierre Janelle ed. (Cambridge: Cambridge University Press, 1930), D vi^v, D iii^r–iii^v, D iv^r–iv^v; Richard Taverner, *The Second Book of the Garden of Wysdome* (London, 1539), fol. 14; Anon., cited in F.L. Baumer, *The Early Tudor Theory of Kingship* (New Haven, CT: Yale University Press, 1940), p. 86.

34 For the remarkable endurance of the intellectual tradition in question, see Oakley, *The Conciliarist Tradition*, pp. 217–49.

35 John Neville Figgis, *The Divine Right of Kings* (New York and London: Harper Torchbooks, 1965), pp. 5–6.

36 Drawing here not only on the speech of 1610 but also on his later "Speech in the Starre-Chamber . . . Anno 1616," both printed in *The Political Works of James I*, C. H. McIlwain ed. (Cambridge, MA: Harvard University Press, 1918), words cited at pp. 307–8, 333. What James appears to be doing in these pieces is conflating the *potentia absoluta/ordinaria* distinction with an even older scholastic

distinction between the secret and revealed wills of God (*voluntas beneplaciti/ signi*, or, in the Reformed terminology, Secret/Hidden and Revealed Will of God. For a detailed analysis of these texts, see Francis Oakley, *Omnipotence, Covenant, and Order: An Excursion in the History of Ideas from Abelard to Leibniz* (Ithaca, NY: Cornell University Press, 1984), pp. 93–118.

37 The numbers in parentheses refer to the pagination of Jacques-Benigne Bossuet, *Politics Drawn from the Very Words of Holy Scripture*, trans. and ed. Patrick Riley (Cambridge: Cambridge University Press, 1990).

38 Stephanus Junius Brutus (ps.), *Vindiciae contra tyrannos: or, concerning the legitimate power of a prince over the people and of the people over a prince*, Qu. 3; ed. and trans. George Garnett (Cambridge: Cambridge University Press, 1994), pp. 122–9. Cf. 1 Samuel, 8:4–21.

39 *Hegel's Philosophy of Right*, trans. T.M. Knox (London, Oxford, New York: Oxford University Press, 1971), pp. 12–13.

6 The Fading Nimbus

1 For this, and for the sacrality of the early modern French kingship in general, see Dale K. Van Kley, *The Religious Origins of the French Revolution: From Calvin to the Civil Constitution, 1560–1791* (New Haven, CT and London: Yale University Press, 1996), esp. pp. 292–3.

2 David Cannadine, "The Context, Performance and Meaning of Ritual: The British Monarchy and the 'Invention of Tradition'," in *The Invention of Tradition*, eds. Eric Hobsbawm and Terence Ranger (Cambridge: Cambridge University Press, pp. 101–67; and, for the critics, Ian Bradley, *God Save the Queen: The Spiritual Dimension of Monarchy* (London: Darton, Longman and Todd, 2002), pp. 142–3.

3 Walter Bagehot, *The English Constitution* (London, New York, Toronto: Oxford University Press, 1928), pp. 35–9.

4 Thus E. Shils and M. Young, "The Meaning of the Coronation," *Sociological Review*, new ser., 1 (1953), 63–81; critical response by N. Birnbaum, "Monarchies and Sociologists: A Reply to Professors Shils and Young," ibid., 3 (1955), 5–23. For the development across time of the English coronation rite, see Percy Ernst Schramm, *A History of the English Coronation*, trans. Leopold G. Wickham Legg (Oxford: Clarendon Press, 1937).

5 Thus the theologian Ian Bradley, *God Save the Queen*, esp. pp. 185 and 87, where he cites Grace Davie's words from the *Church Times*, April 14, 2000.

6 Bagehot, *The English Constitution*, p. 38.

7 Following here Cannadine, "The Context, Performance and Meaning of Ritual," pp. 101–64 (at pp. 110 and 117).

8 Eric Hobsbawm, "Mass-Producing Tradition: Europe, 1870–1914," in Hobsbawm and Ranger, *The Invention of Tradition*, pp. 263–307 (at p. 282).

9 This being the claim made by Gerald Straka, "The Final Phase of Divine Right Theory in England, 1688–1702," *English Historical Review*, 77 (1962), 638–58.

10 Bagehot, *The English Constitution*, pp. 37–8.

11 Paul Kléber Monod, *The Power of Kings: Monarchy and Religion in Europe*

1589–1715 (New Haven, CT, and London: Yale University Press, 1999), pp. 1–31. Subsequent references to this book are given in parentheses in the text.

12 This being the title of H.R. Trevor-Roper's contribution to *Crisis in Europe, 1560–1660*, T.H. Aston ed. (London: Routledge and Kegan Paul, 1965), pp. 59–95; cf. the general statement at pp. 5–58.

13 Montesquieu, *Lettres persanes*, no. 24; in *Oeuvres complètes de Montesquieu* (Paris: Firmin Didot Frères, 1866–79), vol. 1, pp. 16–17.

14 Jeffrey W. Merrick, *Desacralization of the French Monarchy in the Eighteenth Century* (Baton Rouge, LA, and London: Louisiana State University Press, 1990), p. 166.

15 Monod, *The Power of Kings*, pp. 83–5.

16 Van Kley, *Religious Origins of the French Revolution*, p. 12; cf. p. 8, where he adds: "What outright religious civil war failed to fell in the sixteenth century, religious controversy in an era of public opinion effectively undid in the century of lights."

17 Thus, e.g. Roger Chartier, *The Cultural Origins of the French Revolution*, trans. Lydia G. Cochrane (Durham, NC, and London: Duke University Press, 1991), esp. pp. 109–35. Cf. Van Kley, *Religious Origins of the French Revolution* and Merrick, *Desacralization of the French Monarchy*.

18 The words are drawn (in order), from Chartier, pp. 123, 134, 118, 120; Merrick, pp. 167, 26 (cf. pp. 24–5); Van Kley, pp. 129, 294, 392; Robert Darnton, *The Literary Underground of the Old Regime* (Cambridge, MA: Harvard University Press, 1982), esp. pp. 202–5; idem, *The Forbidden Bestsellers of Pre-Revolutionary France* (New York and London: W.W. Norton, 1995), esp. pp. 198–246.

19 Chartier, *Cultural Origins of the French Revolution*, p. 113; cf. Van Kley, *Religious Origins of the French Revolution*, p. 292.

20 Sergio Bertelli, *The King's Body: Sacred Rituals of Power in Medieval and Early Modern Europe*, trans. R. Burr Litchfield (University Park, PA: Pennsylvania State University Press, 2001), pp. 267–9.

21 Ibid., p. 269.

22 Echoing here the distinction which William J. Bouwsma framed in "Christian Adulthood," *Daedalus* (Spring, 1976), 72–92 (at 77); and Peter Berger, *The Sacred Canopy: Elements of a Sociological Theory of Religion* (Garden City, NY: Doubleday Anchor Books, 1969), pp. 105–25 (words quoted at p. 124; cf. pp. 110–12).

23 Berger, *The Sacred Canopy*, p. 111.

24 Ibid., p. 110.

25 Brian Tierney, "Medieval Canon Law and Western Constitutionalism," *Catholic Historical Review*, 52, 1 (1966), 7–8.

26 *Hegel's Philosophy of Right*, trans. T.M. Knox (New York: Oxford University Press, 1967), pp. 84 §124, 124§185; cf. pp. 51§62, 133§206, 195§299, and 267–8, *Add.* 118; G.W.F. Hegel, *Reason in History: A General Introduction to the Philosophy of History*, trans. Robert S. Hartman (New York: Liberal Arts Press, 1953), pp. 23–4; idem, *Philosophy of History*, trans. J. Sibrec (New York: The Colonial Press, 1899), pp. 379, 412.

27 See the essays gathered together in *Creation: The Impact of an Idea*, Daniel O'Connor and Francis Oakley eds. (New York: Charles Scribner's Sons, 1969).

28 Ernst Troeltsch, *The Social Teaching of the Christian Churches*, trans. Olive Wyon, 2 vols. (New York: Harper Torchbooks, 1960), vol. 1, pp. 331–43, 378–82; vol. II, pp. 461–5, 656–65.

29 Ibid.

30 Harry Höpfl and Marilyn P. Thompson, "The History of Contract as a Motif in Political Thought," *American Historial Review*, 94 (1979), 919–44 (at p. 938).

31 John Lilburne, *Regall Tyrannie Discovered* (London, 1647), pp. 6–7; Richard Overton, *An Arrowe Against All Tyrants and Tyranny*, October 12, 1646; cited from the section printed in *The Levellers in the English Revolution*, G.E. Aylmer ed. (Ithaca, NY: Cornell University Press, 1975), 68–9.

32 Erwin Panofsky, *Gothic Architecture and Scholasticism* (New York: Meridian Books, 1976).

33 Plato, *Timaeus* §34B, translated in F.M. Cornford, *Plato's Cosmology: The Timaeus of Plato* (New York: Bobbs-Merrill, nd.), p. 58; Aristotle, *Metaphysics* 12:10; ed. and trans. W.D. Ross, *The Works of Aristotle Translated into English*, 12 vols. (Oxford: Clarendon Press, 1908–52), vol. 12, p. 1074b, 1–15.

34 Thus Étienne Gilson, *History of Christian Philosophy in the Middle Ages* (New York: Random House, 1955), p. 498.

35 Robert Boyle, *A Free Enquiry into the Vulgarly receiv'd Notion of Nature*, in *The Works of the Honorable Robert Boyle*, Thomas Birch ed., 6 vols. (London, 1772), vol. 5, pp. 163–4.

36 R.G. Collingwood, *The Idea of Nature* (Oxford: Oxford University Press, 1945).

37 Thomas Hobbes, *Leviathan*, Michael Oakeshott ed. (Oxford: Basil Blackwell, 1946), Editor's Introduction, pp. xx–xxi, xxvi–ix, xliv–vi, lii–lv.

38 *Leviathan*, Pt. 4, ch. 45; in ibid., p. 435.

Epilogue

1 Sandra Barnes, "Political Ritual and the Public Sphere in Contemporary West Africa," in *The Politics of Cultural Performance*, D. Parkin, L. Caplan, and H. Fisher eds. (Oxford: Berghan, 1996), pp. 19–40 (at pp. 20–1); cf. Michelle Gilbert, "The Person of the King: Ritual Power in a Ghanaian State," in *Rituals of Royalty: Power and Ceremonial in Traditional Societies*, David Cannadine and Simon Price eds. (Cambridge: Cambridge University Press, 1987), 298–330.

2 *Lumen gentium*, cap. 3, §22; in *Decrees of the Ecumenical Councils*, Giuseppe Alberigo and Norman Tanner, eds., 2 vols. (London and Washington, DC: Sheed and Ward and Georgetown University Press, 1990), vol. 2, pp. 866–7; cf. *Nota explicativa praevia*, ibid., pp. 899–900.

3 Albert Camus, *The Rebel: An Essay on Man in Revolt*, trans. Anthony Bower (New York: Vintage Books, 1991), pp. 112–13, 120–1. Judicious discussion of Camus's position and of the multiple French interpretations of the regicide in Susan Dunn, *The Death of Louis XVI: Regicide and the French Political Imagination* (Princeton, NJ: Princeton University Press, 1994).

Suggestions for Further Reading

Al-Azmeh, Aziz, *Muslim Kingship: Power and the Sacred in Muslim, Christian and Pagan Polities* (London and New York: I.B. Tauris, 1997).

Anderson, Thornton, *Russian Political Thought: An Introduction* (Ithaca, NY: Cornell University Press, 1967).

Arquillière, H.-X., *L'Augustinisme politique*, 2nd edn. (Paris: J. Vrin, 1955).

Bendix, Reinhard, *Kings or People: Power and the Mandate to Rule* (Berkeley, Los Angeles, London: University of California Press, 1978).

Berger, Peter, *The Sacred Canopy: Elements of a Sociological Theory of Religion* (Garden City, NY: Doubleday Anchor Books, 1969).

Bertelli, Sergio, *The King's Body: Sacred Rituals of Power in Medieval and Early Modern Europe*, trans. R. Burr Litchfield (University Park, PA: Pennsylvania State University Press, 2001).

Binchy, D.A., *Celtic and Anglo-Saxon Kingship* (Oxford: Clarendon Press, 1970).

Black, Antony, *The History of Islamic Political Thought: From the Prophet to the Present* (New York: Routledge, 2001).

Bloch, Marc, *Les Rois thaumaturges: Étude sur le caractère surnaturel attribué à la puissance royale particulièrement en France et en Angleterre* (Strasburg: Librairie Istra, 1924).

Bradley, Ian, *God Save the Queen: The Spiritual Dimension of Monarchy* (London: Darton, Longman and Todd, 2002).

Burns, J.H., *Lordship, Kingship, and Empire: The Idea of Monarchy 1400–1525* (Oxford: Clarendon Press, 1992).

Cannadine, David, and Price, Simon, eds., *Rituals of Royalty: Power and Ceremonial in Traditional Societies* (Cambridge: Cambridge University Press, 1987).

Chaney, William A., *The Cult of Kingship in Anglo-Saxon England: The Transition from Paganism to Christianity* (Manchester: Manchester University Press, 1970).

Claessen, Henri J.M., and Skalnik, Peter, eds., *The Early State* (The Hague, Paris, New York: Mouton Publishers, 1978).

Crone, Patricia, *God's Rule: Six Centuries of Islamic Political Thought* (New York: Columbia University Press, 2004).

Dunn, Susan, *The Death of Louis XVI: Regicide and the French Political Imagination* (Princeton, NJ: Princeton University Press, 1994).

Dvornik, Francis, *Early Christian and Byzantine Political Philosophy: Origins and Background*, 2 vols. (Washington, DC: Dumbarton Oaks Center for Byzantine Studies, 1966).

Eliade, Mircea, *Cosmos and History: The Myth of the Eternal Return* (New York: Harper and Row, 1959).

Figgis, John Neville, *The Divine Right of Kings* (New York and London: Harper Torchbooks, 1965).

Folz, Robert, *The Concept of Empire in Western Europe from the Fifth to the Fourteenth Century*, trans. Sheila Ann Ogilvie (New York and Evanston, IL: Harper and Row, 1969).

Frankfort, Henri, *Kingship and the Gods: A Study of Near Eastern Religion as the Integration of Society and Nature* (Chicago: University of Chicago Press, 1948).

Fujitani, T., *Splendid Monarchy: Power and Pageantry in Modern Japan* (Berkeley, Los Angeles, London: University of California Press, 1996).

Fustel de Coulanges, Numa D., *The Ancient City*, trans. Willard Small, 12th edn. (Garden City, NY: Doubleday Anchor Books, 1955).

Gauchet, Marcel, *The Disenchantment of the World*, trans. Oscar Burge (Princeton, NJ: Princeton University Press, 1997).

Geertz, Clifford, *Negara: The Theatre State in Nineteenth-Century Bali* (Princeton, NJ: Princeton University Press, 1988).

Hobsbawm, Eric, and Ranger, Terence, eds., *The Invention of Tradition* (Cambridge: Cambridge University Press, 1983).

Hocart, A.M., *Kings and Councillors: An Essay in the Comparative Anatomy of Human Society*, ed. Rodney Needham (Chicago and London: University of Chicago Press, 1970).

Hooke, S.H. ed., *Myth, Ritual and Kingship: Essays on the Theory and Practice of Kingship in the Ancient Near East and in Israel* (Oxford: Clarendon Press, 1958).

Kantorowicz, Ernst, *The King's Two Bodies: A Study in Medieval Political Theology* (Princeton, NJ: Princeton University Press, 1957).

Klaniczay, Gábor, *Holy Rulers and Blessed Princesses: Dynastic Cults in Medieval Central Europe* (Cambridge: Cambridge University Press, 2002).

Merrick, Jeffrey W., *Desacralization of the French Monarchy in the Eighteenth Century* (Baton Rouge, LA, and London: Louisiana State University Press, 1990).

Monod, Paul Kléber, *The Power of Kings: Monarchy and Religion in Europe 1589–1715* (New Haven, CT, and London: Yale University Press, 1999).

Mousnier, Roger, *Monarchies et royautés de la préhistoires à nos jours* (Paris: Librairie Académique Perrin, 1989).

Nelson, Janet L., *The Frankish World 790–900* (London and Rio Grande: The Hambledon Press, 1996).

Oakley, Francis, *The Conciliarist Tradition: Constitutionalism in the Catholic Church 1300–1870* (Oxford: Oxford University Press, 2003).

184

Schele, Linda, and Freidel, David, *A Forest of Kings: The Untold Story of the Ancient Maya* (New York: William Morrow, 1990).

The Sacral Kingship: Contributions to the Central Theme of the VIIIth International Congress for the History of Religions, Rome, April, 1955 (Leiden: E.J. Brill, 1959).

Van Kley, Dale K., *The Religious Origins of the French Revolution: From Calvin to the Civil Constitution, 1560–1791* (New Haven, CT, and London: Yale University Press, 1996).

Voegelin, Eric, *Order and History: I Israel and Revelation* (Baton Rouge, LA: Louisiana State University Press, 1956).

Wallace-Hadrill, J.M., *Early Germanic Kingship in England and on the Continent* (Oxford: Clarendon Press, 1971).

Williams, George H., *The Norman Anonymous of 1100 AD. Toward the Identification and Evaluation of the So-Called Anonymous of York* (Cambridge, MA: Harvard University Press, 1951).

Index

legitimacy, crisis of *see* modern kingship
Leo I, Pope 77, 111
Leo III, Emperor 79
Leo IX, Pope 111, 112
Leopold, King of Belgium 160
Levelers 148–9
Libya 160
Lilburne, John 148–9
liturgical kingship 100–7
Locke, John 149
logos 70–6
Lombards 88, 95
longevity of kingship 10–14
Louis the Pious, Emperor 90
Louis XIII, King of France 138
Louis XIV, King of France 13, 137, 138, 139
Louis XV, King of France 140
Louis XVI, King of France 132, 140, 141–2,
    161, 163
Luke, St: Lukan tradition 73, 120
Lutherans 126

Maistre, Joseph de 115
mana 37
Manegold of Lautenbach 114
Marcellinus, Ammianus 37
marginalization of kingship 4
Marlowe, Christopher 12
Martin V, Pope 123
Matoon dynasty, Kuba 23
Maxentius 74
Maya 11, 16, 27–33
Mazarin, Cardinal 128
Mbop Mábííŋc maMbéky, King of Kuba 27
medieval period 6, 12, 78–125
Mediterranean region 10, 44, 45
Meiji restoration, Japan 19, 20, 23
Melchizedek, King 77, 81, 97, 104
Melito of Sardis 73
Merovingian dynasty 12, 95–6
Mesoamerica 11, 13, 16, 17, 27–33
Mesopotamia 10, 16, 38–43, 51
    see also Babylon/Babylonians; Iraq
Messianic kingdom 57–8, 59
Mexico 28, 158
military role of kings 11–12
ministerial character of kingship 109
Minoans 11, 45
Mishe miShyaang maMbul, King of Kuba 24
modern kingship 132–57
    change 142–57
        in Britain 135–6, 138
        in France 136–7, 138–42
        in Holland 138
        in Italy 138
        in Scandinavia 136
        in Spain 138

de-mystification of European monarchy
    and crisis of legitimacy 133–42
    Anglicans 148
    Calvinism 144, 146
    Catholicism 143–4, 146
    Christianity 143–7, 151–5
    Dominicans 146
    Franciscans 148
    Gregorian reform 144
    Hellenism 150–6
    Islam 151
    Jesuits 146
    Judaism 150–4
    Levelers 148–9
    paganism 147
    Protestant Reformation 143, 145–8
    Puritans 148
    Neoplatonism 152–3, 155
monarchy:
    definition 1–2
    and kingship, distinction between 2
Mongols 14, 84
monocracy, definition 1–2
Monod, P.K. 136–40
Montesquieu, Charles de Secondat, Baron de
    139
Morocco 160
Moses 97
Mousnier, R. 2
Mowinckel, S. 53, 55
Muhammad 63–4, 65
Mycenaeans 11, 12, 45, 46

Naples 137, 138
Napoleon I, Emperor of France 158
Nara era, Japan 22
Nelson, J. 109
Neoplatonism 152–3, 155
Nepal 13, 160
New Testament 56, 58, 59, 60, 61, 62, 63,
    110
    Byzantine *basileus* 78
    Carolingian, Anglo-Saxon and Ottonian
        kingship 95, 99
    Christocentric or "liturgical" kingship 104,
        107
    desacralization of kingship 144, 146
    imperial sacrality 119
    modern kingship 132
    papal monarchy 113–14
    "political Augustinianism" 89, 90, 91
    transition at Rome to Christian monarchy
        69, 70, 71, 74
Newton, Sir Isaac 155
ngesh (Kuba nature-spirits) 26
Nicholas I, Pope 90, 111